1-1 WORK TOGETHER, p. 8

M000239193

Completing the accounting equation

Assets	=	Liabilities	+	Owner's Equity
11,000		3,000		8,000
10,000		4000		6,000
63,000		35,000		28,000

Extra form

Assets	=	Liabilities	+	Owner's Equity

Completing the accounting equation

Assets	=	Liabilities	+	Owner's Equity
23,000		10,000		13,000
100,000		70,000		30,000
48,000		25,000		23,000

Extra form

Assets	=	Liabilities	+	Owner's Equity

1-2 WORK TOGETHER, p. 12

Determining how transactions change an accounting equation

Trans. No.	Assets	=	Liabilities	+	Owner's Equity
1.	+		+		
2.	+				+
3.	+ −				
4.	−		−		

Extra form

Trans. No.	Assets	=	Liabilities	+	Owner's Equity
1.					
2.					
3.					
4.					
5.					
6.					

Determining how transactions change an accounting equation

Trans. No.	Assets	=	Liabilities	+	Owner's Equity
1.	+				+
2.	− +				
3.	− +				
4.	+		+		
5.	−		−		

Extra form

Trans. No.	Assets	=	Liabilities	+	Owner's Equity
1.					
2.					
3.					
4.					
5.					
6.					

1-3 WORK TOGETHER, p. 15

Preparing a balance sheet from information in an accounting equation

Use Cursive writing

HESS COMPANY
BALANCE SHEET
31 OCT 2007

ASSETS			LIABILITIES		
CASH	2900	00	A/P - HULETT Co.	250	00
SUPPLIES	300	00	OWNER'S EQUITY		
PREPAID INSURANCE	600	00	JIM HESS, CAPITOL	3050	00
TOTAL ASSETS	3300	00	TOTAL LIABILITIES / Owners Eq.	3300	00

Extra form

Preparing a balance sheet from information in an accounting equation

Goldstein Company
Balance Sheet
July 31, 2007

Assets			Liabilities		
Cash	2500	00	A/P - Heino Company	500	00
Supplies	800	00	Owners Equity		
Prepaid Insurance	1200	00	Mary Goldstein, capital	4000	00
Total Assets	4500	00	Total Liab. and Owners Eq.	4500	00

Extra form

1-1 APPLICATION PROBLEM, p. 17

Completing the accounting equation

Assets	=	Liabilities	+	Owner's Equity
90,000		49,000		41,000
98,000		68,000		30,000
3,000		1000		2,000
108,000		60,000		48,000
19,000		8000		11,000
16,000		4,000		12,000
25,000		13,000		
162,000		113,000		49,000
4,000		2,000		2,000
86,000		48,000		38,000
12,000		5000		7,000
19000		5,000		14,000
47,000		24,000		23,000
42,000		29,000		13,000
38,000		17,000		21,000
125,000		69,000		56,000
11,000		5,000		6,000
4,000		1,000		3,000

Extra form

Assets	=	Liabilities	+	Owner's Equity

1-2 APPLICATION PROBLEM, p. 17

Determining how transactions change an accounting equation

Trans. No.	Assets			=	Liabilities		+	Owner's Equity
	Cash	+	Supplies +	Prepaid Insurance =	Accts. Pay.— Swan's Supply	+	Accts. Pay.— York Co. +	Frank Mori, Capital
Beg. Bal.	0		0	0	0		0	0
1.	+2,000							+2,000
New Bal.	2,000		0	0	0		0	2,000
2.	-600			+600				
New Bal.	1400		0	600	0		0	2000
3.			+100		+100			
New Bal.	1400		100	600	100		0	2000
4.			+500				+500	
New Bal.	1400		600	600	100		500	2000
5.	-100				-100			
New Bal.	1300		600	600	0		500	2000
6.	-300						-300	
New Bal.	1000		600	600	0		200	2000
7.	-500		+500					
New Bal.	500		1100	600	0		200	2000
8.	+500							+500
New Bal.	1000		1100	600	0		200	2500

Extra form

Trans. No.	Assets			=	Liabilities		+	Owner's Equity
	Cash	+	Supplies +	Prepaid Insurance =		+	+	
Beg. Bal. 1.								
New Bal. 2.								
New Bal. 3.								
New Bal. 4.								
New Bal. 5.								
New Bal. 6.								
New Bal. 7.								
New Bal. 8.								
New Bal.								

Extra form

Trans. No.	Assets			=	Liabilities	+	Owner's Equity
	Cash	+ Supplies	+ Prepaid Insurance	=	+	+	
Beg. Bal. 1.							
New Bal. 2.							
New Bal. 3.							
New Bal. 4.							
New Bal. 5.							
New Bal. 6.							
New Bal. 7.							
New Bal. 8.							
New Bal. 9.							
New Bal. 10.							
New Bal. 11.							
New Bal. 12.							
New Bal. 13.							
New Bal. 14.							
New Bal. 15.							
New Bal. 16.							
New Bal.							

1-3 APPLICATION PROBLEM, p. 18

Determining how transactions change an accounting equation

Trans. No.	Assets			=	Liabilities		+	Owner's Equity
	Cash	+ Supplies	+ Prepaid Insurance	=	Accts. Pay. — Seiler Supply	+ Accts. Pay.— Miles Co.	+	Ellie VonSpreecken, Capital
Beg. Bal.	0	0	0		0	0		0
1.	+3,000							+3,000
New Bal.	3,000	0	0		0	0		3,000
2.	−1200		+1200					
New Bal.	1800	0	1200		0	0		3000
3.		+800			+800			
New Bal.	1800	800	1200		800	0		3000
4.		+500				+500		
New Bal.	1800	1300	1200		800	500		3000
5.	−400				−400			
New Bal.	1400	1300	1200		400	500		3000
6.	+1000							+1000
New Bal.	2400	1300	1200		400	500		4000

Extra form

Trans. No.	Assets			=	Liabilities	+		Owner's Equity
	Cash	+ Supplies	+ Prepaid Insurance	=		+	+	
Beg. Bal. 1.								
New Bal. 2.								
New Bal. 3.								
New Bal. 4.								
New Bal. 5.								
New Bal. 6.								
New Bal.								

Extra form

Trans. No.	Assets			=	Liabilities	+	Owner's Equity
	Cash	+ Supplies	+ Prepaid Insurance	=		+	+
Beg. Bal. 1.							
New Bal. 2.							
New Bal. 3.							
New Bal. 4.							
New Bal. 5.							
New Bal. 6.							
New Bal. 7.							
New Bal. 8.							
New Bal. 9.							
New Bal. 10.							
New Bal. 11.							
New Bal. 12.							
New Bal. 13.							
New Bal. 14.							
New Bal. 15.							
New Bal. 16.							
New Bal.							

1-4 APPLICATION PROBLEM, p. 19

Determining where items are listed on a balance sheet

	1	2	3
		Balance Sheet	
	Items	**Left Side**	**Right Side**
1. Cash		Asset	
2. Michelle Sullivan, Capital			Owner's Eq
3. Supplies		Asset	
4. Prepaid Insurance		Asset	
5. Accounts Payable—Action Laundry			Liability
6. Anything owned		Asset	
7. Any amount owed			Liability
8. Owner's capital account			Owner's Eq

Extra form

	1	2	3
		Balance Sheet	
	Items	**Left Side**	**Right Side**
1.			
2.			
3.			
4.			
5.			
6.			
7.			
8.			

Extra form

1	2	3
	Balance Sheet	
Items	Left Side	Right Side
1.		
2.		
3.		
4.		
5.		
6.		
7.		
8.		
9.		
10.		
11.		
12.		
13.		
14.		
15.		
16.		
17.		
18.		
19.		
20.		
21.		
22.		
23.		
24.		
25.		
26.		
27.		
28.		
29.		
30.		

1-5 APPLICATION PROBLEM, p. 19

Preparing a balance sheet from information in an accounting equation

Steffens Company
Balance Sheet
September 30, 2007

Assets		Liabilities	
Cash	1 20 0 00	A/P - Morton Co.	2 50 00
Supplies	1 50 00	Owner's Equity	
Prepaid Insurance	3 00 00	Steven Steffens, Capital	1 4 00 00
Total Assets	1 6 50 00	Total Liabilities & Owners Eq	1 6 50 00

Extra form

1-6 MASTERY PROBLEM, p. 19

Determining how transactions change an accounting equation and preparing a balance sheet

1.

Trans. No.	Assets			=	Liabilities	+	Owner's Equity
	Cash	+ Supplies	+ Prepaid Insurance	=	Accts. Pay.— Helfrey Co.	+	Nancy Dirks, Capital
Beg. Bal. 1.	0 +350	0	0		0		0 +350
New Bal. 2.	350	0 +100	0		0 +100		350
New Bal. 3.	350 −150	100	0 +150		100		350
New Bal. 4.	~~150~~ 200 −50	100 +50	150		100		350
New Bal. 5.	~~100~~ 150 +300	150	150		100		350 +300
New Bal. 6.	450 −75	150	150		100 −75		650
New Bal.	375	150	150		25		650

2.

Dirks Company
Balance Sheet
July 31, 2007

Assets			Liabilities		
Cash	375 00		A/P – Helfrey Co.	25 00	
Supplies	150 00		Owner's Equity		
Prepaid Insurance	150 00		Nancy Dirks, Capital	650 00	
Total Assets	675 00		Total Liabilities and Owners Eq	675 00	

Extra forms

Trans. No.	Assets			=	Liabilities	+	Owner's Equity
	Cash	+	Supplies	+	Prepaid Insurance	=	+
Beg. Bal. 1.							
New Bal. 2.							
New Bal. 3.							
New Bal. 4.							
New Bal. 5.							
New Bal. 6.							
New Bal.							

1-7 CHALLENGE PROBLEM, p. 20

Applying accounting concepts to determine how transactions change the accounting equation

Trans. No.	Assets			=	Liabilities		+	Owner's Equity
	Cash	+ Supplies	+ Prepaid Insurance	=	Accts. Pay.— Mutual Sav. Bank	+ Accts. Pay. — Nelson Supply Company	+	Gregory Morgan, Capital
Beg. Bal. 1.	0 +1,500	0	0		0	0		0 +1,500
New Bal. 2.	1,500 -400	0 +400	0		0	0		1,500
New Bal. 3.	1100 -240	400	0 +240		0	0		1500
New Bal. 4.	860	400 +80	240		0	0 +80		1500
New Bal. 5.	860	480	240		0	80		1500
New Bal. 6.	860 -100	480 +100	240		0	80		1500
New Bal. 7.	760	580 +300	240		0	80		1500 +300
New Bal.	760	880	240		0	80		1800

Extra form

Trans. No.	Assets			=	Liabilities		+	Owner's Equity
	Cash	+ Supplies	+ Prepaid Insurance	=		+	+	
Beg. Bal. 1.								
New Bal. 2.								
New Bal. 3.								
New Bal. 4.								
New Bal. 5.								
New Bal. 6.								
New Bal. 7.								
New Bal.								

Extra form

Trans. No.	Assets			=	Liabilities	+	Owner's Equity
	Cash	+ Supplies	+ Prepaid Insurance	=	+	+	
Beg. Bal. 1.							
New Bal. 2.							
New Bal. 3.							
New Bal. 4.							
New Bal. 5.							
New Bal. 6.							
New Bal. 7.							
New Bal. 8.							
New Bal. 9.							
New Bal. 10.							
New Bal. 11.							
New Bal. 12.							
New Bal. 13.							
New Bal. 14.							
New Bal. 15.							
New Bal.							

2-1 WORK TOGETHER, p. 29

Determining how transactions change an accounting equation

Trans. No.	Assets				=	Liabilities	+	Owner's Equity
	Cash	+ Accts. Rec.—Bowman Co.	+ Supplies	+ Prepaid Insurance	=	Accts. Pay.—Maxwell Co.	+	Susan Sanders, Capital
1.	+							+
2.		+						+
3.	−							−
4.	+	−						

Extra form

Trans. No.	Assets				=	Liabilities	+	Owner's Equity
	Cash	+	+ Supplies	+ Prepaid Insurance	=		+	
1.								
2.								
3.								
4.								
5.								
6.								
7.								
8.								

Determining how transactions change an accounting equation

Trans. No.	Assets				= Liabilities +	Owner's Equity
	Cash	Accts. Rec.— + O'Leary Co. +	Supplies +	Prepaid Insurance =	Accts. Pay.— Barrett Co. +	Sue Marist, Capital
1.		+				+
2.	−					−
3.	+					+
4.	+	−				

Extra form

Trans. No.	Assets				= Liabilities +	Owner's Equity
	Cash +	+	Supplies +	Prepaid Insurance =	+	
1.						
2.						
3.						
4.						
5.						
6.						
7.						
8.						

2-2 WORK TOGETHER, p. 31

Preparing a balance sheet

Marier Company
Balance Sheet
Oct 31, 2007

Assets		Liabilities	
Cash	7733 00	A/P - Alvarez Co.	250 00
Accts. Rec. - Poole Co.	5000 00	Owner's Equity	
Supplies	800 00	Joel Marier, Capital	15683 00
Prepaid Insurance	2400 00		
Total Assets	15933 00	Total Liabilts & Owners Eq.	15933 00

Extra form

Preparing a balance sheet

Lynum Company
Balance Sheet
Dec 31, 2008

Assets			Liabilities		
Cash	5400 00		Accts. Pay. - Kelly Co.	2250 00	
Accts. Rec. - Meyer Co.	600 00		Owner's Equity	5900 00	
Supplies	350 00		Tanya Lynum, Capital	5900 00	
Prepaid Insurance	1800 00				
Total Assets	8150 00		Total Liabilities & Owners Eq.	8150 00	

Extra form

Name _____ Date _____ Class _____

Determining how revenue, expense, and withdrawal transactions change an accounting equation

Trans. No.	Assets				= Liabilities	+ Owner's Equity
	Cash	+ Accts. Rec.—Lisa Lee	+ Supplies	+ Prepaid Insurance	= Accts. Pay.—Kline Co.	+ Peter Smith, Capital
Beg. Bal. 1.	625 −300	–0–	375	300	200	1,100 −300 (expense)
New Bal. 2.	325 −150	–0–	375	300	200	800 −150 (draw)
New Bal. 3.	175 +800	0	375	300	200	650 +800 (revenue)
New Bal. 4.	975 −100	0	375	300	200	1450 −100 (expense)
New Bal. 5.	875	0 +400	375	300	200	1350 +400 (revenue)
New Bal. 6.	875 +650	400	375	300	200	1750 +650 (revenue)
New Bal. 7.	1525 −35	400	375	300	200	2400 −35 (expense)
New Bal. 8.	1490 +300	400 −300	375	300	200	2365
New Bal.	1790	100	375	300	200	2365

Extra form

Trans. No.	Assets				= Liabilities	+ Owner's Equity
	Cash	+	+ Supplies	+ Prepaid Insurance	=	+
Beg. Bal. 1.						
New Bal. 2.						
New Bal. 3.						
New Bal. 4.						
New Bal. 5.						
New Bal. 6.						
New Bal.						

Extra form

Trans. No.	Assets					=	Liabilities	+	Owner's Equity
	Cash	+		+	Supplies	+	Prepaid Insurance	=	+
Beg. Bal. 1.									
New Bal. 2.									
New Bal. 3.									
New Bal. 4.									
New Bal. 5.									
New Bal. 6.									
New Bal. 7.									
New Bal. 8.									
New Bal. 9.									
New Bal. 10.									
New Bal. 11.									
New Bal. 12.									
New Bal. 13.									
New Bal. 14.									
New Bal. 15.									
New Bal.									

2-2 APPLICATION PROBLEM, p. 34

Determining how transactions change an accounting equation

Trans. No.	Assets				= Liabilities	+ Owner's Equity
	Cash +	Accts. Rec.—Suburban Rental +	Supplies +	Prepaid Insurance =	Accts. Pay.—Teale Co. +	Doris Becker, Capital
Beg. Bal. 1.	500 −50	−0−	260	300	100	960 −50 (expense)
New Bal. 2.	450 +325	−0−	260	300	100	910 +325 (revenue)
New Bal. 3.	775 −200	0	260 +200	300	100	1235 −200 (expense)
New Bal. 4.	575	0	260 +1200	300	100 +1200	1035
New Bal. 5.	575 −200	0	1460	300	1300	1035 −200 (expense)
New Bal. 6.	375 +280	0	1460	300	1300	835 +280 (revenue)
New Bal. 7.	655 −60	0	1460	300	1300	1115 −10 (expense)
New Bal. 8.	595	0 +320	1460	300	1300	1055 +320 (revenue)
New Bal. 9.	595 −125	320	1460	300	1300	1375 −125 (draw)
New Bal. 10.	470 +250	320 −250	1460	300	1300	1250
New Bal. 11.	720 −100	70	1460	300	1300 −100	1250
New Bal. 12.	620 +1000	70	1460	300	1200	1250 +1000 (capital contr.)
New Bal.	1620	70	1460	300	1200	2250 ?
	1660					2450

Extra form

Trans. No.	Assets				= Liabilities	+ Owner's Equity
	Cash +	+	Supplies +	Prepaid Insurance =		+
Beg. Bal. 1.						
New Bal. 2.						
New Bal. 3.						
New Bal. 4.						
New Bal. 5.						
New Bal. 6.						
New Bal. 7.						
New Bal. 8.						
New Bal. 9.						
New Bal. 10.						
New Bal. 11.						
New Bal. 12.						
New Bal. 13.						
New Bal. 14.						
New Bal. 15.						
New Bal.						

2-3 APPLICATION PROBLEM, p. 35

Preparing a balance sheet

Balance Sheet
Heil Company
June 30, 2008

Assets		Liabilities	
Cash	8655 00	A/P-Franco Supplies	665 00
A/R – Jana Friested	942 00	Owner's Equity	
Supplies	475 00	Kevin Heil, Capital	10157 00
Prepaid Insurance	750 00		
Total Assets	10822 00	Total Liabilities / Owner's Eq	10822 00

Extra form

2-4 MASTERY PROBLEM, p. 35

Determining how transactions change an accounting equation and preparing a balance sheet

1.

Trans. No.	Assets				= Liabilities +	Owner's Equity
	Cash	+ Accts. Rec.— + Dorothy Romano	Supplies +	Prepaid Insurance	= Accts. Pay.— Sickle Co. +	Mikaela Mundt, Capital
Beg. Bal. 1.	1,400 −100	–0–	300	400	1,500	600 −100 (expense)
New Bal. 2.	1,300 +200	–0–	300	400	1,500	500 +200 (cap. contr. ?)
New Bal. 3.	1500 -500	0	300	400	1500	700 -500 (expense)
New Bal. 4.	1000 +895	0	300	400	1500	200 +895 (revenue)
New Bal. 5.	1895	0	300 +600	400	1500 +600	1095
New Bal. 6.	1895	0 +920	900	400	2100	1095 +920 (revenue)
New Bal. 7.	1895 -400	920	900 +400	400	2100	2015
New Bal. 8.	1495 -250	920	1300	400	2100	2015 -250 (expense)
New Bal. 9.	1245 +800	920 -800	1300	400	2100	1765
New Bal. 10.	2045 -1500	120	1300	400	2100 -1500	1765
New Bal. 11.	545 -250	120	1300	400 +250	600	1765
New Bal. 12.	295 +1960	120	1300	650	600	1765 +1960 (revenue)
New Bal. 13.	2255 -1000	120	1300	650	600	3725 -1000 (draw)
New Bal.	1255	120	1300	650	600	2725

2.

Balance Sheet
Mundt Company
April 30, 2008

Assets		Liabilities	
Cash	1255 00	A/P - Sickle Co.	600 00
A/R - Dorothy Romano	120 00	Owner's Equity	
Supplies	1300 00	Mikaela Mundt, Capital	2725 00
Prepaid Insurance	650 00		
Total Assets	3325 00	Total Liabilities / Owner's Eq.	3325 00

Extra form

2-5 CHALLENGE PROBLEM, p. 36

Determining how transactions change an accounting equation

1.

Trans. No.	Assets				= Liabilities +	Owner's Equity
	Cash	Accts. Rec.— + Mary Lou Pier +	Supplies +	Prepaid Insurance	Accts. Pay.— = Kollasch Co. +	Zachary Martin, Capital
Beg. Bal. 1.	8,552	1,748	1,485 -400	615	3,145	9,255 -400 (draw)
New Bal. 2.	8552	1748	1085	615	3145 +250	8855 -250 (expense)
New Bal. 3.	8552	1748	1085	615	3395	8605
New Bal. 4.	8552 -120	1748	1085	615	3395 -120	8605
New Bal.	8432	1748	1085	615	3275	8605

2.

_____

_____

_____

_____

_____

_____

_____

_____

_____

_____

_____

_____

_____

_____

_____

_____

_____

Extra form

Trans. No.	Assets				= Liabilities +	Owner's Equity
	Cash +	+	Supplies +	Prepaid Insurance =	+	
Beg. Bal. 1.						
New Bal. 2.						
New Bal. 3.						
New Bal. 4.						
New Bal. 5.						
New Bal. 6.						
New Bal. 7.						
New Bal. 8.						
New Bal. 9.						
New Bal. 10.						
New Bal. 11.						
New Bal. 12.						
New Bal. 13.						
New Bal. 14.						
New Bal. 15.						
New Bal.						

3-1 WORK TOGETHER, p. 44

Determining the normal balance, increase, and decrease sides for accounts

Cash

DR	CR
↑ NB	↓

A/R

DR	CR
↑ NB	↓

Supplies

DR	CR
↑ NB	↓

Prepaid Insurance

DR	CR
↑ NB	↓

A/P – Miller Supplies

DR	CR
↓	NB ↑

A/P – Wayne Office Supplies

DR	CR
↓	NB ↑

Jeff Dixon, Capital

DR	CR
↓	NB ↑

Extra forms

Determining the normal balance, increase, and decrease sides for accounts

Cash	
DR	CR
↑ NB	↓

Prepaid Ins.	
DR	CR
↑ NB	↓

A/R – Brianlee	
DR	CR
↑ NB	↓

A/P – Golf Tees	
DR	CR
↓	NB ↑

Supplies	
DR	CR
↑ NB	↓

Vickie Haskins, Capital	
DR	CR
↓	NB ↑

Extra forms

3-2 WORK TOGETHER, p. 50

Analyzing a transaction into its debit and credit parts

April

1. Cash	1. Kathy Bergum, Capital
5000	5000

2. Cash	2. Supplies
50	50

5. Cash	5. Prepaid Ins.
75	75

6. Supplies	6. A/P – Bales Supplies
100	100

9. Cash	9. A/P – Bales Supplies
50	50

Extra forms

Analyzing a transaction into its debit and credit parts

Sept.

1.

Cash	
DR	CR
3000	

1.

Jens Puckett, Capital	
DB	CR
	3000

4.

Cash	
	100

4.

Prepaid Ins.	
100	

5.

Cash	
	90

5.

Supplies	
90	

6.

Supplies	
200	

6.

A/P – Computer Supply	
	200

11.

Cash	
	150

11.

A/P – Computer Supply	
150	

Extra forms

3-3 WORK TOGETHER, p. 56

Analyzing revenue, expense, and withdrawal transactions into debit and credit parts

April

10.	Cash		10.	Sales
	600			600

11.	A/R – Sam Erickson		11.	Sales
	850			850

14.	Cash		14.	Rent Expense
		250		250

18.	Cash		18.	A/R – Sam Erickson
	425			425

20.	Cash		20.	Kathy Bergen, Drawing
		300		300

Extra forms

Analyzing revenue, expense, and withdrawal transactions into debit and credit parts

Sept.

13.	Cash		13.	Sales
	1000			1000

15.	A/R - King Company		15.	Sales
	~~1000~~ 1500			~~1000~~ 1500

16.	Cash		16.	Utilities Expense
		500		500

18.	Cash		18.	A/R - King Company
	750			750

21.	Cash		21.	Jens Puckett, Drawing
		650		650

Extra forms

3-1 APPLICATION PROBLEM, p. 58

Test

Determining the normal balance, increase, and decrease sides for accounts

	1	2	3	4	5	6	7	8
	Account	Account Classification	Account's Normal Balance		Increase Side		Decrease Side	
			Debit	Credit	Debit	Credit	Debit	Credit
Cash	Asset	✔		✔				✔
A/R - Laurie Menz	Asset	✓		✓				✓
Supplies	Asset	✓		✓				✓
Prepaid Ins	Asset	✓		✓				✓
A/P - Comrcl B/s	Liability		✓		✓	✓		
A/P - Van Dyke Co.	Liability		✓		✓	✓		
Vivian Marx, Capital	Owner's Eq		✓		✓	✓		

Extra form

1	2	3	4	5	6	7	8
Account	Account Classification	Account's Normal Balance		Increase Side		Decrease Side	
		Debit	Credit	Debit	Credit	Debit	Credit

3-2 APPLICATION PROBLEM, p. 58

Analyzing transactions into debit and credit parts

March

1.

Cash	
1,500.00	

John Burke, Capital	
	1,500.00

March

1.

Cash	
600.00	

Prepaid Insurance	
600.00	

March

3.

A/P – D&S Co.	
800.00	

Supplies ~~John Burke, Capital~~	
800.00	

March

5.

Cash	
	200.00

Supplies	
200.00	

March

8.

Cash	
	400.00

A/P – D&S Co.	
400.00	

Extra forms

3-3 APPLICATION PROBLEM, p. 59

Analyzing revenue, expense, and withdrawal transactions into debit and credit parts

March

11.

Cash	
2200.00	

John Burke, Capital	
	2200.00

March

12.

Cash	
	150.00

Advertising Expense	
150.00	

March

14.

A/R - Oru Grant	
1700.00	

John Burke, Capital	
	1700.00

March

18.

Cash	
	500.00

John Burke, Drawing	
500.00	

March

19.

A/R - Oru Grant	
~~1000.00~~	1000.00

Cash	
1000.00	

Extra forms

3-4 APPLICATION PROBLEM, p. 59

Analyzing revenue, expense, and withdrawal transactions into debit and credit parts

March 25.

Cash	
900.00	

Sales	
	900.00

March 26.

A/R – Orv Grant	
750.00	

Sales	
	750.00

March 27.

Advertising Expense	
25.00	

Cash	
	25.00

March 28.

Cash	
	450.00

John Durke, Capital	
	450.00

March 29.

Cash	
375.00	

A/R – Orv Grant	
	375.00

Extra forms

3-5 MASTERY PROBLEM, p. 60

Analyzing transactions into debit and credit parts

CASH

(1) 3000.00	
(4) 350.00	(2) 60.00
(11) 900.00	(4) 200.00
(11) 300.00	(5) 10.00
(13) 125.00	(10) 100.00
(30) 100.00	(15) 5.00
	(16) 50.00
	(22) 35.00
	(23) 30.00
	(26) 600.00

Mark Lands, Capital

	(1) 3000.00
	(11) 900.00

Rent Expense

(4) 200.00	

Supplies

(2) 60.00	
(9) 500.00	
(12) 50.00	

Sales

	(4) 350.00
	(8) 200.00
	(11) 300.00
	(25) 220.00

A/R – Joe Corbett

(8) 200.00	(13) 125.00

Repair Expense

(5) 10.00	

A/P – Janitor Supplies

(16) 50.00	(9) 500.00

Prepaid Insurance

(10) 100.00	

A/P – Dorner Office Supplies

	(12) 50.00

Misc. Expense

(15) 5.00	

Utilities Expense

(22) 35.00	

Advertising Expense

(23) 30.00	

A/R – Vera Rice

(25) 220.00	(30) 100.00

Mark Lands, Drawing

(26) 600.00	

Extra forms

Name _____ Date _____ Class _____

3-6 CHALLENGE PROBLEM, p. 61

Analyzing transactions recorded in T accounts

1	2	3	4	5	6
Trans. No.	Accounts Affected	Account Classification	Entered in Account as a		Description of Transaction
			Debit	Credit	
1.	Cash	Asset	✔		Received cash from owner as an investment
	Carol Burns, Capital	Owner's Equity		✔	
2.	Cash	Asset	✔		Cash to owner for personal use
	Carol Burns, Drawing	Owner's Equity		✔	
3.	Supplies	Asset	✔		Paid cash Bought supplies on account
	A/P – Midwest Supplies	Liability		✔	
4.	Cash	Asset		✔	Cash for Misc. Expense
	Misc Expense	Owners Eq.	✔		
5.					
6.					
7.					
8.					
9.					
10.					
11.					
12.					
13.					

Extra form

1	2	3	4	5	6
Trans. No.	Accounts Affected	Account Classification	Entered in Account as a		Description of Transaction
			Debit	Credit	
1.					
2.					
3.					
4.					
5.					
6.					
7.					
8.					
9.					
10.					
11.					
12.					
13.					

Name _____ Date _____ Class _____

4-1 Journalizing entries into a general journal
4-2 Journalizing entries into a general journal
4-3 Journalizing transactions that affect owner's equity into a general journal
4-4 Journalizing transactions and starting a new general journal page

GENERAL JOURNAL   PAGE 1

	DATE 2007	ACCOUNT TITLE	DOC. NO.	POST. REF.	DEBIT	CREDIT	
1	Apr 1	Cash	R1		7 0 0 0 00		1
2		Ruth Muldoon, Capital				7 0 0 0 00	2
3	2	Supplies	C1		4 2 5 00		3
4		Cash				4 2 5 00	4
5	5	Supplies	M1		3 0 0 00		5
6		A/P - Ron's Supplies				3 0 0 00	6
7	7	Prepaid Insurance	C2		6 0 0 00		7
8		Cash				6 0 0 00	8
9	9	Accts. Pay - Ron's Supplies	C3		3 0 0 00		9
10		Cash				3 0 0 00	10
11	12	Rent Expenses	C4		9 5 0 00		11
12		Cash				9 5 0 00	12
13	13	Cash	T13		2 2 0 0 00		13
14		Sales				2 2 0 0 00	14
15	14	A/R - Lester Dodge	S1		6 2 5 00		15
16		Sales				6 2 5 00	16
17	A	Utilities Expense	C5		1 5 7 00		17
18		Cash				1 5 7 00	18
19	20	Cash	R2		3 0 0 00		19
20		A/R - Lester Dodge				3 0 0 00	20
21	21	Ruth Muldoon, Capital	C6		1 4 0 0 00		21
22		Cash				1 4 0 0 00	22
23	22	Utilities Expense	C7		1 5 0 00		23
24		Cash				1 5 0 00	24
25	23	A/R - Lester Dodge	S2		3 1 7 00		25
26		Sales				3 1 7 00	26
27	26	Cash	T26		1 5 6 0 00		27
28		Sales				1 5 6 0 00	28
29	27	Ruth Muldoon, Capital Drawing	C8		7 5 0 00		29
30		Cash				7 5 0 00	30
31	27	Supplies	C9		2 4 00		31
32		Cash				2 4 00	32
33	27	Miscellaneous Expenses	40		3 5 00		33
34		Cash				3 5 00	34

GENERAL JOURNAL   PAGE 2

	DATE	ACCOUNT TITLE	DOC. NO.	POST. REF.	DEBIT	CREDIT	
1	29	Cash	R3		75 00		1
2		A/R – Lester Dodge				75 00	2
3	30	Cash	T30		743 00		3
4		Sales				743 00	4
5							5
6							6
7							7
8							8
9							9
10							10
11							11
12							12
13							13
14							14
15							15
16							16
17							17
18							18
19							19
20							20
21							21
22							22
23							23
24							24
25							25
26							26
27							27
28							28
29							29
30							30
31							31
32							32
33							33
34							34

4-1, 4-2, 4-3, and 4-4 ON YOUR OWN, pp. 71, 75, 81, 85

4-1 Journalizing entries into a general journal
4-2 Journalizing entries into a general journal
4-3 Journalizing transactions that affect owner's equity into a general journal
4-4 Journalizing transactions and starting a new general journal page

GENERAL JOURNAL   PAGE 1

	DATE 20--	ACCOUNT TITLE	DOC. NO.	POST. REF.	DEBIT	CREDIT	
1	Jun 2	Cash	R1		1500.00		1
2		Gale Klein, Capital				1500.00	2
3	3	Supplies	C1		35.00		3
4		Cash				35.00	4
5	5	Prepaid Insurance	C2		100.00		5
6		Cash				100.00	6
7	9	Supplies	M1		155.00		7
8		A/P – Osamu Supply Co.				155.00	8
9	10	A/P – Osamu Supply Co.	C3		155.00		9
10		Cash				155.00	10
11	11	Rent Expense	C4		200.00		11
12		Cash				200.00	12
13	12	A/R – Connie Vaughn	S1		200.00		13
14		Sales				200.00	14
15	16	Cash	T16		1050.00		15
16		Sales				1050.00	16
17	17	Miscellaneous Expense	C5		32.00		17
18		Cash				32.00	18
19	19	Cash	R2		100.00		19
20		A/R – Connie Vaughn				100.00	20
21	20	Gale Klein, Drawing	C6		250.00		21
22		Cash				250.00	22
23	23	A/R – Connie Vaughn	S2		135.00		23
24		Sales				135.00	24
25	24	Advertising Expense	C7		48.00		25
26		Cash				48.00	26
27	25	Cash	T25		850.00		27
28		Sales				850.00	28
29	26	Miscellaneous Expense	C8		17.00		29
30		Cash				17.00	30
31	26	Cash	R3		100.00		31
32		A/R – Connie Vaughn				100.00	32
33	26	Miscellaneous Expense	C9		15.00		33
34		Cash				15.00	34

GENERAL JOURNAL

PAGE 2

	DATE	ACCOUNT TITLE	DOC. NO.	POST. REF.	DEBIT	CREDIT	
1	27	Supplies	C10		21 00		1
2		Cash				21 00	2
3	30	Cash	T30		235 00		3
4		Sales				235 00	4
5							5
6							6
7							7
8							8
9							9
10							10
11							11
12							12
13							13
14							14
15							15
16							16
17							17
18							18
19							19
20							20
21							21
22							22
23							23
24							24
25							25
26							26
27							27
28							28
29							29
30							30
31							31
32							32
33							33
34							34

4-1, 4-2, 4-3, and 4-4   APPLICATION PROBLEMS, pp. 87, 88

4-1 Journalizing transactions into a general journal
4-2 Journalizing buying insurance, buying on account, and paying on account into a general journal
4-3 Journalizing transactions that affect owner's equity into a general journal
4-4 Journalizing transactions and starting a new page of a general journal

GENERAL JOURNAL   PAGE 1

	DATE 20--	ACCOUNT TITLE	DOC. NO.	POST. REF.	DEBIT	CREDIT	
1	Feb 1	Cash	R1		10 000 00		1
2		Dennis Filbert, Capital				10 000 00	2
3	4	Supplies	C1		1 000 00		3
4		Cash				1 000 00	4
5	6	Prepaid Insurance	C2		1 200 00		5
6		Cash				1 200 00	6
7	7	Supplies	M1		1 400 00		7
8		A/P - Rankin Supplies				1 400 00	8
9	8	A/P - Rankin Supplies	C3		700 00		9
10		Cash				700 00	10
11	12	A/P - Rankin Supplies	C4		700 00		11
12		Cash				700 00	12
13	12	Rent Expense	C5		600 00		13
14		Cash				600 00	14
15	13	Cash	T13		500 00		15
16		Sales				500 00	16
17	14	A/R - Hetland Company	S1		450 00		17
18		Sales				450 00	18
19	15	Dennis Filbert, Drawing	C6		1 800 00		19
20		Cash				1 800 00	20
21	18	Cash	T18		278 00		21
22		Sales				278 00	22
23	19	Miscellaneous Expense	C7		64 00		23
24		Cash				64 00	24
25	21	Cash	R2		250 00		25
26		A/R - Hetland Company				250 00	26
27	22	Cash	T22		342 00		27
28		Sales				342 00	28
29	22	Utilities Expense	C8		329 00		29
30		Cash				329 00	30
31	25	Cash	R3		200 00		31
32		A/R - Hetland Company				200 00	32
33	25	Miscellaneous Expense			18 00		33
34		Cash				18 00	34

GENERAL JOURNAL PAGE 2

	DATE	ACCOUNT TITLE	DOC. NO.	POST. REF.	DEBIT	CREDIT	
1	26	A/R - Holland Company	52		1 3 6 00		1
2		Sales				1 3 6 00	2
3	26	Supplies	C10		4 4 00		3
4		Cash				4 4 00	4
5	27	Rent Expense	C11		6 0 0 00		5
6		Cash				6 0 0 00	6
7	27	Miscellaneous Expense	C12		1 0 00		7
8		Cash				1 0 00	8
9	28	Cash	T28		1 3 6 5 00		9
10		Sales				1 3 6 5 00	10
11	28	Dennis Gilbert, Drawing	C13		1 0 0 0 00		11
12		Cash				1 0 0 0 00	12
13							13
14							14
15							15
16							16
17							17
18							18
19							19
20							20
21							21
22							22
23							23
24							24
25							25
26							26
27							27
28							28
29							29
30							30
31							31
32							32
33							33
34							34

4-5 APPLICATION PROBLEM, p. 88

Journalizing transactions

GENERAL JOURNAL   PAGE   1

	DATE 20--		ACCOUNT TITLE	DOC. NO.	POST. REF.	DEBIT	CREDIT	
1	Apr	1						1
2								2
3								3
4								4
5								5
6								6
7								7
8								8
9								9
10								10
11								11
12								12
13								13
14								14
15								15
16								16
17								17
18								18
19								19
20								20
21								21
22								22
23								23
24								24
25								25
26								26
27								27
28								28
29								29
30								30
31								31
32								32
33								33

Extra form

GENERAL JOURNAL

PAGE

	DATE		ACCOUNT TITLE	DOC. NO.	POST. REF.	DEBIT	CREDIT	
1								1
2								2
3								3
4								4
5								5
6								6
7								7
8								8
9								9
10								10
11								11
12								12
13								13
14								14
15								15
16								16
17								17
18								18
19								19
20								20
21								21
22								22
23								23
24								24
25								25
26								26
27								27
28								28
29								29
30								30
31								31
32								32
33								33

4-6 MASTERY PROBLEM, p. 89

Journalizing transactions

GENERAL JOURNAL   PAGE 1

	DATE 2008		ACCOUNT TITLE	DOC. NO.	POST. REF.	DEBIT	CREDIT	
1	Jun	1	Cash	R1		17 500 00		1
2			Jill Statsholt, Capital				17 500 00	2
3		2	Rent Expense	C1		400 00		3
4			Cash				400 00	4
5		3	Supplies	C2		1 200 00		5
6			Cash				1 200 00	6
7		4	Supplies	M1		2 000 00		7
8			A/P - Akita Supplies				2 000 00	8
9		5	Prepaid Insurance	C3		4 500 00		9
10			Cash				4 500 00	10
11		8	A/P - Akita Supplies	C4		1 500 00		11
12			Cash				1 500 00	12
13		8	Cash	T8		750 00		13
14			Sales				750 00	14
15		8	A/R - David's Limos	S1		200 00		15
16			Sales				200 00	16
17		9	Utilities Expense	C5		75 00		17
18			Cash				75 00	18
19		10	Miscellaneous Expense	C6		7 00		19
20			Cash				7 00	20
21		10	Cash	T10		750 00		21
22			Sales				750 00	22
23		11	Repair Expense	C7		100 00		23
24			Cash				100 00	24
25		11	Cash	T11		850 00		25
26			Sales				850 00	26
27		12	Cash	T12		700 00		27
28			Sales				700 00	28
29		15	Jill Statsholt, Drawing	C8		350 00		29
30			Cash				350 00	30
31		15	Cash	T15		750 00		31
32			Sales				750 00	32
33		16	Supplies	C9		1 500 00		33
34			Cash				1 500 00	34

GENERAL JOURNAL   PAGE 2

	DATE	ACCOUNT TITLE	DOC. NO.	POST. REF.	DEBIT	CREDIT	
1	17	Cash	R2		200 00		1
2		A/R - David's Limos				200 00	2
3	17	Supplies	M2		750 00		3
4		A/P - Long Supplies				750 00	4
5	17	Cash	T17		600 00		5
6		Sales				600 00	6
7	18	Cash	T18		800 00		7
8		Sales				800 00	8
9	19	Cash	T19		750 00		9
10		Sales				750 00	10
11	22	Supplies	M3		80 00		11
12		A/P - Long Supplies				80 00	12
13	22	Cash	T22		700 00		13
14		Sales				700 00	14
15	23	Advertising Expense	C10		130 00		15
16		Cash				130 00	16
17	23	A/R - David's Limos	S2		650 00		17
18		Sales				650 00	18
19	24	Utility Expense	C11		60 00		19
20		Cash				60 00	20
21	24	Cash	T24		600 00		21
22		Sales				600 00	22
23	25	Cash	T25		550 00		23
24		Sales				550 00	24
25	26	Supplies	C12		70 00		25
26		Cash				70 00	26
27	26	Cash	T26		600 00		27
28		Sales				600 00	28
29	29	Cash	R3		650 00		29
30		A/R - David's Limos				650 00	30
31	30	Jill Stetsholt, Drawing	C13		375 00		31
32		Cash				375 00	32
33	30	Cash	T30		800 00		33
34		Sales				800 00	34

4-7 CHALLENGE PROBLEM, p. 90

Journalizing transactions using a variation of the general journal

GENERAL JOURNAL

PAGE 1

	DEBIT		DATE 2008		ACCOUNT TITLE	DOC. NO.	POST. REF.	CREDIT	
1	17 0 0 0 00	Jan	1	Cash	R1			1
2				Tony Wirth, Capital			17 0 0 0 00	2
3	3 0 0 0 00		2	Prepaid Insurance	C1			3
4				Cash			3 0 0 0 00	4
5	2 5 0 0 00		3	Supplies	M1			5
6				A/P - Marker Supplies			2 5 0 0 00	6
7	1 4 0 0 00		4	Supplies	C2			7
8				Cash			1 4 0 0 00	8
9	1 3 0 0 00		8	A/P - Marker Supplies	C3			9
10				Cash			1 3 0 0 00	10
11	8 0 0 00		9	Rent Expense	C4			11
12				Cash			8 0 0 00	12
13	5 5 0 00		12	Cash	T12			13
14				Sales			5 5 0 00	14
15	3 0 0 00		15	A/R - Amy's Uniforms	S1			15
16				Sales			3 0 0 00	16
17	7 0 00		16	Utilities Expense	C5			17
18				Cash			7 0 00	18
19	3 0 0 00		22	Cash	R2			19
20				A/R - Amy's Uniforms			3 0 0 00	20
21	9 0 0 00		25	Tony Wirth, Drawing	C6			21
22				Cash			9 0 0 00	22
23								23
24								24
25								25
26								26
27								27
28								28
29								29
30								30
31								31
32								32
33								33

Extra form

GENERAL JOURNAL

PAGE

	DEBIT		DATE		ACCOUNT TITLE	DOC. NO.	POST. REF.	CREDIT		
1										1
2										2
3										3
4										4
5										5
6										6
7										7
8										8
9										9
10										10
11										11
12										12
13										13
14										14
15										15
16										16
17										17
18										18
19										19
20										20
21										21
22										22
23										23
24										24
25										25
26										26
27										27
28										28
29										29
30										30
31										31
32										32
33										33

5-1 WORK TOGETHER, p. 100

Preparing a chart of accounts and opening an account

3.

Roseman Services
Chart of Accounts

Balance Sheet Accounts	Income Statement Accounts
(100) Assets	(400) Revenue
110 Cash	410 Sales
120 A/R - Amber Jorgenson	(500) Expenses
130 A/R - Tyler Cobb	510 Automobile Expense
140 Supplies	520 Insurance Expense
150 Prepaid Insurance	530 Miscellaneous Expense
(200) Liabilities	540 Rent Expense
210 A/P - Campbell Office Supplies	
220 A/P - Kammerer Supplies	
(300) Owner's Equity	
310 Clara Roseman, Capital	
320 Clara Roseman, Drawing	

4.

New Accounts

Account No.	Account Title
515	Gasoline Expense
550	Utilities Expense

5.

ACCOUNT **Cash**   ACCOUNT NO. **110**

DATE	ITEM	POST. REF.	DEBIT	CREDIT	BALANCE DEBIT	BALANCE CREDIT

Preparing a chart of accounts and opening an account

6.

_____
_____
_____
_____
_____
_____
_____
_____
_____
_____
_____
_____
_____

7.

_____
_____
_____
_____
_____
_____
_____
_____

8.

ACCOUNT   ACCOUNT NO.

DATE	ITEM	POST. REF.	DEBIT	CREDIT	BALANCE	
					DEBIT	CREDIT

5-2 WORK TOGETHER, p. 105

Posting to a general ledger

GENERAL JOURNAL
PAGE 1

	DATE		ACCOUNT TITLE	DOC. NO.	POST. REF.	DEBIT	CREDIT	
1	Mar.	1	Cash	R1	110	5 0 0 0 00		1
2			Leonard Witkowski, Capital		310		5 0 0 0 00	2
3		3	Prepaid Insurance	C1	140	6 6 0 00		3
4			Cash		110		6 6 0 00	4
5		4	Supplies	M1	130	7 8 00		5
6			Accounts Payable—Joshua's Supplies		210		7 8 00	6
7		8	Cash	T8	110	6 7 5 00		7
8			Sales		410		6 7 5 00	8
9		9	Accounts Receivable—Danielle Braastad	S1	120	1 6 3 00		9
10			Sales		410		1 6 3 00	10
11		12	Rent Expense	C2	510	3 7 5 00		11
12			Cash		110		3 7 5 00	12
13		15	Accounts Payable—Joshua's Supplies	C3	210	5 0 00		13
14			Cash		110		5 0 00	14
15		16	Cash	R2	110	1 0 0 00		15
16			Accounts Receivable—Danielle Braastad		120		1 0 0 00	16
17		25	Leonard Witkowski, Drawing	C4	320	1 0 0 0 00		17
18			Cash		110		1 0 0 0 00	18
19								19
20								20
21								21
22								22
23								23
24								24
25								25
26								26
27								27
28								28
29								29
30								30
31								31
32								32
33								33

Extra form

GENERAL JOURNAL

PAGE

	DATE		ACCOUNT TITLE	DOC. NO.	POST. REF.	DEBIT	CREDIT	
1								1
2								2
3								3
4								4
5								5
6								6
7								7
8								8
9								9
10								10
11								11
12								12
13								13
14								14
15								15
16								16
17								17
18								18
19								19
20								20
21								21
22								22
23								23
24								24
25								25
26								26
27								27
28								28
29								29
30								30
31								31
32								32
33								33

5-2 WORK TOGETHER (continued)

GENERAL LEDGER

ACCOUNT Cash   ACCOUNT NO. 110

DATE 2007	ITEM	POST. REF.	DEBIT	CREDIT	BALANCE DEBIT	BALANCE CREDIT
Mar 1		G1	5000 00		5000 00	
3		G1		660 00	4340 00	
8		G1	675 00		5015 00	
12		G1		375 00	4640 00	
15		G1		50 00	4590 00	
16		G1	100 00		4690 00	
25		G1		1000 00	3690 00	

ACCOUNT Accounts Receivable—Danielle Braastad   ACCOUNT NO. 120

DATE 2007	ITEM	POST. REF.	DEBIT	CREDIT	BALANCE DEBIT	BALANCE CREDIT
Mar 9		G1	163 00		163 00	
16		G1		100 00	63 00	

ACCOUNT Supplies   ACCOUNT NO. 130

DATE	ITEM	POST. REF.	DEBIT	CREDIT	BALANCE DEBIT	BALANCE CREDIT
Mar 4		G1	78 00		78 00	

ACCOUNT Prepaid Insurance   ACCOUNT NO. 140

DATE 2007	ITEM	POST. REF.	DEBIT	CREDIT	BALANCE DEBIT	BALANCE CREDIT
Mar 3		G1	660 00		660 00	

GENERAL LEDGER

ACCOUNT Accounts Payable—Joshua's Supplies   ACCOUNT NO. 210

DATE 2007	ITEM	POST. REF.	DEBIT	CREDIT	BALANCE DEBIT	BALANCE CREDIT
Mar 4		G1		78 00		78 00
15		G1	50 00			28 00

ACCOUNT Leonard Witkowski, Capital   ACCOUNT NO. 310

DATE 2007	ITEM	POST. REF.	DEBIT	CREDIT	BALANCE DEBIT	BALANCE CREDIT
Mar 1		G1		5 000 00		5 000 00

ACCOUNT Leonard Witkowski, Drawing   ACCOUNT NO. 320

DATE 2007	ITEM	POST. REF.	DEBIT	CREDIT	BALANCE DEBIT	BALANCE CREDIT
Mar 25		G1	1 000 00		1 000 00	

ACCOUNT Sales   ACCOUNT NO. 410

DATE 2007	ITEM	POST. REF.	DEBIT	CREDIT	BALANCE DEBIT	BALANCE CREDIT
Mar 8		G1		675 00		675 00
9		G1		163 00		838 00

ACCOUNT Rent Expense   ACCOUNT NO. 510

DATE 2007	ITEM	POST. REF.	DEBIT	CREDIT	BALANCE DEBIT	BALANCE CREDIT
Mar 12		G1	375 00		375 00	

Name _____ Date _____ Class _____

Posting to a general ledger

GENERAL JOURNAL   PAGE 1

	DATE		ACCOUNT TITLE	DOC. NO.	POST. REF.	DEBIT	CREDIT	
1	Sept.	1	Cash	R1	110	2 5 0 0 00		1
2			Melanie Komoko, Capital		310		2 5 0 0 00	2
3		4	Supplies	M1	130	6 7 00		3
4			Accounts Payable—Signs Plus		210		6 7 00	4
5		7	Prepaid Insurance	C1	140	3 3 3 00		5
6			Cash		110		3 3 3 00	6
7		10	Accounts Receivable—Brenden Otto	S1	120	1 9 5 00		7
8			Sales		410		1 9 5 00	8
9		13	Cash	T13	110	1 1 0 0 00		9
10			Sales		410		1 1 0 0 00	10
11		18	Utilities Expense	C2	510	4 9 00		11
12			Cash		110		4 9 00	12
13		21	Accounts Payable—Signs Plus	C3	210	3 5 00		13
14			Cash		110		3 5 00	14
15		27	Cash	R2	110	1 0 0 00		15
16			Accounts Receivable—Brenden Otto		120		1 0 0 00	16
17		30	Melanie Komoko, Drawing	C4	320	3 0 0 00		17
18			Cash		110		3 0 0 00	18
19								19
20								20
21								21
22								22
23								23
24								24
25								25
26								26
27								27
28								28
29								29
30								30
31								31
32								32
33								33

Extra form

GENERAL JOURNAL PAGE

	DATE		ACCOUNT TITLE	DOC. NO.	POST. REF.	DEBIT	CREDIT	
1								1
2								2
3								3
4								4
5								5
6								6
7								7
8								8
9								9
10								10
11								11
12								12
13								13
14								14
15								15
16								16
17								17
18								18
19								19
20								20
21								21
22								22
23								23
24								24
25								25
26								26
27								27
28								28
29								29
30								30
31								31
32								32
33								33

5-2 ON YOUR OWN (continued)

GENERAL LEDGER

ACCOUNT Cash   ACCOUNT NO. 110

DATE 2007	ITEM	POST. REF.	DEBIT	CREDIT	BALANCE DEBIT	BALANCE CREDIT
Sep 1		G1	2500 00		2500 00	
7		G1		333 00	2167 00	
13		G1	1100 00		3267 00	
18		G1		49 00	3218 00	
21		G1		35 00	3183 00	
27		G1	100 00		3283 00	
30		G1		300 00	2983 00	

ACCOUNT Accounts Receivable—Brenden Otto   ACCOUNT NO. 120

DATE 2007	ITEM	POST. REF.	DEBIT	CREDIT	BALANCE DEBIT	BALANCE CREDIT
Sep 10		G1	195 00		195 00	
27		G1		100 00	95 00	

ACCOUNT Supplies   ACCOUNT NO. 130

DATE 2007	ITEM	POST. REF.	DEBIT	CREDIT	BALANCE DEBIT	BALANCE CREDIT
Sep 4		G1	67 00		67 00	

ACCOUNT Prepaid Insurance   ACCOUNT NO. 140

DATE 2007	ITEM	POST. REF.	DEBIT	CREDIT	BALANCE DEBIT	BALANCE CREDIT
Sp 7		G1	333 00		333 00	

GENERAL LEDGER

ACCOUNT Accounts Payable—Signs Plus   ACCOUNT NO. 210

DATE 2007	ITEM	POST. REF.	DEBIT	CREDIT	BALANCE DEBIT	BALANCE CREDIT
Sep 4		G1		67 00		67 00
21		G1	35 00			32 00

ACCOUNT Melanie Komoko, Capital   ACCOUNT NO. 310

DATE 2007	ITEM	POST. REF.	DEBIT	CREDIT	BALANCE DEBIT	BALANCE CREDIT
Sep 1		G1		2500 00		2500 00

ACCOUNT Melanie Komoko, Drawing   ACCOUNT NO. 320

DATE 2007	ITEM	POST. REF.	DEBIT	CREDIT	BALANCE DEBIT	BALANCE CREDIT
Sep 30		G1	300 00		300 00	

ACCOUNT Sales   ACCOUNT NO. 410

DATE 2007	ITEM	POST. REF.	DEBIT	CREDIT	BALANCE DEBIT	BALANCE CREDIT
Sep 10		G1		195 00		195 00
13		G1		1100 00		1295 00

ACCOUNT Utilities Expense   ACCOUNT NO. 510

DATE 2007	ITEM	POST. REF.	DEBIT	CREDIT	BALANCE DEBIT	BALANCE CREDIT
Sep 18		G1	49 00		49 00	

5-3 WORK TOGETHER, p. 111

Journalizing correcting entries

GENERAL JOURNAL

PAGE

	DATE		ACCOUNT TITLE	DOC. NO.	POST. REF.	DEBIT	CREDIT	
1								1
2								2
3								3
4								4
5								5
6								6
7								7
8								8
9								9
10								10
11								11

Extra form

GENERAL JOURNAL

PAGE

	DATE		ACCOUNT TITLE	DOC. NO.	POST. REF.	DEBIT	CREDIT	
1								1
2								2
3								3
4								4
5								5
6								6
7								7
8								8
9								9
10								10
11								11

Journalizing correcting entries

GENERAL JOURNAL

PAGE

	DATE		ACCOUNT TITLE	DOC. NO.	POST. REF.	DEBIT	CREDIT	
1								1
2								2
3								3
4								4
5								5
6								6
7								7
8								8
9								9
10								10
11								11

Extra form

GENERAL JOURNAL

PAGE

	DATE		ACCOUNT TITLE	DOC. NO.	POST. REF.	DEBIT	CREDIT	
1								1
2								2
3								3
4								4
5								5
6								6
7								7
8								8
9								9
10								10
11								11

5-1 APPLICATION PROBLEM, p. 113

TEST

Preparing a chart of accounts and opening an account

1. _____

_____
_____
_____
_____
_____
_____
_____
_____
_____
_____
_____
_____
_____

2. _____

_____
_____
_____
_____
_____

3.

ACCOUNT _____ ACCOUNT NO. _____

DATE	ITEM	POST. REF.	DEBIT	CREDIT	BALANCE DEBIT	BALANCE CREDIT

ACCOUNT _____ ACCOUNT NO. _____

DATE	ITEM	POST. REF.	DEBIT	CREDIT	BALANCE DEBIT	BALANCE CREDIT

Extra forms

ACCOUNT _____   ACCOUNT NO. _____

DATE		ITEM	POST. REF.	DEBIT	CREDIT	BALANCE	
						DEBIT	CREDIT

ACCOUNT _____   ACCOUNT NO. _____

DATE		ITEM	POST. REF.	DEBIT	CREDIT	BALANCE	
						DEBIT	CREDIT

5-2 APPLICATION PROBLEM, p. 113

Posting to a general ledger

GENERAL JOURNAL   PAGE 1

	DATE		ACCOUNT TITLE	DOC. NO.	POST. REF.	DEBIT	CREDIT	
1	20-- Oct.	1	Cash	R1		1 5 0 0 00		1
2			Michael Byrum, Capital				1 5 0 0 00	2
3		4	Prepaid Insurance	C1		6 0 00		3
4			Cash				6 0 00	4
5		10	Supplies	M1		5 5 00		5
6			Accounts Payable—Golden Gate Supply				5 5 00	6
7		12	Cash	T12		3 8 2 00		7
8			Sales				3 8 2 00	8
9		15	Accounts Receivable—Cheri Frank	S1		4 2 00		9
10			Sales				4 2 00	10
11		19	Advertising Expense	C2		2 5 00		11
12			Cash				2 5 00	12
13		20	Accounts Payable—Golden Gate Supply	C3		3 0 00		13
14			Cash				3 0 00	14
15		27	Cash	R2		2 1 00		15
16			Accounts Receivable—Cheri Frank				2 1 00	16
17		31	Michael Byrum, Drawing	C4		1 5 0 00		17
18			Cash				1 5 0 00	18
19								19
20								20
21								21
22								22
23								23
24								24
25								25
26								26
27								27
28								28
29								29
30								30
31								31
32								32
33								33

Extra form

GENERAL JOURNAL

PAGE

	DATE		ACCOUNT TITLE	DOC. NO.	POST. REF.	DEBIT	CREDIT	
1								1
2								2
3								3
4								4
5								5
6								6
7								7
8								8
9								9
10								10
11								11
12								12
13								13
14								14
15								15
16								16
17								17
18								18
19								19
20								20
21								21
22								22
23								23
24								24
25								25
26								26
27								27
28								28
29								29
30								30
31								31
32								32
33								33

5-2 **APPLICATION PROBLEM (continued)**

GENERAL LEDGER

ACCOUNT Cash   ACCOUNT NO. 110

DATE	ITEM	POST. REF.	DEBIT	CREDIT	BALANCE DEBIT	BALANCE CREDIT

ACCOUNT Accounts Receivable—Cheri Frank   ACCOUNT NO. 120

DATE	ITEM	POST. REF.	DEBIT	CREDIT	BALANCE DEBIT	BALANCE CREDIT

ACCOUNT Supplies   ACCOUNT NO. 130

DATE	ITEM	POST. REF.	DEBIT	CREDIT	BALANCE DEBIT	BALANCE CREDIT

ACCOUNT Prepaid Insurance   ACCOUNT NO. 140

DATE	ITEM	POST. REF.	DEBIT	CREDIT	BALANCE DEBIT	BALANCE CREDIT

GENERAL LEDGER

ACCOUNT Accounts Payable—Golden Gate Supply ACCOUNT NO. 210

DATE	ITEM	POST. REF.	DEBIT	CREDIT	BALANCE	
					DEBIT	CREDIT

ACCOUNT Michael Byrum, Capital ACCOUNT NO. 310

DATE	ITEM	POST. REF.	DEBIT	CREDIT	BALANCE	
					DEBIT	CREDIT

ACCOUNT Michael Byrum, Drawing ACCOUNT NO. 320

DATE	ITEM	POST. REF.	DEBIT	CREDIT	BALANCE	
					DEBIT	CREDIT

ACCOUNT Sales ACCOUNT NO. 410

DATE	ITEM	POST. REF.	DEBIT	CREDIT	BALANCE	
					DEBIT	CREDIT

ACCOUNT Advertising Expense ACCOUNT NO. 510

DATE	ITEM	POST. REF.	DEBIT	CREDIT	BALANCE	
					DEBIT	CREDIT

5-3   APPLICATION PROBLEM, p. 113

Journalizing correcting entries

GENERAL JOURNAL   PAGE _____

	DATE	ACCOUNT TITLE	DOC. NO.	POST. REF.	DEBIT	CREDIT	
1							1
2							2
3							3
4							4
5							5
6							6
7							7
8							8
9							9
10							10
11							11
12							12
13							13
14							14
15							15
16							16
17							17
18							18
19							19
20							20
21							21
22							22
23							23
24							24
25							25
26							26
27							27
28							28
29							29
30							30
31							31
32							32
33							33

Extra form

GENERAL JOURNAL

PAGE

	DATE		ACCOUNT TITLE	DOC. NO.	POST. REF.	DEBIT	CREDIT	
1								1
2								2
3								3
4								4
5								5
6								6
7								7
8								8
9								9
10								10
11								11
12								12
13								13
14								14
15								15
16								16
17								17
18								18
19								19
20								20
21								21
22								22
23								23
24								24
25								25
26								26
27								27
28								28
29								29
30								30
31								31
32								32
33								33

Name _____ Date _____ Class _____

5-4 **MASTERY PROBLEM, p. 114**

Journalizing transactions and posting to a general ledger

2., 3.
GENERAL JOURNAL   PAGE ____

	DATE		ACCOUNT TITLE	DOC. NO.	POST. REF.	DEBIT	CREDIT	
1								1
2								2
3								3
4								4
5								5
6								6
7								7
8								8
9								9
10								10
11								11
12								12
13								13
14								14
15								15
16								16
17								17
18								18
19								19
20								20
21								21
22								22
23								23
24								24
25								25
26								26
27								27
28								28
29								29
30								30
31								31
32								32
33								33
34								34

Extra form

GENERAL JOURNAL

PAGE

	DATE		ACCOUNT TITLE	DOC. NO.	POST. REF.	DEBIT	CREDIT	
1								1
2								2
3								3
4								4
5								5
6								6
7								7
8								8
9								9
10								10
11								11
12								12
13								13
14								14
15								15
16								16
17								17
18								18
19								19
20								20
21								21
22								22
23								23
24								24
25								25
26								26
27								27
28								28
29								29
30								30
31								31
32								32
33								33
34								34

5-4 MASTERY PROBLEM (continued)

1., 3., 4.   **GENERAL LEDGER**

ACCOUNT Cash   ACCOUNT NO. 110

DATE	ITEM	POST. REF.	DEBIT	CREDIT	BALANCE DEBIT	BALANCE CREDIT

ACCOUNT Accounts Receivable—Alphonse Gutenberg   ACCOUNT NO. 120

DATE	ITEM	POST. REF.	DEBIT	CREDIT	BALANCE DEBIT	BALANCE CREDIT

ACCOUNT Supplies   ACCOUNT NO. 130

DATE	ITEM	POST. REF.	DEBIT	CREDIT	BALANCE DEBIT	BALANCE CREDIT

ACCOUNT Accounts Payable—Major Supplies   ACCOUNT NO. 210

DATE	ITEM	POST. REF.	DEBIT	CREDIT	BALANCE DEBIT	BALANCE CREDIT

1., 3., 4.   **GENERAL LEDGER**

ACCOUNT Allan Derner, Capital   ACCOUNT NO. 310

DATE	ITEM	POST. REF.	DEBIT	CREDIT	BALANCE DEBIT	BALANCE CREDIT

ACCOUNT Allan Derner, Drawing   ACCOUNT NO. 320

DATE	ITEM	POST. REF.	DEBIT	CREDIT	BALANCE DEBIT	BALANCE CREDIT

ACCOUNT Sales   ACCOUNT NO. 410

DATE	ITEM	POST. REF.	DEBIT	CREDIT	BALANCE DEBIT	BALANCE CREDIT

ACCOUNT Advertising Expense   ACCOUNT NO. 510

DATE	ITEM	POST. REF.	DEBIT	CREDIT	BALANCE DEBIT	BALANCE CREDIT

ACCOUNT Miscellaneous Expense   ACCOUNT NO. 520

DATE	ITEM	POST. REF.	DEBIT	CREDIT	BALANCE DEBIT	BALANCE CREDIT

ACCOUNT Rent Expense   ACCOUNT NO. 530

DATE	ITEM	POST. REF.	DEBIT	CREDIT	BALANCE DEBIT	BALANCE CREDIT

ACCOUNT   ACCOUNT NO.

DATE	ITEM	POST. REF.	DEBIT	CREDIT	BALANCE DEBIT	BALANCE CREDIT

5-5 CHALLENGE PROBLEM, p. 114

Posting using a variation of the general journal

GENERAL JOURNAL

PAGE 1

	DEBIT	DATE	ACCOUNT TITLE	DOC. NO.	POST. REF.	CREDIT	
1	8 0 0 0 00	20-- Mar. 1	Cash	R1			1
2			Nathan Jackson, Capital			8 0 0 0 00	2
3	3 5 0 00	3	Rent Expense	C1			3
4			Cash			3 5 0 00	4
5	5 00	5	Miscellaneous Expense	C2			5
6			Cash			5 00	6
7	2 5 0 00	9	Accounts Receivable—Joelle Chu	S1			7
8			Sales			2 5 0 00	8
9	4 0 0 00	11	Supplies	C3			9
10			Cash			4 0 0 00	10
11	4 5 0 00	13	Cash	T13			11
12			Sales			4 5 0 00	12
13	7 0 0 00	16	Supplies	M1			13
14			Accounts Payable—Hartwood Supplies			7 0 0 00	14
15	3 5 0 00	18	Accounts Payable—Hartwood Supplies	C4			15
16			Cash			3 5 0 00	16
17	6 0 00	19	Utilities Expense	C5			17
18			Cash			6 0 00	18
19	1 1 0 0 00	20	Cash	T20			19
20			Sales			1 1 0 0 00	20
21	5 0 00	23	Advertising Expense	C6			21
22			Cash			5 0 00	22
23	1 5 0 00	23	Supplies	C7			23
24			Cash			1 5 0 00	24
25	1 5 0 00	27	Supplies	C8			25
26			Cash			1 5 0 00	26
27	1 8 3 0 00	27	Cash	T27			27
28			Sales			1 8 3 0 00	28
29	4 0 0 00	30	Nathan Jackson, Drawing	C9			29
30			Cash			4 0 0 00	30
31	4 1 0 00	31	Cash	T31			31
32			Sales			4 1 0 00	32
33							33

Extra form

GENERAL JOURNAL

	DEBIT		DATE		ACCOUNT TITLE	DOC. NO.	POST. REF.	CREDIT		
1										1
2										2
3										3
4										4
5										5
6										6
7										7
8										8
9										9
10										10
11										11
12										12
13										13
14										14
15										15
16										16
17										17
18										18
19										19
20										20
21										21
22										22
23										23
24										24
25										25
26										26
27										27
28										28
29										29
30										30
31										31
32										32
33										33

5-5 CHALLENGE PROBLEM (continued)

GENERAL LEDGER

ACCOUNT Cash — ACCOUNT NO. 110

DATE	ITEM	POST. REF.	DEBIT	CREDIT	BALANCE DEBIT	BALANCE CREDIT

ACCOUNT Accounts Receivable—Joelle Chu — ACCOUNT NO. 120

DATE	ITEM	POST. REF.	DEBIT	CREDIT	BALANCE DEBIT	BALANCE CREDIT

ACCOUNT Supplies — ACCOUNT NO. 130

DATE	ITEM	POST. REF.	DEBIT	CREDIT	BALANCE DEBIT	BALANCE CREDIT

ACCOUNT Accounts Payable—Hartwood Supplies — ACCOUNT NO. 210

DATE	ITEM	POST. REF.	DEBIT	CREDIT	BALANCE DEBIT	BALANCE CREDIT

ACCOUNT Nathan Jackson, Capital — ACCOUNT NO. 310

DATE	ITEM	POST. REF.	DEBIT	CREDIT	BALANCE DEBIT	BALANCE CREDIT

GENERAL LEDGER

ACCOUNT Nathan Jackson, Drawing   ACCOUNT NO. 320

DATE	ITEM	POST. REF.	DEBIT	CREDIT	BALANCE DEBIT	BALANCE CREDIT

ACCOUNT Sales   ACCOUNT NO. 410

DATE	ITEM	POST. REF.	DEBIT	CREDIT	BALANCE DEBIT	BALANCE CREDIT

ACCOUNT Advertising Expense   ACCOUNT NO. 510

DATE	ITEM	POST. REF.	DEBIT	CREDIT	BALANCE DEBIT	BALANCE CREDIT

ACCOUNT Miscellaneous Expense   ACCOUNT NO. 520

DATE	ITEM	POST. REF.	DEBIT	CREDIT	BALANCE DEBIT	BALANCE CREDIT

ACCOUNT Rent Expense   ACCOUNT NO. 530

DATE	ITEM	POST. REF.	DEBIT	CREDIT	BALANCE DEBIT	BALANCE CREDIT

ACCOUNT Utilities Expense   ACCOUNT NO. 540

DATE	ITEM	POST. REF.	DEBIT	CREDIT	BALANCE DEBIT	BALANCE CREDIT

6-1 WORK TOGETHER, p. 124

Endorsing and writing checks

4. **a.**

ENDORSE HERE
X
DO NOT WRITE, STAMP, OR SIGN BELOW THIS LINE RESERVED FOR FINANCIAL INSTITUTION USE

b.

ENDORSE HERE
X
DO NOT WRITE, STAMP, OR SIGN BELOW THIS LINE RESERVED FOR FINANCIAL INSTITUTION USE

c.

ENDORSE HERE
X
DO NOT WRITE, STAMP, OR SIGN BELOW THIS LINE RESERVED FOR FINANCIAL INSTITUTION USE

5., 6., 7a.

NO. 78 $ 162.00
Date: 10/30 2008
To: Corner Garage
For: Repairs

BAL. BRO'T. FOR'D.	1805	75
AMT. DEPOSITED .... 10 30 08 Date	489	00
SUBTOTAL	2294	75
OTHER:	0	00
SUBTOTAL	2294	75
AMT. THIS CHECK	162	00
BAL. CAR'D. FOR'D.	2132	75

Balsam Lake Accounting
154 Main Street
Balsam Lake, WI 54810

NO. 78   93-109/929

October 30 20 08

PAY TO THE ORDER OF Corner Garage $ 162 00/100

One Hundred Sixty Two and 00/100 _____ DOLLARS

Peoples national bank
Balsam Lake, WI 54810

For Classroom Use Only

FOR Repairs

⑆0929010941⑆ 291⑈36118⑈

7b.

NO. 79 $ 92.00
Date: October 30 20 08
To: St. Croix Supply
For: Supplies

BAL. BRO'T. FOR'D.	2132	75
AMT. DEPOSITED .... Date	0	00
SUBTOTAL	2132	75
OTHER:	0	00
SUBTOTAL	2132	75
AMT. THIS CHECK	92	00
BAL. CAR'D. FOR'D.	2040	75

Balsam Lake Accounting
154 Main Street
Balsam Lake, WI 54810

NO. 79   93-109/929

October 30 20 08

PAY TO THE ORDER OF St. Croix Supply $ 92 00/100

Ninety Two and 00/100 _____ DOLLARS

Peoples national bank
Balsam Lake, WI 54810

For Classroom Use Only

FOR Supplies

⑆0929010941⑆ 291⑈36118⑈

Endorsing and writing checks

8. **a.**

```
ENDORSE HERE

X
_____

_____

_____

DO NOT WRITE, STAMP, OR SIGN BELOW THIS LINE
RESERVED FOR FINANCIAL INSTITUTION USE
```

b.

```
ENDORSE HERE

X
_____

_____

_____

DO NOT WRITE, STAMP, OR SIGN BELOW THIS LINE
RESERVED FOR FINANCIAL INSTITUTION USE
```

9., 10., 11a.

```
NO. 345          $ _____
Date: _____ 20 ___
To: _____
For: _____
_____
BAL. BRO'T. FOR'D. . . . . . . . . .
AMT. DEPOSITED . . . .
SUBTOTAL . . . . . . . . . . . . . . . .   Date
OTHER:
    _____
    _____
SUBTOTAL . . . . . . . . . . . . . . . .
AMT. THIS CHECK . . . . . . . . . . .
BAL. CAR'D. FOR'D. . . . . . . . . . .
```

```
DRESSER HAIR CARE                    NO. 345   79-1058
1250 State Street                              981
Dresser, WI  54009           _____ 20 _____

PAY TO THE
ORDER OF _____ $ _____

_____ DOLLARS
∴∴∴ County Bank          For Classroom Use Only
    Dresser, WI 54009

FOR _____   _____
⑆098110588⑆  291⑈36118⑈
```

11b.

```
NO. 346          $ _____
Date: _____ 20 ___
To: _____
For: _____
_____
BAL. BRO'T. FOR'D. . . . . . . . . . .
AMT. DEPOSITED . . . .
SUBTOTAL . . . . . . . . . . . . . . . .   Date
OTHER:
    _____
    _____
SUBTOTAL . . . . . . . . . . . . . . . .
AMT. THIS CHECK . . . . . . . . . . .
BAL. CAR'D. FOR'D. . . . . . . . . . .
```

```
DRESSER HAIR CARE                    NO. 346   79-1058
1250 State Street                              981
Dresser, WI  54009           _____ 20 _____

PAY TO THE
ORDER OF _____ $ _____

_____ DOLLARS
∴∴∴ County Bank          For Classroom Use Only
    Dresser, WI 54009

FOR _____   _____
⑆098110588⑆  291⑈36118⑈
```

6-2 WORK TOGETHER, p. 129

Reconciling a bank statement and recording a bank service charge

3.

RECONCILIATION OF BANK STATEMENT

_____
(Date)

Balance On Check Stub No. ____ .... $ 1575 00

DEDUCT BANK CHARGES:

Description	Amount	
Service	$ 2 00	

Total bank charges ▶ 2 00

Balance On Bank Statement .... $ 1528 00

ADD OUTSTANDING DEPOSITS:

Date	Amount	
July 28 2008	$ 150 00	

Total outstanding deposits ▶ 150 00

SUBTOTAL .... $ 1678 00

DEDUCT OUTSTANDING CHECKS:

Ck. No.	Amount	Ck. No.	Amount
103	70 00		
105	35 00		

Total outstanding checks ▶ 105 00

Adjusted Check Stub Balance .... $ 1573 00

Adjusted Bank Balance .... $ 1573 00

TEST

4.

```
NO. 106              $ _____
Date: _____ 20 - -
To: _____
   _____
For: _____
   _____

BAL. BRO'T. FOR'D. .............  1,575 | 00
AMT. DEPOSITED .... [    ]
                        Date
SUBTOTAL ....................   1,575 | 00
OTHER:
   Service Charge               2 | 00
SUBTOTAL ....................   1573 00
AMT. THIS CHECK .............
BAL. CAR'D. FOR'D. ...........
```

5.

GENERAL JOURNAL

PAGE 14

	DATE	ACCOUNT TITLE	DOC. NO.	POST. REF.	DEBIT	CREDIT	
14	Jul 29	Miscellaneous Expense	M44		2 00		14
15		Cash				2 00	15
16							16

Reconciling a bank statement and recording a bank service charge

6.

RECONCILIATION OF BANK STATEMENT

_____
(Date)

Balance On Check Stub No. ____ . . . . $
DEDUCT BANK CHARGES:

Description	Amount	
	$	

Total bank charges ▶

Adjusted Check Stub Balance . . . . $

Balance On Bank Statement . . . . $
ADD OUTSTANDING DEPOSITS:

Date	Amount	
	$	

Total outstanding deposits ▶

SUBTOTAL . . . . $
DEDUCT OUTSTANDING CHECKS:

Ck. No.	Amount	Ck. No.	Amount

Total outstanding checks ▶

Adjusted Bank Balance . . . . $

7.

NO. **218**	$ _____	
Date: _____ 20 - -		
To: _____		
For: _____		
BAL. BRO'T. FOR'D.	3,578	00
AMT. DEPOSITED . . . . [ ] Date		
SUBTOTAL	3,578	00
OTHER:		
SUBTOTAL		
AMT. THIS CHECK		
BAL. CAR'D. FOR'D.		

8.

GENERAL JOURNAL

PAGE

	DATE	ACCOUNT TITLE	DOC. NO.	POST. REF.	DEBIT	CREDIT	
17							17
18							18
19							19

6-3 WORK TOGETHER, p. 134

Recording dishonored checks, electronic funds transfers, and debit card purchases

GENERAL JOURNAL

PAGE _____

	DATE	ACCOUNT TITLE	DOC. NO.	POST. REF.	DEBIT	CREDIT	
3							3
4							4
5							5
6							6
7							7
8							8
9							9
10							10
11							11
12							12
13							13

Extra form

GENERAL JOURNAL

PAGE _____

	DATE	ACCOUNT TITLE	DOC. NO.	POST. REF.	DEBIT	CREDIT	
1							1
2							2
3							3
4							4
5							5
6							6
7							7
8							8
9							9
10							10
11							11
12							12

Recording dishonored checks, electronic funds transfers, and debit card purchases

GENERAL JOURNAL

PAGE

	DATE	ACCOUNT TITLE	DOC. NO.	POST. REF.	DEBIT	CREDIT	
15							15
16							16
17							17
18							18
19							19
20							20
21							21
22							22
23							23
24							24
25							25

Extra form

GENERAL JOURNAL

PAGE

	DATE	ACCOUNT TITLE	DOC. NO.	POST. REF.	DEBIT	CREDIT	
1							1
2							2
3							3
4							4
5							5
6							6
7							7
8							8
9							9
10							10
11							11
12							12

6-4 WORK TOGETHER, p. 138

Establishing and replenishing a petty cash fund

GENERAL JOURNAL

PAGE _____

	DATE	ACCOUNT TITLE	DOC. NO.	POST. REF.	DEBIT	CREDIT	
1							1
2							2
3							3
4							4
5							5
6							6
7							7
8							8
9							9
10							10
11							11
12							12

Extra form

GENERAL JOURNAL

PAGE _____

	DATE	ACCOUNT TITLE	DOC. NO.	POST. REF.	DEBIT	CREDIT	
1							1
2							2
3							3
4							4
5							5
6							6
7							7
8							8
9							9
10							10
11							11
12							12

Establishing and replenishing a petty cash fund

GENERAL JOURNAL PAGE

	DATE		ACCOUNT TITLE	DOC. NO.	POST. REF.	DEBIT	CREDIT	
1								1
2								2
3								3
4								4
5								5
6								6
7								7
8								8
9								9
10								10
11								11
12								12

Extra form

GENERAL JOURNAL PAGE

	DATE		ACCOUNT TITLE	DOC. NO.	POST. REF.	DEBIT	CREDIT	
1								1
2								2
3								3
4								4
5								5
6								6
7								7
8								8
9								9
10								10
11								11
12								12

6-1 APPLICATION PROBLEM, p. 140

Endorsing and writing checks

1. **a.**

ENDORSE HERE

X *[signature]*

DO NOT WRITE, STAMP, OR SIGN BELOW THIS LINE
RESERVED FOR FINANCIAL INSTITUTION USE

b.

ENDORSE HERE

X *Pay to the order of*
Bryan Astrup
[signature]

DO NOT WRITE, STAMP, OR SIGN BELOW THIS LINE
RESERVED FOR FINANCIAL INSTITUTION USE

c.

ENDORSE HERE

X *For deposit only to the*
account of Accounting
Tutors
[signature]

DO NOT WRITE, STAMP, OR SIGN BELOW THIS LINE
RESERVED FOR FINANCIAL INSTITUTION USE

Extra forms

ENDORSE HERE

X

DO NOT WRITE, STAMP, OR SIGN BELOW THIS LINE
RESERVED FOR FINANCIAL INSTITUTION USE

ENDORSE HERE

X

DO NOT WRITE, STAMP, OR SIGN BELOW THIS LINE
RESERVED FOR FINANCIAL INSTITUTION USE

2., 3., 4a.

NO. **608**	$ *1050·00*	
Date: *September 30,*		20 *08*
To: *Oak St. Supplies*		
For: *Supplies*		

BAL. BRO'T. FOR'D.	9811	71
AMT. DEPOSITED .... 9 30 08 Date	1359	00
SUBTOTAL	11170	71
OTHER:		
SUBTOTAL	11170	71
AMT. THIS CHECK	1050	00
BAL. CAR'D. FOR'D.	10120	71

Accounting Tutors
707 Oak Street
Minneapolis, MN 55447

NO. **608**   17-432⁄910

September 30 20 *08*

PAY TO THE ORDER OF *Oak Street Supplies* $ *1050 00/100*

One Thousand fifty and 00/100 ——————— DOLLARS

First National Bank
Minneapolis, MN 55447

For Classroom Use Only

FOR *Supplies*

⑴091004329⑴ 291 ⑾ 36118 ⑾

4b.

NO. **609**	$ _____	
Date: _____		20 __
To: _____		
For: _____		

BAL. BRO'T. FOR'D.		
AMT. DEPOSITED .... Date		
SUBTOTAL		
OTHER:		
SUBTOTAL		
AMT. THIS CHECK		
BAL. CAR'D. FOR'D.		

Accounting Tutors
707 Oak Street
Minneapolis, MN 55447

NO. **609**   17-432⁄910

_____ 20 ____

PAY TO THE ORDER OF _____ $ _____

_____ DOLLARS

First National Bank
Minneapolis, MN 55447

For Classroom Use Only

FOR _____

⑴091004329⑴ 291 ⑾ 36118 ⑾

4c.

NO. **610**	$ _____	
Date: _____		20 __
To: _____		
For: _____		

BAL. BRO'T. FOR'D.		
AMT. DEPOSITED .... Date		
SUBTOTAL		
OTHER:		
SUBTOTAL		
AMT. THIS CHECK		
BAL. CAR'D. FOR'D.		

Accounting Tutors
707 Oak Street
Minneapolis, MN 55447

NO. **610**   17-432⁄910

_____ 20 ____

PAY TO THE ORDER OF _____ $ _____

_____ DOLLARS

First National Bank
Minneapolis, MN 55447

For Classroom Use Only

FOR _____

⑴091004329⑴ 291 ⑾ 36118 ⑾

6-2 APPLICATION PROBLEM, p. 140

Reconciling a bank statement and recording a bank service charge

1.

RECONCILIATION OF BANK STATEMENT

May 31, 2008
(Date)

Balance On Check Stub No. 312	$ 2675	99

DEDUCT BANK CHARGES:

Description	Amount	
Bank Service Chrg	$ 10	00

Total bank charges ▶	10	00

Balance On Bank Statement	$ 2482	00

ADD OUTSTANDING DEPOSITS:

Date	Amount	
May 30, 2008	$ 756	25

Total outstanding deposits ▶	756	25
SUBTOTAL	$ 3238	25

DEDUCT OUTSTANDING CHECKS:

Ck. No.	Amount		Ck. No.	Amount	
310	421	76			
311	150	50			

Total outstanding checks ▶	572	26

Adjusted Check Stub Balance	$ 2665	99

Adjusted Bank Balance	$ 2665	99

2.

NO. **312** $ _____		
Date: _____ 20--		
To: _____		
_____		
For: _____		
BAL. BRO'T. FOR'D.	2,675	99
AMT. DEPOSITED .... [Date]		
SUBTOTAL	2,675	99
OTHER: Service Chrg 10.00	10	00
SUBTOTAL		
AMT. THIS CHECK		
BAL. CAR'D. FOR'D.		

3.

GENERAL JOURNAL

PAGE

	DATE	ACCOUNT TITLE	DOC. NO.	POST. REF.	DEBIT	CREDIT	
21	May 31	Miscellaneous Expense	M58		10 00		21
22		Cash				10 00	22
23							23

Extra forms

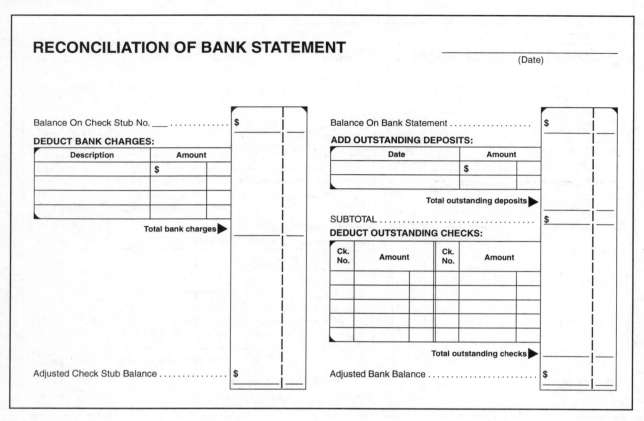

RECONCILIATION OF BANK STATEMENT

_____
(Date)

Balance On Check Stub No. ___ .... $

DEDUCT BANK CHARGES:

Description	Amount	
	$	

Total bank charges ▶

Balance On Bank Statement .... $

ADD OUTSTANDING DEPOSITS:

Date	Amount	
	$	

Total outstanding deposits ▶

SUBTOTAL .... $

DEDUCT OUTSTANDING CHECKS:

Ck. No.	Amount	Ck. No.	Amount

Total outstanding checks ▶

Adjusted Check Stub Balance .... $

Adjusted Bank Balance .... $

GENERAL JOURNAL

PAGE

	DATE	ACCOUNT TITLE	DOC. NO.	POST. REF.	DEBIT	CREDIT	
1							1
2							2
3							3
4							4
5							5
6							6
7							7
8							8
9							9
10							10
11							11
12							12
13							13

6-3 APPLICATION PROBLEM, p. 140

Recording dishonored checks, electronic funds transfers, and debit card purchases

GENERAL JOURNAL   PAGE

	DATE		ACCOUNT TITLE	DOC. NO.	POST. REF.	DEBIT	CREDIT	
12	Feb	15	A/R - Patricia Dubay	M217		1 2 5 00		12
13			Cash				1 2 5 00	13
14		16	A/P - Alec Hongo	M218		3 5 4 00		14
15			Cash				3 5 4 00	15
16		17	Supplies	M219		8 9 00		16
17			Cash				8 9 00	17
18								18
19								19
20								20
21								21
22								22

Extra form

GENERAL JOURNAL   PAGE

	DATE		ACCOUNT TITLE	DOC. NO.	POST. REF.	DEBIT	CREDIT	
1								1
2								2
3								3
4								4
5								5
6								6
7								7
8								8
9								9
10								10
11								11
12								12

Extra form

GENERAL JOURNAL

	DATE		ACCOUNT TITLE	DOC. NO.	POST. REF.	DEBIT	CREDIT	
1								1
2								2
3								3
4								4
5								5
6								6
7								7
8								8
9								9
10								10
11								11
12								12
13								13
14								14
15								15
16								16
17								17
18								18
19								19
20								20
21								21
22								22
23								23
24								24
25								25
26								26
27								27
28								28
29								29
30								30
31								31
32								32
33								33

6-4 APPLICATION PROBLEM, p. 141

Establishing and replenishing a petty cash fund

GENERAL JOURNAL   PAGE 22

	DATE	ACCOUNT TITLE	DOC. NO.	POST. REF.	DEBIT	CREDIT	
4	Nov 5	Petty Cash	C527		300 00		4
5		Cash				300 00	5
6	30	Supplies	C555		57 00		6
7		Miscellaneous Expense			58 00		7
8		Repairs			40 00		8
9		Postage Expense			10 00		9
10		Cash				165 00	10
11							11
12							12
13							13
14							14

Extra form

GENERAL JOURNAL   PAGE

	DATE	ACCOUNT TITLE	DOC. NO.	POST. REF.	DEBIT	CREDIT	
1							1
2							2
3							3
4							4
5							5
6							6
7							7
8							8
9							9
10							10
11							11
12							12
13							13

Extra form

GENERAL JOURNAL

	DATE		ACCOUNT TITLE	DOC. NO.	POST. REF.	DEBIT	CREDIT	
1								1
2								2
3								3
4								4
5								5
6								6
7								7
8								8
9								9
10								10
11								11
12								12
13								13
14								14
15								15
16								16
17								17
18								18
19								19
20								20
21								21
22								22
23								23
24								24
25								25
26								26
27								27
28								28
29								29
30								30
31								31
32								32
33								33

6-5 MASTERY PROBLEM, p. 141

Reconciling a bank statement; journalizing a bank service charge, a dishonored check, and petty cash transactions

1., 3.

GENERAL JOURNAL   PAGE 20

	DATE	ACCOUNT TITLE	DOC. NO.	POST. REF.	DEBIT	CREDIT	
1	Aug 21	Petty Cash	C61		200 00		1
2		Cash				200 00	2
3	24	Repair Expense	C62		235 00		3
4		Cash				235 00	4
5	26	Supplies	C63		40 00		5
6		Cash				40 00	6
7	27	A/R – Stacy Griffith	M22		50 00		7
8		Cash				50 00	8
9	28	Miscellaneous Expense	C64		12 00		9
10		Cash				12 00	10
11	31	Joseph Cruz, Drawing	C65		300 00		11
12		Cash				300 00	12
13	31	Supplies	C66		35 00		13
14		Miscellaneous Expense			20 00		14
15		Cash				55 00	15
16	31	Miscellaneous Expense	M23		5 00		16
17		Cash				5 00	17
18							18
19							19
20							20
21							21
22							22
23							23
24							24
25							25
26							26
27							27
28							28
29							29
30							30

2.

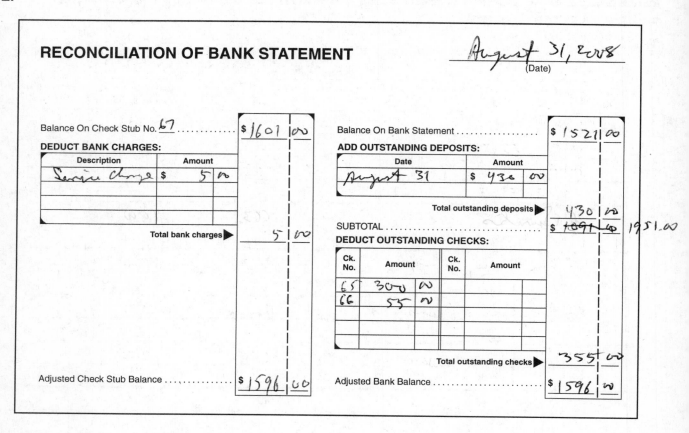

RECONCILIATION OF BANK STATEMENT   August 31, 2008
(Date)

Balance On Check Stub No. 67		$ 1607	00
DEDUCT BANK CHARGES:			

Description	Amount		
Service Charge	$ 5	00	

Total bank charges ▶   5 | 00

Balance On Bank Statement		$ 1521	00
ADD OUTSTANDING DEPOSITS:			

Date	Amount	
August 31	$ 430	00

Total outstanding deposits ▶   430 | 00

SUBTOTAL .... $ 1091 00   1951.00

DEDUCT OUTSTANDING CHECKS:

Ck. No.	Amount		Ck. No.	Amount	
65	300	00			
66	55	00			

Total outstanding checks ▶   355 | 00

Adjusted Check Stub Balance		$ 1596	00

Adjusted Bank Balance		$ 1596	00

Extra form

GENERAL JOURNAL   PAGE

	DATE	ACCOUNT TITLE	DOC. NO.	POST. REF.	DEBIT	CREDIT	
1							1
2							2
3							3
4							4
5							5
6							6
7							7
8							8
9							9
10							10
11							11

6-6 CHALLENGE PROBLEM, p. 142

Reconciling a bank statement and recording a bank service charge

1., 2.

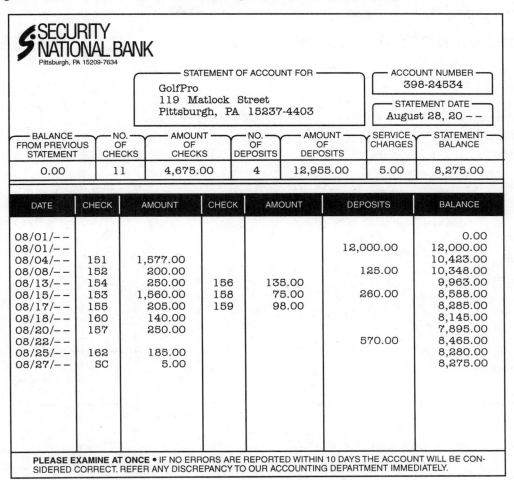

SECURITY NATIONAL BANK
Pittsburgh, PA 15209-7634

STATEMENT OF ACCOUNT FOR
GolfPro
119 Matlock Street
Pittsburgh, PA 15237-4403

ACCOUNT NUMBER
398-24534

STATEMENT DATE
August 28, 20 – –

BALANCE FROM PREVIOUS STATEMENT	NO. OF CHECKS	AMOUNT OF CHECKS	NO. OF DEPOSITS	AMOUNT OF DEPOSITS	SERVICE CHARGES	STATEMENT BALANCE
0.00	11	4,675.00	4	12,955.00	5.00	8,275.00

DATE	CHECK	AMOUNT	CHECK	AMOUNT	DEPOSITS	BALANCE
08/01/– –						0.00
08/01/– –					12,000.00	12,000.00
08/04/– –	151	1,577.00				10,423.00
08/08/– –	152	200.00			125.00	10,348.00
08/13/– –	154	250.00	156	135.00		9,963.00
08/15/– –	153	1,560.00	158	75.00	260.00	8,588.00
08/17/– –	155	205.00	159	98.00		8,285.00
08/18/– –	160	140.00				8,145.00
08/20/– –	157	250.00				7,895.00
08/22/– –					570.00	8,465.00
08/25/– –	162	185.00				8,280.00
08/27/– –	SC	5.00				8,275.00

PLEASE EXAMINE AT ONCE • IF NO ERRORS ARE REPORTED WITHIN 10 DAYS THE ACCOUNT WILL BE CONSIDERED CORRECT. REFER ANY DISCREPANCY TO OUR ACCOUNTING DEPARTMENT IMMEDIATELY.

GolfPro
119 Matlock Street
Pittsburgh, PA 15237–4403
NO. 151   8-17/430
August 1, 20 – –
PAY TO THE ORDER OF *Montag Company* $ 1,577.00

GolfPro
119 Matlock Street
Pittsburgh, PA 15237–4403
NO. 152   8-17/430
August 5, 20 – –
PAY TO THE ORDER OF *Plain Company* $ 200.00

GolfPro
119 Matlock Street
Pittsburgh, PA 15237–4403
NO. 153   8-17/430
August 8, 20 – –
PAY TO THE ORDER OF *Thomson Company* $ 1,560.00

GolfPro
119 Matlock Street
Pittsburgh, PA 15237–4403
NO. 154   8-17/430
August 8, 20 – –
PAY TO THE ORDER OF *Metro Insurance Co.* $ 250.00

GolfPro
119 Matlock Street
Pittsburgh, PA 15237–4403
NO. 155   8-17/430
August 10, 20 – –
PAY TO THE ORDER OF *City Electric Company* $ 205.00

GolfPro
119 Matlock Street
Pittsburgh, PA 15237–4403
NO. 156   8-17/430
August 10, 20 – –
PAY TO THE ORDER OF *Patterson Supplies* $ 135.00
One hundred thirty-five dollars ———— 00/XX DOLLARS
SECURITY NATIONAL BANK
Pittsburgh, PA 15209-7634
FOR *payment on account*   John Walker
⑆043000177⑆ 398⑈ 24534⑇

GolfPro
119 Matlock Street
Pittsburgh, PA 15237–4403
NO. 157   8-17/430
August 13, 20 – –
PAY TO THE ORDER OF *John Walker* $ 250.00

GolfPro
119 Matlock Street
Pittsburgh, PA 15237–4403
NO. 158   8-17/430
August 14, 20 – –
PAY TO THE ORDER OF *Pennsylvania Telephone Co.* $ 75.00

GolfPro
119 Matlock Street
Pittsburgh, PA 15237–4403
NO. 159   8-17/430
August 15, 20 – –
PAY TO THE ORDER OF *Ace Cleaning Company* $ 98.00

GolfPro
119 Matlock Street
Pittsburgh, PA 15237–4403
NO. 160   8-17/430
August 15, 20 – –
PAY TO THE ORDER OF *Tri-State Agency* $ 140.00

GolfPro
119 Matlock Street
Pittsburgh, PA 15237–4403
NO. 162   8-17/430
August 22, 20 – –
PAY TO THE ORDER OF *Dowd Company* $ 185.00
One hundred eighty-five dollars ———— 00/XX DOLLARS
SECURITY NATIONAL BANK
Pittsburgh, PA 15209-7634
FOR *payment on account*   John Walker
⑆043000177⑆ 398⑈ 24534⑇

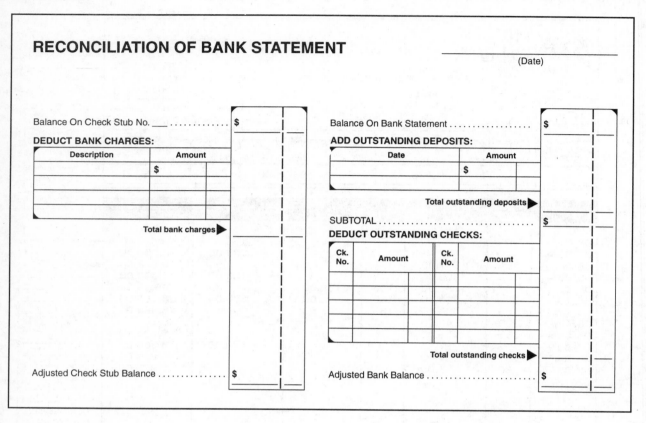

RECONCILIATION OF BANK STATEMENT

_____
(Date)

Balance On Check Stub No. ___ .... $

DEDUCT BANK CHARGES:

Description	Amount	
	$	

Total bank charges ▶

Adjusted Check Stub Balance .... $

Balance On Bank Statement .... $

ADD OUTSTANDING DEPOSITS:

Date	Amount	
	$	

Total outstanding deposits ▶

SUBTOTAL .... $

DEDUCT OUTSTANDING CHECKS:

Ck. No.	Amount	Ck. No.	Amount

Total outstanding checks ▶

Adjusted Bank Balance .... $

GENERAL JOURNAL

PAGE

	DATE	ACCOUNT TITLE	DOC. NO.	POST. REF.	DEBIT	CREDIT	
1							1
2							2
3							3
4							4
5							5
6							6
7							7
8							8
9							9
10							10
11							11
12							12

6-6 CHALLENGE PROBLEM (continued)

1., 2., 4.

NO. **151**	$ 1,577.00	
Date: August 1, 20 --		
To: Montag Company		
For: Supplies		
BAL. BRO'T. FOR'D.	0	00
AMT. DEPOSITED .... 8/1 --	12,000	00
SUBTOTAL	12,000	00
OTHER:		
SUBTOTAL	12,000	00
AMT. THIS CHECK	1,577	00
BAL. CAR'D. FOR'D.	10,423	00

NO. **152**	$ 200.00	
Date: August 5, 20 --		
To: Plain Company		
For: Rent		
BAL. BRO'T. FOR'D.	10,423	00
AMT. DEPOSITED		
SUBTOTAL	10,423	00
OTHER:		
SUBTOTAL	10,423	00
AMT. THIS CHECK	200	00
BAL. CAR'D. FOR'D.	10,223	00

NO. **153**	$ 1,560.00	
Date: August 8, 20 --		
To: Thomson Company		
For: Supplies		
BAL. BRO'T. FOR'D.	10,223	00
AMT. DEPOSITED .... 8/8 --	125	00
SUBTOTAL	10,348	00
OTHER:		
SUBTOTAL	10,348	00
AMT. THIS CHECK	1,560	00
BAL. CAR'D. FOR'D.	8,788	00

NO. **154**	$ 250.00	
Date: August 8, 20 --		
To: Metro Insurance Company		
For: Insurance		
BAL. BRO'T. FOR'D.	8,788	00
AMT. DEPOSITED		
SUBTOTAL	8,788	00
OTHER:		
SUBTOTAL	8,788	00
AMT. THIS CHECK	250	00
BAL. CAR'D. FOR'D.	8,538	00

NO. **155**	$ 205.00	
Date: August 10, 20 --		
To: City Electric Company		
For: Utilities		
BAL. BRO'T. FOR'D.	8,538	00
AMT. DEPOSITED		
SUBTOTAL	8,538	00
OTHER:		
SUBTOTAL	8,538	00
AMT. THIS CHECK	205	00
BAL. CAR'D. FOR'D.	8,333	00

NO. **156**	$ 135.00	
Date: August 10, 20 --		
To: Patterson Supplies		
For: Payment on account		
BAL. BRO'T. FOR'D.	8,333	00
AMT. DEPOSITED		
SUBTOTAL	8,333	00
OTHER:		
SUBTOTAL	8,333	00
AMT. THIS CHECK	135	00
BAL. CAR'D. FOR'D.	8,198	00

NO. **157**	$ 250.00	
Date: August 13, 20 --		
To: John Walker		
For: Owner's withdrawal		
BAL. BRO'T. FOR'D.	8,198	00
AMT. DEPOSITED		
SUBTOTAL	8,198	00
OTHER:		
SUBTOTAL	8,198	00
AMT. THIS CHECK	250	00
BAL. CAR'D. FOR'D.	7,948	00

NO. **158**	$ 75.00	
Date: August 14, 20 --		
To: Pennsylvania Telephone Company		
For: Utilities		
BAL. BRO'T. FOR'D.	7,948	00
AMT. DEPOSITED		
SUBTOTAL	7,948	00
OTHER:		
SUBTOTAL	7,948	00
AMT. THIS CHECK	75	00
BAL. CAR'D. FOR'D.	7,873	00

NO. **159**	$ 98.00	
Date: August 15, 20 --		
To: Ace Cleaning Company		
For: Cleaning		
BAL. BRO'T. FOR'D.	7,873	00
AMT. DEPOSITED		
SUBTOTAL	7,873	00
OTHER:		
SUBTOTAL	7,873	00
AMT. THIS CHECK	98	00
BAL. CAR'D. FOR'D.	7,775	00

1., 2., 4.

NO. 160	$ 140.00	
Date: August 15,		20--
To: Tri-State Agency		
For: Miscellaneous		

BAL. BRO'T. FOR'D.	7,775	00
AMT. DEPOSITED .... 8 15 --	260	00
SUBTOTAL	8,035	00
OTHER:		
SUBTOTAL	8,035	00
AMT. THIS CHECK	140	00
BAL. CAR'D. FOR'D.	7,895	00

NO. 161	$ 375.00	
Date: August 19,		20--
To: Pittsburgh Enquirer		
For: Advertising		

BAL. BRO'T. FOR'D.	7,895	00
AMT. DEPOSITED		
SUBTOTAL	7,895	00
OTHER:		
SUBTOTAL	7,895	00
AMT. THIS CHECK	375	00
BAL. CAR'D. FOR'D.	7,520	00

NO. 162	$ 185.00	
Date: August 22,		20--
To: Dowd Company		
For: Payment on account		

BAL. BRO'T. FOR'D.	7,520	00
AMT. DEPOSITED .... 8 22 --	570	00
SUBTOTAL	8,090	00
OTHER:		
SUBTOTAL	8,090	00
AMT. THIS CHECK	185	00
BAL. CAR'D. FOR'D.	7,905	00

NO. 163	$ 17.00	
Date: August 23,		20--
To: Jason North		
For: Miscellaneous		

BAL. BRO'T. FOR'D.	7,905	00
AMT. DEPOSITED		
SUBTOTAL	7,905	00
OTHER:		
SUBTOTAL	7,905	00
AMT. THIS CHECK	17	00
BAL. CAR'D. FOR'D.	7,888	00

NO. 164	$ 250.00	
Date: August 28,		20--
To: John Walker		
For: Owner's withdrawal		

BAL. BRO'T. FOR'D.	7,888	00
AMT. DEPOSITED .... 8 28 --	430	00
SUBTOTAL	8,318	00
OTHER:		
SUBTOTAL	8,318	00
AMT. THIS CHECK	250	00
BAL. CAR'D. FOR'D.	8,068	00

NO. 165	$	
Date:		20--
To:		
For:		

BAL. BRO'T. FOR'D.	8,068	00
AMT. DEPOSITED		
SUBTOTAL	8,068	00
OTHER:		
SUBTOTAL		
AMT. THIS CHECK		
BAL. CAR'D. FOR'D.		

6-6 **CHALLENGE PROBLEM (concluded)**

2.

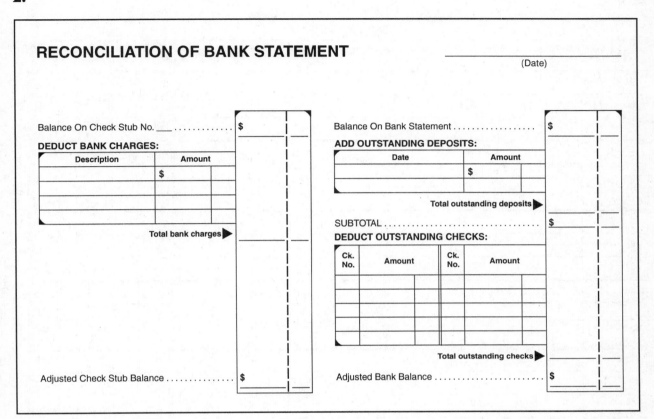

RECONCILIATION OF BANK STATEMENT

_____ (Date)

Balance On Check Stub No. ____ .... $ | |

DEDUCT BANK CHARGES:

Description	Amount	
	$	

Total bank charges ▶

Adjusted Check Stub Balance .... $ | |

Balance On Bank Statement .... $ | |

ADD OUTSTANDING DEPOSITS:

Date	Amount	
	$	

Total outstanding deposits ▶

SUBTOTAL .... $ | |

DEDUCT OUTSTANDING CHECKS:

Ck. No.	Amount	Ck. No.	Amount

Total outstanding checks ▶

Adjusted Bank Balance .... $ | |

3.

GENERAL JOURNAL

PAGE

	DATE	ACCOUNT TITLE	DOC. NO.	POST. REF.	DEBIT	CREDIT	
1							1
2							2
3							3
4							4
5							5
6							6
7							7
8							8
9							9
10							10
11							11

Extra form

GENERAL JOURNAL

	DATE		ACCOUNT TITLE	DOC. NO.	POST. REF.	DEBIT	CREDIT	
1								1
2								2
3								3
4								4
5								5
6								6
7								7
8								8
9								9
10								10
11								11
12								12
13								13
14								14
15								15
16								16
17								17
18								18
19								19
20								20
21								21
22								22
23								23
24								24
25								25
26								26
27								27
28								28
29								29
30								30
31								31
32								32
33								33

REINFORCEMENT ACTIVITY 1

PART A, p. 145

An Accounting Cycle for a Proprietorship: Journalizing and Posting Transactions

1., 2.

GENERAL JOURNAL   PAGE 1

	DATE	ACCOUNT TITLE	DOC. NO.	POST. REF.	DEBIT	CREDIT	
1							1
2							2
3							3
4							4
5							5
6							6
7							7
8							8
9							9
10							10
11							11
12							12
13							13
14							14
15							15
16							16
17							17
18							18
19							19
20							20
21							21
22							22
23							23
24							24
25							25
26							26
27							27
28							28
29							29
30							30
31							31
32							32
33							33
34							34

REINFORCEMENT ACTIVITY 1

PART A (continued)

3., 5., 6.

GENERAL JOURNAL

	DATE		ACCOUNT TITLE	DOC. NO.	POST. REF.	DEBIT	CREDIT	
1								1
2								2
3								3
4								4
5								5
6								6
7								7
8								8
9								9
10								10
11								11
12								12
13								13
14								14
15								15
16								16
17								17
18								18
19								19
20								20
21								21
22								22
23								23
24								24
25								25
26								26
27								27
28								28
29								29
30								30
31								31
32								32
33								33
34								34

REINFORCEMENT ACTIVITY 1 PART A (continued)

The general ledger prepared in Reinforcement Activity 1, Part A, is needed to complete Reinforcement Activity 1, Part B.

2., 6., 7., 15., 16.   GENERAL LEDGER

ACCOUNT Cash   ACCOUNT NO. 110

DATE		ITEM	POST. REF.	DEBIT	CREDIT	BALANCE DEBIT	CREDIT

REINFORCEMENT ACTIVITY 1

PART A (continued)

2., 6., 15., 16.   GENERAL LEDGER

ACCOUNT Petty Cash   ACCOUNT NO. 120

DATE		ITEM	POST. REF.	DEBIT	CREDIT	BALANCE	
						DEBIT	CREDIT

ACCOUNT Accounts Receivable—Breck School   ACCOUNT NO. 130

DATE		ITEM	POST. REF.	DEBIT	CREDIT	BALANCE	
						DEBIT	CREDIT

ACCOUNT Accounts Receivable—Lincoln School   ACCOUNT NO. 140

DATE		ITEM	POST. REF.	DEBIT	CREDIT	BALANCE	
						DEBIT	CREDIT

ACCOUNT Supplies   ACCOUNT NO. 150

DATE		ITEM	POST. REF.	DEBIT	CREDIT	BALANCE	
						DEBIT	CREDIT

Name _____ Date _____ Class _____

REINFORCEMENT ACTIVITY 1

PART A (continued)

2., 6., 15., 16.   **GENERAL LEDGER**

ACCOUNT Prepaid Insurance   ACCOUNT NO. 160

DATE	ITEM	POST. REF.	DEBIT	CREDIT	BALANCE DEBIT	BALANCE CREDIT

ACCOUNT Accounts Payable—Dunnel Supplies   ACCOUNT NO. 210

DATE	ITEM	POST. REF.	DEBIT	CREDIT	BALANCE DEBIT	BALANCE CREDIT

ACCOUNT Accounts Payable—Voiles Office Supplies   ACCOUNT NO. 220

DATE	ITEM	POST. REF.	DEBIT	CREDIT	BALANCE DEBIT	BALANCE CREDIT

ACCOUNT Caleb Christianson, Capital   ACCOUNT NO. 310

DATE	ITEM	POST. REF.	DEBIT	CREDIT	BALANCE DEBIT	BALANCE CREDIT

REINFORCEMENT ACTIVITY 1
PART A (concluded)

2., 6., 15., 16.   **GENERAL LEDGER**

ACCOUNT Caleb Christianson, Drawing   ACCOUNT NO. 320

DATE	ITEM	POST. REF.	DEBIT	CREDIT	BALANCE DEBIT	BALANCE CREDIT

ACCOUNT Income Summary   ACCOUNT NO. 330

DATE	ITEM	POST. REF.	DEBIT	CREDIT	BALANCE DEBIT	BALANCE CREDIT

ACCOUNT Sales   ACCOUNT NO. 410

DATE	ITEM	POST. REF.	DEBIT	CREDIT	BALANCE DEBIT	BALANCE CREDIT

ACCOUNT Advertising Expense   ACCOUNT NO. 510

DATE	ITEM	POST. REF.	DEBIT	CREDIT	BALANCE DEBIT	BALANCE CREDIT

NOTE: May 31 postings from page 3 of the journal are part of the solution to Part B.

REINFORCEMENT ACTIVITY 1

PART A (continued)

The general ledger prepared in Reinforcement Activity 1, Part A, is needed to complete Reinforcement Activity 1, Part B.

2., 6., 15., 16. 　　　　　　　　**GENERAL LEDGER**

ACCOUNT Insurance Expense　　　　　　　　　　　　ACCOUNT NO. 520

DATE	ITEM	POST. REF.	DEBIT	CREDIT	BALANCE DEBIT	BALANCE CREDIT

ACCOUNT Miscellaneous Expense　　　　　　　　　　ACCOUNT NO. 530

DATE	ITEM	POST. REF.	DEBIT	CREDIT	BALANCE DEBIT	BALANCE CREDIT

ACCOUNT Rent Expense　　　　　　　　　　　　　　ACCOUNT NO. 540

DATE	ITEM	POST. REF.	DEBIT	CREDIT	BALANCE DEBIT	BALANCE CREDIT

ACCOUNT Repair Expense　　　　　　　　　　　　　ACCOUNT NO. 550

DATE	ITEM	POST. REF.	DEBIT	CREDIT	BALANCE DEBIT	BALANCE CREDIT

ACCOUNT Supplies Expense　　　　　　　　　　　　ACCOUNT NO. 560

DATE	ITEM	POST. REF.	DEBIT	CREDIT	BALANCE DEBIT	BALANCE CREDIT

PART A (concluded)

2., 6., 15., 16.   GENERAL LEDGER

ACCOUNT Utilities Expense   ACCOUNT NO. 570

DATE	ITEM	POST. REF.	DEBIT	CREDIT	BALANCE	
					DEBIT	CREDIT

4.

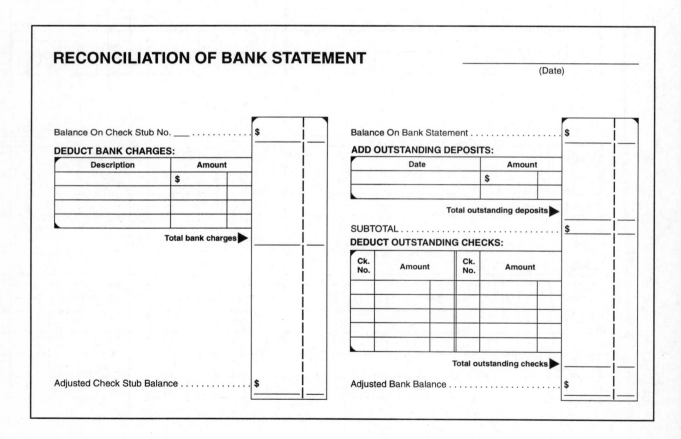

RECONCILIATION OF BANK STATEMENT

_____ (Date)

Balance On Check Stub No. ____ . . . . $

DEDUCT BANK CHARGES:

Description	Amount
	$

Total bank charges ▶

Adjusted Check Stub Balance . . . . $

Balance On Bank Statement . . . . $

ADD OUTSTANDING DEPOSITS:

Date	Amount
	$

Total outstanding deposits ▶

SUBTOTAL . . . . $

DEDUCT OUTSTANDING CHECKS:

Ck. No.	Amount	Ck. No.	Amount

Total outstanding checks ▶

Adjusted Bank Balance . . . . $

7-1, 7-2, and 7-3 WORK TOGETHER, pp. 152, 158, 163

7-1 Recording the trial balance on a work sheet
7-2 Planning adjustments on a work sheet
7-3 Completing a work sheet

Golden Tan
Work Sheet
For Month Ended February 28, 2008

	Trial Balance Debit	Trial Balance Credit	Adjustments Debit	Adjustments Credit	Income Statement Debit	Income Statement Credit	Balance Sheet Debit	Balance Sheet Credit
1 Cash	9800 00						9800 00	
2 Petty Cash	150 00						150 00	
3 A/R—Becky Price	2795 00						2795 00	
4 Supplies	4560 00			(b) 2250 00			2310 00	
5 Prepaid Insurance	7500 00			(a) 1310 00			6190 00	
6 A/P—Richard Navarro		555 00						555 00
7 Gary Balghin, Capital		14885 00						14885 00
8 Gary Balghin, Drawing	3400 00						3400 00	
9 Income Summary								
10 Sales		4320 00				4320 00		
11 Advertising Expense	931 00				931 00			
12 Insurance Expense			(a) 2250 00		2250 00			
13 Miscellaneous Expense	378 00				378 00			
14 Supplies Expense			(b) 1310 00		1310 00			
15 Utilities Expense	1100 00				1100 00			
16	19760 00	19760 00	3810 00	3810 00	16910 00	4320 00	16970 00	15470 00
17					27910 00			1530 00
18					4320 00	4320 00	16970 00	16970 00
19								
20								

7-1 Recording the trial balance on a work sheet
7-2 Planning adjustments on a work sheet
7-3 Completing a work sheet

ACCOUNT TITLE		TRIAL BALANCE		ADJUSTMENTS		INCOME STATEMENT		BALANCE SHEET	
		1 DEBIT	2 CREDIT	3 DEBIT	4 CREDIT	5 DEBIT	6 CREDIT	7 DEBIT	8 CREDIT
1									
2									
3									
4									
5									
6									
7									
8									
9									
10									
11									
12									
13									
14									
15									
16									
17									
18									
19									
20									

Name _____ Date _____ Class _____

7-4 WORK TOGETHER, p. 167

Finding and correcting errors in accounting records

4., 5.   **GENERAL LEDGER**

ACCOUNT Cash   ACCOUNT NO. 110

DATE		ITEM	POST. REF.	DEBIT	CREDIT	BALANCE DEBIT	BALANCE CREDIT
20-- Sept.	1		G1	4 0 0 0 00		4 0 0 0 00	
	30		G2	7 0 0 0 00		15 0 0 0 00	
	30		G2		6 7 5 0 00	8 0 0 0 00	

ACCOUNT Accounts Receivable—Sharon Mann   ACCOUNT NO. 120

DATE		ITEM	POST. REF.	DEBIT	CREDIT	BALANCE DEBIT	BALANCE CREDIT
20-- Sept.	12		G1	1 0 0 0 00		1 0 0 0 00	

ACCOUNT Supplies   ACCOUNT NO. 130

DATE		ITEM	POST. REF.	DEBIT	CREDIT	BALANCE DEBIT	BALANCE CREDIT
20-- Sept.	2		G1	6 0 0 00		6 0 0 00	
	25		G2	4 2 5 00		7 2 5 00	

ACCOUNT Prepaid Insurance   ACCOUNT NO. 140

DATE		ITEM	POST. REF.	DEBIT	CREDIT	BALANCE DEBIT	BALANCE CREDIT
20-- Sept.	3		G1	1 5 0 00		1 5 0 00	
	20		G2	1 5 0 00		4 0 0 00	

ACCOUNT Accounts Payable—Powers Supply   ACCOUNT NO. 210

DATE		ITEM	POST. REF.	DEBIT	CREDIT	BALANCE DEBIT	BALANCE CREDIT
20-- Sept.	4		G1		3 0 0 00		3 0 0 00
	15		G2	1 5 0 00			1 5 0 00

ACCOUNT Paul Coty, Capital   ACCOUNT NO. 310

DATE		ITEM	POST. REF.	DEBIT	CREDIT	BALANCE DEBIT	BALANCE CREDIT
20-- Sept.	1		G1		5 0 0 0 00		5 0 0 0 00

4., 5.   **GENERAL LEDGER**

ACCOUNT Paul Coty, Drawing   ACCOUNT NO. 320

DATE	ITEM	POST. REF.	DEBIT	CREDIT	BALANCE DEBIT	BALANCE CREDIT
20-- Sept. 30		G2	3 0 0 00		3 0 0 00	

ACCOUNT Income Summary   ACCOUNT NO. 330

DATE	ITEM	POST. REF.	DEBIT	CREDIT	BALANCE DEBIT	BALANCE CREDIT

ACCOUNT Sales   ACCOUNT NO. 410

DATE	ITEM	POST. REF.	DEBIT	CREDIT	BALANCE DEBIT	BALANCE CREDIT
20-- Sept. 30		G2		1 9 0 0 00		1 8 7 5 00

ACCOUNT Insurance Expense   ACCOUNT NO. 510

DATE	ITEM	POST. REF.	DEBIT	CREDIT	BALANCE DEBIT	BALANCE CREDIT

ACCOUNT Miscellaneous Expense   ACCOUNT NO. 520

DATE	ITEM	POST. REF.	DEBIT	CREDIT	BALANCE DEBIT	BALANCE CREDIT
20-- Sept. 9		G1	1 5 0 00		1 5 0 00	
27		G2	2 5 00		1 2 5 00	

ACCOUNT Supplies Expense   ACCOUNT NO. 530

DATE	ITEM	POST. REF.	DEBIT	CREDIT	BALANCE DEBIT	BALANCE CREDIT

7-4 **WORK TOGETHER (continued)**

4. **ERRORS**

4. ERRORS

7-4 WORK TOGETHER (continued)

4.

LeafyLift

Work Sheet

For Month Ended September 30, 20 - -

#	ACCOUNT TITLE	TRIAL BALANCE DEBIT	TRIAL BALANCE CREDIT	ADJUSTMENTS DEBIT	ADJUSTMENTS CREDIT	INCOME STATEMENT DEBIT	INCOME STATEMENT CREDIT	BALANCE SHEET DEBIT	BALANCE SHEET CREDIT
1	Cash	8000.00						8000.00	
2	Accts. Rec.—Sharon Mann	1000.00						1000.00	
3	Supplies	725.00		(a) 390.00				1115.00	
4	Prepaid Insurance	400.00		(b) 95.00				495.00	
5	Accts. Pay.—Powers Supply		150.00						150.00
6	Paul Coty, Capital		5000.00						5000.00
7	Paul Coty, Drawing	300.00							300.00
8	Income Summary								
9	Sales		1875.00				1875.00		
10	Insurance Expense				(b) 95.00		95.00		
11	Miscellaneous Expense	125.00				152.00			
12	Supplies Expense				(a) 390.00		390.00		
13		10550.00	7025.00	485.00	485.00	152.00	2360.00	10610.00	5450.00
14	Net Income					2208.00			5160.00
15						2360.00	2360.00	10610.00	10610.00

Extra form

	ACCOUNT TITLE		TRIAL BALANCE		ADJUSTMENTS		INCOME STATEMENT		BALANCE SHEET	
			1 DEBIT	2 CREDIT	3 DEBIT	4 CREDIT	5 DEBIT	6 CREDIT	7 DEBIT	8 CREDIT
1										
2										
3										
4										
5										
6										
7										
8										
9										
10										
11										
12										
13										
14										
15										
16										
17										
18										
19										
20										
21										
22										
23										

7-4   WORK TOGETHER (concluded)

6.

#	ACCOUNT TITLE	TRIAL BALANCE DEBIT	TRIAL BALANCE CREDIT	ADJUSTMENTS DEBIT	ADJUSTMENTS CREDIT	INCOME STATEMENT DEBIT	INCOME STATEMENT CREDIT	BALANCE SHEET DEBIT	BALANCE SHEET CREDIT
1	Cash	4250 00						4250 00	
2	A/R – Sharon Mann	1000 00						1000 00	
3	Supplies	1025 00			(a) 390 00			635 00	
4	Prepaid Insurance	300 00			(b) 95 00			205 00	
5	A/P – Bons Supply		150 00						150 00
6	Paul Coty, Capital		5000 00						5000 00
7	Paul Coty, Drawing	300 00						300 00	
8	Income Summary								
9	Sales		1900 00				1900 00		
10	Insurance Expense			(b) 95 00		95 00			
11	Misc. Expense	175 00				175 00			
12	Supplies Expense			(a) 390 00		390 00			
13		7050 00	7050 00	485 00	485 00	660 00	1900 00	6390 00	5150 00
14	Net Income					1240 00			1240 00
15						1900 00	1900 00	6390 00	6390 00
16									
17									
18									
19									
20									
21									

Extra form

ACCOUNT TITLE		TRIAL BALANCE		ADJUSTMENTS		INCOME STATEMENT		BALANCE SHEET	
		DEBIT	CREDIT	DEBIT	CREDIT	DEBIT	CREDIT	DEBIT	CREDIT
1									
2									
3									
4									
5									
6									
7									
8									
9									
10									
11									
12									
13									
14									
15									
16									
17									
18									
19									
20									
21									
22									
23									

Name _____ Date _____ Class _____

7-4 ON YOUR OWN, p. 167

Finding and correcting errors in accounting records

7., 8.   **GENERAL LEDGER**

ACCOUNT Cash   ACCOUNT NO. 110

DATE		ITEM	POST. REF.	DEBIT	CREDIT	BALANCE	
						DEBIT	CREDIT
20-- Nov.	1		G1	11 000 00		11 000 00	
	30		G2	6 495 00		17 945 00	
	30		G2		5 550 00	12 395 00	

ACCOUNT Supplies   ACCOUNT NO. 120

DATE		ITEM	POST. REF.	DEBIT	CREDIT	BALANCE	
						DEBIT	CREDIT
20-- Nov.	2		G1	400 00		400 00	
	25		G2	100 00		140 00	

ACCOUNT Prepaid Insurance   ACCOUNT NO. 130

DATE		ITEM	POST. REF.	DEBIT	CREDIT	BALANCE	
						DEBIT	CREDIT
20-- Nov.	3		G1	250 00		520 00	

ACCOUNT Accounts Payable—NW Electric   ACCOUNT NO. 210

DATE		ITEM	POST. REF.	DEBIT	CREDIT	BALANCE	
						DEBIT	CREDIT
20-- Nov.	4		G1		500 00		500 00
	15		G2	150 00			650 00

ACCOUNT Marlene Lewis, Capital   ACCOUNT NO. 310

DATE		ITEM	POST. REF.	DEBIT	CREDIT	BALANCE	
						DEBIT	CREDIT
20-- Nov.	1		G1		11 000 00		11 000 00

7., 8.   **GENERAL LEDGER**

ACCOUNT Marlene Lewis, Drawing   ACCOUNT NO. 320

DATE	ITEM	POST. REF.	DEBIT	CREDIT	BALANCE DEBIT	BALANCE CREDIT
Nov. 20-- 30		G2	4 0 0 00		4 0 0 00	

ACCOUNT Income Summary   ACCOUNT NO. 330

DATE	ITEM	POST. REF.	DEBIT	CREDIT	BALANCE DEBIT	BALANCE CREDIT

ACCOUNT Sales   ACCOUNT NO. 410

DATE	ITEM	POST. REF.	DEBIT	CREDIT	BALANCE DEBIT	BALANCE CREDIT
Nov. 20-- 30		G2		1 9 0 0 00		1 9 0 0 00

ACCOUNT Insurance Expense   ACCOUNT NO. 510

DATE	ITEM	POST. REF.	DEBIT	CREDIT	BALANCE DEBIT	BALANCE CREDIT

ACCOUNT Miscellaneous Expense   ACCOUNT NO. 520

DATE	ITEM	POST. REF.	DEBIT	CREDIT	BALANCE DEBIT	BALANCE CREDIT
Nov. 20-- 9		G1	1 0 0 00		1 0 0 00	
27		G2	5 5 00		4 5 00	

ACCOUNT Supplies Expense   ACCOUNT NO. 530

DATE	ITEM	POST. REF.	DEBIT	CREDIT	BALANCE DEBIT	BALANCE CREDIT

7-4 **ON YOUR OWN (continued)**

7. **ERRORS**

7.   ERRORS

7-4   **ON YOUR OWN (continued)**

7.

Internet Access
Work Sheet
For Month Ended November 30, 20 – –

#	ACCOUNT TITLE	TRIAL BALANCE DEBIT	TRIAL BALANCE CREDIT	ADJUSTMENTS DEBIT	ADJUSTMENTS CREDIT	INCOME STATEMENT DEBIT	INCOME STATEMENT CREDIT	BALANCE SHEET DEBIT	BALANCE SHEET CREDIT
1	Cash	12395 00						12395 00	
2	Supplies	140 00			(b) 104 00			230 00	
3	Prepaid Insurance	520 00			(a) 90 00			430 00	
4	Accts. Pay.—NW Electric		650 00						650 00
5	Marlene Lewis, Capital		11000 00						11000 00
6	Marlene Lewis, Drawing	400 00						400 00	
7	Income Summary								
8	Sales		1900 00				1900 00		
9	Insurance Expense			(a) 90 00		90 00			
10	Miscellaneous Expense	54 00				54 00			
11	Supplies Expense			(b) 104 00		104 00			
12		13500 00	13550 00	194 00	194 00	54 00	2094 00	13267 00	12050 00
13	Net Income					2040 00			1217 00
14						2094 00	2094 00	13267 00	13267 00
15									
16									
17									
18									
19									
20									
21									

Extra form

ACCOUNT TITLE	TRIAL BALANCE		ADJUSTMENTS		INCOME STATEMENT		BALANCE SHEET	
	1 DEBIT	2 CREDIT	3 DEBIT	4 CREDIT	5 DEBIT	6 CREDIT	7 DEBIT	8 CREDIT
1								
2								
3								
4								
5								
6								
7								
8								
9								
10								
11								
12								
13								
14								
15								
16								
17								
18								
19								
20								
21								
22								
23								

7-4 **ON YOUR OWN (concluded)**

9.

ACCOUNT TITLE	TRIAL BALANCE		ADJUSTMENTS		INCOME STATEMENT		BALANCE SHEET	
	DEBIT	CREDIT	DEBIT	CREDIT	DEBIT	CREDIT	DEBIT	CREDIT
1								
2								
3								
4								
5								
6								
7								
8								
9								
10								
11								
12								
13								
14								
15								
16								
17								
18								
19								
20								
21								

Extra form

ACCOUNT TITLE	TRIAL BALANCE		ADJUSTMENTS		INCOME STATEMENT		BALANCE SHEET	
	DEBIT	CREDIT	DEBIT	CREDIT	DEBIT	CREDIT	DEBIT	CREDIT
	1	2	3	4	5	6	7	8
1								
2								
3								
4								
5								
6								
7								
8								
9								
10								
11								
12								
13								
14								
15								
16								
17								
18								
19								
20								
21								
22								
23								

7-1, 7-2, and 7-3 APPLICATION PROBLEMS, p. 169

7-1 Recording the trial balance on a work sheet
7-2 Planning adjustments on a work sheet
7-3 Completing a work sheet

Roseville Rental

Worksheet

For month ending June 30, 2008

	TRIAL BALANCE		ADJUSTMENTS		INCOME STATEMENT		BALANCE SHEET	
ACCOUNT TITLE	DEBIT	CREDIT	DEBIT	CREDIT	DEBIT	CREDIT	DEBIT	CREDIT
1 Cash								
2 Petty Cash								
3 A/R – Kip Teslow								
4 A/R – Laura N Day								
5 Supplies								
6 Prepaid Insurance								
7 A/P – Ling Music Supplies								
8 A/P – Sullivan Office Supply								
9 Barbara Trevino Capital								
10 Barbara Trevino, Drawing								
11 Income Summary								
12 Sales								
13 Advertising Expense								
14 Insurance Expense								
15 Miscellaneous Expense								
16 Rent Expense								
17 Supplies Expense								
18 Utilities Expense								
19								
20								

Extra form

Lewisville Rental
Work Sheet
For Month Ended June 30, 200 8

	ACCOUNT TITLE	TRIAL BALANCE DEBIT	TRIAL BALANCE CREDIT	ADJUSTMENTS DEBIT	ADJUSTMENTS CREDIT	INCOME STATEMENT DEBIT	INCOME STATEMENT CREDIT	BALANCE SHEET DEBIT	BALANCE SHEET CREDIT	
1	Cash	10610 00						10610 00		1
2	Petty Cash	100 00						100 00		2
3	A/R—Nachfelder	805 00						805 00		3
4	Supplies	750 00			(a) 150 00			600 00		4
5	Prepaid Insurance	800 00			(b) 100 00			700 00		5
6	A/P—Faith Miltman		555 00						555 00	6
7	Rebecca Chin, Capital		11926 00						11926 00	7
8	Rebecca Chin, Drawing	700 00						700 00		8
9	Income Summary									9
10	Sales		2220 00				2220 00			10
11	Advertising Expense	480 00				480 00				11
12	Insurance Expense			(b) 100 00		100 00				12
13	Miscellaneous Expense	144 00				144 00				13
14	Supplies Expense			(a) 150 00		150 00				14
15	Utilities Expense	312 00				312 00				15
16		14701 00	14701 00	250 00	250 00	1186 00	2220 00	13515 00	12481 00	16
17	Net Income					1034 00			1034 00	17
18						2220 00	2220 00	13515 00	13515 00	18
19										19
20										20
21										21
22										22
23										23

7-4 APPLICATION PROBLEM, p. 170

Finding and correcting errors in accounting records

1., 2.   **GENERAL LEDGER**

ACCOUNT Cash   ACCOUNT NO. 110

DATE		ITEM	POST. REF.	DEBIT	CREDIT	BALANCE DEBIT	BALANCE CREDIT
20-- Apr.	1		G1	8 5 0 0 00		8 5 0 0 00	
	30		G2	1 5 3 5 00		10 3 0 5 00	
	30		G2		2 3 4 0 00	7 9 6 5 00	

ACCOUNT Supplies   ACCOUNT NO. 120

DATE		ITEM	POST. REF.	DEBIT	CREDIT	BALANCE DEBIT	BALANCE CREDIT
20-- Apr.	2		G1	5 0 0 00		5 0 0 00	

ACCOUNT Prepaid Insurance   ACCOUNT NO. 130

DATE		ITEM	POST. REF.	DEBIT	CREDIT	BALANCE DEBIT	BALANCE CREDIT
20-- Apr.	3		G1	6 3 0 00		6 3 0 00	

ACCOUNT Accounts Payable—Archer Supplies   ACCOUNT NO. 210

DATE		ITEM	POST. REF.	DEBIT	CREDIT	BALANCE DEBIT	BALANCE CREDIT
20-- Apr.	4		G1		7 0 0 00		7 0 0 00
	15		G2	2 0 0 00			5 0 0 00

ACCOUNT Ervin Watkins, Capital   ACCOUNT NO. 310

DATE		ITEM	POST. REF.	DEBIT	CREDIT	BALANCE DEBIT	BALANCE CREDIT
20-- Apr.	1		G1		8 5 0 0 00		5 8 0 0 00

1., 2.   **GENERAL LEDGER**

ACCOUNT Ervin Watkins, Drawing   ACCOUNT NO. 320

DATE	ITEM	POST. REF.	DEBIT	CREDIT	BALANCE DEBIT	BALANCE CREDIT
20-- Apr. 30		G2	6 0 0 00		6 0 0 00	

ACCOUNT Income Summary   ACCOUNT NO. 330

DATE	ITEM	POST. REF.	DEBIT	CREDIT	BALANCE DEBIT	BALANCE CREDIT

ACCOUNT Sales   ACCOUNT NO. 410

DATE	ITEM	POST. REF.	DEBIT	CREDIT	BALANCE DEBIT	BALANCE CREDIT
20-- Apr. 30		G2		9 0 0 00		9 9 0 00

ACCOUNT Insurance Expense   ACCOUNT NO. 510

DATE	ITEM	POST. REF.	DEBIT	CREDIT	BALANCE DEBIT	BALANCE CREDIT

ACCOUNT Miscellaneous Expense   ACCOUNT NO. 520

DATE	ITEM	POST. REF.	DEBIT	CREDIT	BALANCE DEBIT	BALANCE CREDIT
20-- Apr. 9		G1	3 5 0 00			3 5 0 00
27		G2	1 2 5 00			2 2 5 00

ACCOUNT Supplies Expense   ACCOUNT NO. 530

DATE	ITEM	POST. REF.	DEBIT	CREDIT	BALANCE DEBIT	BALANCE CREDIT

7-4 **APPLICATION PROBLEM** (continued)

1.   **ERRORS**

1.   **ERRORS**

7-4 **APPLICATION PROBLEM (continued)**

1.

Ever Clean

Work Sheet

For Month Ended April 30, 20 – –

	ACCOUNT TITLE	TRIAL BALANCE DEBIT	TRIAL BALANCE CREDIT	ADJUSTMENTS DEBIT	ADJUSTMENTS CREDIT	INCOME STATEMENT DEBIT	INCOME STATEMENT CREDIT	BALANCE SHEET DEBIT	BALANCE SHEET CREDIT	
1	Cash	7 9 6 5 00						7 9 5 6 00		1
2	Supplies	5 0 00			(b) 3 0 0 00				2 5 0 00	2
3	Prepaid Insurance	6 3 0 00		(b) 2 1 0 00				2 4 0 00		3
4	Accts. Pay.—Archer Supplies		5 0 0 00						5 0 0 00	4
5	Ervin Watkins, Capital		5 8 0 0 00						5 8 0 0 00	5
6	Ervin Watkins, Drawing	6 0 0 00						6 0 0 00		6
7	Income Summary									7
8	Sales		9 9 0 00				9 9 0 00			8
9	Insurance Expense				(b) 2 1 0 00	2 1 0 00				9
10	Miscellaneous Expense	2 2 5 00				2 2 5 00				10
11	Supplies Expense			(b) 3 0 0 00		3 0 0 00				11
12		9 4 7 0 00	7 2 9 0 00	5 1 0 00	5 1 0 00	5 2 5 00	1 2 0 0 00	8 7 9 6 00	6 5 5 0 00	12
13	Net Income					6 7 5 00			2 2 4 6 00	13
14						1 2 0 0 00	1 2 0 0 00	8 7 9 6 00	8 7 9 6 00	14
15										15
16										16
17										17
18										18
19										19
20										20
21										21

Extra form

ACCOUNT TITLE		TRIAL BALANCE		ADJUSTMENTS		INCOME STATEMENT		BALANCE SHEET	
		1 DEBIT	2 CREDIT	3 DEBIT	4 CREDIT	5 DEBIT	6 CREDIT	7 DEBIT	8 CREDIT
1									
2									
3									
4									
5									
6									
7									
8									
9									
10									
11									
12									
13									
14									
15									
16									
17									
18									
19									
20									
21									
22									
23									

7-4 **APPLICATION PROBLEM (concluded)**

ACCOUNT TITLE	TRIAL BALANCE		ADJUSTMENTS		INCOME STATEMENT		BALANCE SHEET	
	1 DEBIT	2 CREDIT	3 DEBIT	4 CREDIT	5 DEBIT	6 CREDIT	7 DEBIT	8 CREDIT

Extra form

| ACCOUNT TITLE | | TRIAL BALANCE | | ADJUSTMENTS | | INCOME STATEMENT | | BALANCE SHEET | |
		1 DEBIT	2 CREDIT	3 DEBIT	4 CREDIT	5 DEBIT	6 CREDIT	7 DEBIT	8 CREDIT
1									
2									
3									
4									
5									
6									
7									
8									
9									
10									
11									
12									
13									
14									
15									
16									
17									
18									
19									
20									
21									
22									
23									

7-5   MASTERY PROBLEM, p. 170

Completing a work sheet

EasyGlo
Work Sheet
For Month Ended April 30, 20--

	Trial Balance Debit	Trial Balance Credit	Adjustments Debit	Adjustments Credit	Income Statement Debit	Income Statement Credit	Balance Sheet Debit	Balance Sheet Credit
1 Cash	1729.00						1729.00	
2 Petty Cash	200.00						200.00	
3 A/R—Lois Mahlin	561.00						561.00	
4 Supplies	895.00			(a)695.00			200.00	
5 Prepaid Insurance	1000.00			(b)250.00			750.00	
6 A/P—Avery Supplies		500.00						500.00
7 Natasha Kabila, Capital		3500.00						3500.00
8 Natasha Kabila, Drawing	400.00						400.00	
9 Income Summary								
10 Sales		2300.00				2300.00		
11 Advertising Expense	425.00				425.00			
12 Insurance Expense			(b)250.00		250.00			
13 Miscellaneous Expense	240.00				240.00			
14 Rent Expense	400.00				400.00			
15 Supplies Expense			(a)695.00		695.00			
16 Utilities Expense	450.00				450.00			
17	6300.00	6300.00	945.00	945.00	2460.00	2300.00	160.00	
18								
19 Net Loss					2460.00	2460.00	4000.00	4000.00
20								
21								

Extra form

ACCOUNT TITLE		TRIAL BALANCE		ADJUSTMENTS		INCOME STATEMENT		BALANCE SHEET	
		1 DEBIT	2 CREDIT	3 DEBIT	4 CREDIT	5 DEBIT	6 CREDIT	7 DEBIT	8 CREDIT
1									
2									
3									
4									
5									
6									
7									
8									
9									
10									
11									
12									
13									
14									
15									
16									
17									
18									
19									
20									
21									
22									
23									

7-6 **CHALLENGE PROBLEM, p. 171**

Completing a work sheet

ACCOUNT TITLE	TRIAL BALANCE		ADJUSTMENTS		INCOME STATEMENT		BALANCE SHEET	
	DEBIT	CREDIT	DEBIT	CREDIT	DEBIT	CREDIT	DEBIT	CREDIT
	1	2	3	4	5	6	7	8

Extra form

ACCOUNT TITLE		TRIAL BALANCE		ADJUSTMENTS		INCOME STATEMENT		BALANCE SHEET	
		1 DEBIT	2 CREDIT	3 DEBIT	4 CREDIT	5 DEBIT	6 CREDIT	7 DEBIT	8 CREDIT
1									
2									
3									
4									
5									
6									
7									
8									
9									
10									
11									
12									
13									
14									
15									
16									
17									
18									
19									
20									
21									
22									
23									

8-1 WORK TOGETHER, p. 180

Preparing an income statement

	ACCOUNT TITLE	5 INCOME STATEMENT DEBIT	6 INCOME STATEMENT CREDIT	7 BALANCE SHEET DEBIT	8 BALANCE SHEET CREDIT	
11	Sales		5 5 1 1 00			11
12	Advertising Expense	8 2 1 00				12
13	Insurance Expense	3 0 0 00				13
14	Miscellaneous Expense	3 4 7 00				14
15	Supplies Expense	7 1 3 00				15
16		2 1 8 1 00	5 5 1 1 00	11 0 6 0 00	7 7 3 0 00	16
17	Net Income	3 3 3 0 00			3 3 3 0 00	17
18		5 5 1 1 00	5 5 1 1 00	11 0 6 0 00	11 0 6 0 00	18
19						19
20						20
21						21
22						22

Darlen's Relivery Source
Income Statement
For Month ended July 31, 2008

				% OF SALES
Revenue:				
Sales			5 5 1 1 00	100
Expenses:				
Advertising Expense	8 2 1 00			
Insurance Expense	3 0 0 00			
Miscellaneous Expense	3 4 7 00			
Supplies Expense	7 1 3 00			
Total Expenses	2 1 8 1 00	2 1 8 1 00		39.6
Net Income			3 3 3 0 00	60.4

Preparing an income statement

	ACCOUNT TITLE	INCOME STATEMENT		BALANCE SHEET		
		5 DEBIT	6 CREDIT	7 DEBIT	8 CREDIT	
12	Sales		6 3 4 7 00			12
13	Insurance Expense	3 0 0 00				13
14	Miscellaneous Expense	9 6 2 00				14
15	Supplies Expense	5 2 0 00				15
16	Utilities Expense	1 4 1 4 00				16
17		3 1 9 6 00	6 3 4 7 00	9 1 9 8 00	6 0 4 7 00	17
18	Net Income	3 1 5 1 00			3 1 5 1 00	18
19		6 3 4 7 00	6 3 4 7 00	9 1 9 8 00	9 1 9 8 00	19
20						20
21						21
22						22
23						23

Keith's Copies

Income Statement

For Month Ended February 28, 2008

			% OF SALES
Revenue:			
Sales		6 3 47 00	100.0
Expenses:			
Insurance Expense	3 0 0 00		
Misc. Expense	9 6 2 00		
Supplies Expense	5 2 0 00		
Utilities Expense	1 4 1 4 00		
Total Expenses		3 1 96 00	50.4
Net Income		3 1 51 00	49.6

8-2 WORK TOGETHER, p. 185

Preparing a balance sheet

	ACCOUNT TITLE	BALANCE SHEET DEBIT	BALANCE SHEET CREDIT	
1	Cash	9 5 0 0 00		1
2	Petty Cash	1 0 0 00		2
3	Accts. Rec.—Betsy Russell	1 6 5 0 00		3
4	Accts. Rec.—Charles Healy	1 4 0 3 00		4
5	Supplies	2 2 0 00		5
6	Prepaid Insurance	6 4 0 00		6
7	Accts. Pay.—Lindgren Supply		5 4 8 00	7
8	Accts. Pay.—Taxes By Thomas		1 1 1 00	8
9	Ken Cherniak, Capital		11 8 1 0 00	9
10	Ken Cherniak, Drawing	8 5 5 00		10
11	Income Summary			11
18		14 3 6 8 00	12 4 6 9 00	18
19	Net Income		1 8 9 9 00	19
20		14 3 6 8 00	14 3 6 8 00	20
21				21
22				22

(handwritten:)

Ken's Carpet Cleaning
Balance Sheet
April 30, 2008

Assets		Liabilities	
Cash	9 500 00	A/P — Lindgren Supply	548 00
Petty Cash	100 00	A/P — Taxes By Thomas	111 00
~~A/R — Betsy Russell~~	~~1650~~	Total Liabilities	659 00
A/R — Charles Healy	1 403 00	Owner's Equity	
A/R — Betsy Russell	1 650 00	Ken Cherniak, Capital	12 854 00
Supplies	220 00		
Prepaid Insurance	640 00		
Total Assets	13 513 00	Total Liab. & Owner's Eq.	13 513 00

Preparing a balance sheet

	ACCOUNT TITLE	BALANCE SHEET DEBIT	BALANCE SHEET CREDIT	
1	Cash	6 4 0 0 00		1
2	Petty Cash	1 0 0 00		2
3	Accts. Rec.—Debbie McDonald	6 5 7 00		3
4	Accts. Rec.—Howard Kiklas	5 9 9 00		4
5	Supplies	1 5 5 00		5
6	Prepaid Insurance	3 0 0 00		6
7	Accts. Pay.—Bailey's Supply		1 8 7 00	7
8	Accts. Pay.—Freida's on Fulton		1 2 6 00	8
9	Jane Wisen, Capital		6 4 3 0 00	9
10	Jane Wisen, Drawing	1 5 0 0 00		10
16		9 7 1 1 00	6 7 4 3 00	16
17	Net Income		2 9 6 8 00	17
18		9 7 1 1 00	9 7 1 1 00	18
19				19
20				20
21				21

Jane's Sewing Machine Repair
Balance Sheet
October 31, 2008

Assets		Liabilities	
Cash	6 400 00	A/P - Bailey's Supply	1 87 00
Petty Cash	1 00 00	A/P - Freida's on Fulton	1 26 00
Accts. Rec. - Debbie McDon.	6 57 00	Total liabilities	3 13 00
A/R - Howard Kiklas	5 99 00	Owner's Equity	
Supplies	1 55 00	Jane Wisen, Capital	7 898 00
Prepaid Insurance	3 00 00		
Total Assets	8 211 00	Total Liabilities & Owner's Eq.	8 211 00

8-1 APPLICATION PROBLEM, p. 187

Preparing an income statement

Robbie's Rugcare
Income Statement
For Month Ended August 31, 2008

				% OF SALES
Revenue:				
Sales			5707 00	
Expenses:				
Advertising Expense		900 00		
Insurance Expense		200 00		
Miscellaneous Expense		267 00		
Supplies Expense		500 00		
Utilities Expense		1592 00		
Total Expenses		3229 00	3229 00	56.6
Net Income			2478 00	43.4

Extra form

											% OF SALES

8-2 APPLICATION PROBLEM, p. 187

Preparing a balance sheet

Robbins Rugcare
Balance Sheet
August 31, 2008

Assets		Liabilities	
Cash	8752 00	A/P – Daniel Supplies	442 00
A/R – Crystal Thompson	200 00	A/P – Francis Irons	676 00
A/R – Robert Bojie	175 00	Total Liabilities	1118 00
Supplies	400 00	Owner's Equity	
Prepaid Insurance	220 00	Roberta Greenstein, Capital	8629 00
~~A/P – Daniel Supplies~~			
~~A/P – Francis Irons~~			
~~Robert~~			
Total Assets	9747 00	Total Liabilities & Own. Eq.	9747 00

Extra form

8-3   MASTERY PROBLEM, p. 188

Preparing financial statements with a net loss

1., 2.

Mancini Hair Care
Income Statement
For Month Ended September 30, 2008

		% OF SALES
Revenue:		
Sales		4 5 9 6 00
Expenses:		
Advertising Expense	5 5 0 00	
Insurance Expense	1 7 5 00	
Miscellaneous Expense	5 8 00	
Supplies Expense	1 5 0 0 00	
Utilities Expense	2 7 1 4 00	
Total Expenses		4 9 9 7 00	108.7
Net Loss		(4 0 1 00)	(8.7)

3.

Mancini Hair Care
Balance Sheet
September 30, 2008

Assets		Liabilities	
Cash	7 6 7 8 00	A/P - Aldo Supplies	7 3 3 00
Petty Cash	1 0 0 00	Owner's Equity	
A/R - Jennifer Baba	1 6 4 00	Jim Mancini, Capital	8 5 9 9 00
Supplies	6 9 0 00		
Prepaid Insurance	7 0 0 00		
Total Assets	9 3 3 2 00	Total Liabilities & O. Eq.	9 3 3 2 00

Extra forms

						% OF SALES

8-4 CHALLENGE PROBLEM, p. 188

Preparing financial statements with two sources of revenue and a net loss

1., 2.

					% OF SALES

3.

Extra forms

		% OF SALES

9-1 Journalizing and posting adjusting entries
9-2 Journalizing and posting closing entries

ACCOUNT TITLE	ADJUSTMENTS DEBIT	ADJUSTMENTS CREDIT	INCOME STATEMENT DEBIT	INCOME STATEMENT CREDIT	BALANCE SHEET DEBIT	BALANCE SHEET CREDIT
1 Cash					7350 00	
2 Accts. Rec.—Romelle Woods					372 00	
3 Accts. Rec.—Wyatt Ames					88 00	
4 Supplies		(a) 713 00			250 00	
5 Prepaid Insurance		(b) 300 00			900 00	
6 Accts. Pay.—Colin Gas						975 00
7 Accts. Pay.—Grand Uniforms						212 00
8 Darlene Wong, Capital						6543 00
9 Darlene Wong, Drawing					2100 00	
10 Income Summary						
11 Sales				5511 00		
12 Advertising Expense			821 00			
13 Insurance Expense	(b) 300 00		300 00			
14 Miscellaneous Expense			347 00			
15 Supplies Expense	(a) 713 00		713 00			
16	1013 00	1013 00	2181 00	5511 00	11060 00	7730 00
17 Net Income			3330 00			3330 00
18			5511 00	5511 00	11060 00	11060 00

9-1 Journalizing and posting adjusting entries
9-2 Journalizing and posting closing entries

	ACCOUNT TITLE	ADJUSTMENTS DEBIT	ADJUSTMENTS CREDIT	INCOME STATEMENT DEBIT	INCOME STATEMENT CREDIT	BALANCE SHEET DEBIT	BALANCE SHEET CREDIT	
1	Cash					6072 00		1
2	Petty Cash					175 00		2
3	Accts. Rec.—Terry Jo Hugo					356 00		3
4	Accts. Rec.—Jean Asmus					128 00		4
5	Supplies		(a) 520 00			117 00		5
6	Prepaid Insurance		(b) 300 00			600 00		6
7	Accts. Pay.—Jaeger Repair						758 00	7
8	Accts. Pay.—Dakota Supply						129 00	8
9	Keith Altobelli, Capital						5160 00	9
10	Keith Altobelli, Drawing					175 0 00		10
11	Income Summary							11
12	Sales				6347 00			12
13	Insurance Expense	(b) 300 00		300 00				13
14	Miscellaneous Expense			962 00				14
15	Supplies Expense	(a) 520 00		520 00				15
16	Utilities Expense			1414 00				16
17		820 00	820 00	3196 00	6347 00	9198 00	6047 00	17
18	Net Income			3151 00			3151 00	18
19				6347 00	6347 00	9198 00	9198 00	19
20								20
21								21
22								22

9-1 and 9-2   WORK TOGETHER (continued)

GENERAL JOURNAL   PAGE   8

	DATE 20--	ACCOUNT TITLE	DOC. NO.	POST. REF.	DEBIT	CREDIT	
1		Adjusting Entries					1
2	Jul 31	Supplies Expense		540	713 00		2
3		Supplies		140		713 00	3
4	31	Insurance Expense		520	300 00		4
5		Prepaid Insurance		150		300 00	5
6		Closing Entries					6
7	31	Sales		410	5711 00		7
8		Income Summary		330		5711 00	8
9	31	Income Summary		330	2181 00		9
10		Advertising Expense		510		821 00	10
11		Insurance Expense		520		300 00	11
12		Miscellaneous Expense		530		347 00	12
13		Supplies Expense		540		713 00	13
14	31	Income Summary		330	3330 00		14
15		Darlene Wong, capital		310		3330 00	15
16	31	Darlene Wong, capital		310	2100 00		16
17		Darlene Wong, drawing		320		2100 00	17
18							18
19							19
20							20
21							21
22							22
23							23
24							24
25							25
26							26
27							27
28							28
29							29
30							30
31							31
32							32
33							33
34							34

(On Your Own is continued on pages 176–178.)

GENERAL JOURNAL   PAGE 8

	DATE 20X8	ACCOUNT TITLE	DOC. NO.	POST. REF.	DEBIT	CREDIT	
1		Adjusting Entries					1
2	Feb 28	Supplies Expense			520 00		2
3		Supplies				520 00	3
4	28	Insurance Expense			300 00		4
5		Prepaid Insurance				300 00	5
6		Closing Entries					6
7	28	Sales			6347 00		7
8		Income Summary				6347 00	8
9	28	Income Summary			3196 00		9
10		Insurance				300 00	10
11		Miscellaneous				962 00	11
12		Supplies				520 00	12
13		Utilities				1414 00	13
14	28	Income Summary			3151 00		14
15		Kieth Altodelli, capital				3151 00	15
16	28	Kieth Altodelli, capital			1750 00		16
17		Keith Altodelli, drawing				1750 00	17
18							18
19							19
20							20
21							21
22							22
23							23
24							24
25							25
26							26
27							27
28							28
29							29
30							30
31							31
32							32
33							33

9-1 and 9-2 WORK TOGETHER (continued)

GENERAL LEDGER

ACCOUNT Cash   ACCOUNT NO. 110

DATE	ITEM	POST. REF.	DEBIT	CREDIT	BALANCE DEBIT	BALANCE CREDIT
20-- July 31	Balance	✔			7 3 5 0 00	

ACCOUNT Accounts Receivable—Romelle Woods   ACCOUNT NO. 120

DATE	ITEM	POST. REF.	DEBIT	CREDIT	BALANCE DEBIT	BALANCE CREDIT
20-- July 31	Balance	✔			3 7 2 00	

ACCOUNT Accounts Receivable—Wyatt Ames   ACCOUNT NO. 130

DATE	ITEM	POST. REF.	DEBIT	CREDIT	BALANCE DEBIT	BALANCE CREDIT
20-- July 31	Balance	✔			8 8 00	

ACCOUNT Supplies   ACCOUNT NO. 140

DATE	ITEM	POST. REF.	DEBIT	CREDIT	BALANCE DEBIT	BALANCE CREDIT
20-- July 31	Balance	✔			9 6 3 00	
31				7 1 3 00	2 5 0 00	

ACCOUNT Prepaid Insurance   ACCOUNT NO. 150

DATE	ITEM	POST. REF.	DEBIT	CREDIT	BALANCE DEBIT	BALANCE CREDIT
20-- July 31	Balance	✔			1 2 0 0 00	
31		6-8		3 0 0 00	9 0 0 00	

ACCOUNT Accounts Payable—Colin Gas   ACCOUNT NO. 210

DATE	ITEM	POST. REF.	DEBIT	CREDIT	BALANCE DEBIT	BALANCE CREDIT
20-- July 31	Balance	✔				9 7 5 00

GENERAL LEDGER

ACCOUNT Accounts Payable—Grand Uniforms   ACCOUNT NO. 220

DATE		ITEM	POST. REF.	DEBIT	CREDIT	BALANCE DEBIT	BALANCE CREDIT
July 20--	31	Balance	✔				2 1 2 00

ACCOUNT Darlene Wong, Capital   ACCOUNT NO. 310

DATE		ITEM	POST. REF.	DEBIT	CREDIT	BALANCE DEBIT	BALANCE CREDIT
July 20--	31	Balance	✔				6 5 4 3 00
	31		G8		3 3 3 0 00		9 8 7 3 00
	31		G8	2 1 0 0 00			7 7 7 3 00

ACCOUNT Darlene Wong, Drawing   ACCOUNT NO. 320

DATE		ITEM	POST. REF.	DEBIT	CREDIT	BALANCE DEBIT	BALANCE CREDIT
July 20--	31	Balance	✔			2 1 0 0 00	
	31				2 1 0 0 00	0 0 0 0 00	

ACCOUNT Income Summary   ACCOUNT NO. 330

DATE		ITEM	POST. REF.	DEBIT	CREDIT	BALANCE DEBIT	BALANCE CREDIT
Jul 31			G8		5 5 1 1 00		5 5 1 1 00
	31		G8	2 1 8 1 00			3 3 3 0 00
	31		G8	3 3 3 0 00			0 0 0 0 00

ACCOUNT Sales   ACCOUNT NO. 410

DATE		ITEM	POST. REF.	DEBIT	CREDIT	BALANCE DEBIT	BALANCE CREDIT
July 20--	31	Balance	✔				5 5 1 1 00
	31		G8	5 5 1 1 00			0 0 0 0 00

ACCOUNT Advertising Expense   ACCOUNT NO. 510

DATE		ITEM	POST. REF.	DEBIT	CREDIT	BALANCE DEBIT	BALANCE CREDIT
July 20--	31	Balance	✔			8 2 1 00	
	31		G8		8 2 1 00	0 0 0 00	

9-1 and 9-2   **WORK TOGETHER (concluded)**

GENERAL LEDGER

ACCOUNT Insurance Expense   ACCOUNT NO. 520

DATE	ITEM	POST. REF.	DEBIT	CREDIT	BALANCE DEBIT	BALANCE CREDIT
Jul 31		68	300 00		300 00	
31		68		300 00	000 00	

ACCOUNT Miscellaneous Expense   ACCOUNT NO. 530

DATE	ITEM	POST. REF.	DEBIT	CREDIT	BALANCE DEBIT	BALANCE CREDIT
20-- July 31	Balance	✔			347 00	
31		68		347 00	000 00	

ACCOUNT Supplies Expense   ACCOUNT NO. 540

DATE 2008	ITEM	POST. REF.	DEBIT	CREDIT	BALANCE DEBIT	BALANCE CREDIT
Jul 31		68	713 00		713 00	
31				713 00	000 00	

ACCOUNT   ACCOUNT NO.

DATE	ITEM	POST. REF.	DEBIT	CREDIT	BALANCE DEBIT	BALANCE CREDIT

ACCOUNT   ACCOUNT NO.

DATE	ITEM	POST. REF.	DEBIT	CREDIT	BALANCE DEBIT	BALANCE CREDIT

ACCOUNT   ACCOUNT NO.

DATE	ITEM	POST. REF.	DEBIT	CREDIT	BALANCE DEBIT	BALANCE CREDIT

GENERAL LEDGER

ACCOUNT Cash   ACCOUNT NO. 110

DATE		ITEM	POST. REF.	DEBIT	CREDIT	BALANCE	
						DEBIT	CREDIT
Feb.	28	Balance	✔			6 0 7 2 00	

ACCOUNT Petty Cash   ACCOUNT NO. 120

DATE		ITEM	POST. REF.	DEBIT	CREDIT	BALANCE	
						DEBIT	CREDIT
Feb.	28	Balance	✔			1 7 5 00	

ACCOUNT Accounts Receivable—Terry Jo Hugo   ACCOUNT NO. 130

DATE		ITEM	POST. REF.	DEBIT	CREDIT	BALANCE	
						DEBIT	CREDIT
Feb.	28	Balance	✔			3 5 6 00	

ACCOUNT Accounts Receivable—Jean Asmus   ACCOUNT NO. 140

DATE		ITEM	POST. REF.	DEBIT	CREDIT	BALANCE	
						DEBIT	CREDIT
Feb.	28	Balance	✔			1 2 8 00	

ACCOUNT Supplies   ACCOUNT NO. 150

DATE		ITEM	POST. REF.	DEBIT	CREDIT	BALANCE	
						DEBIT	CREDIT
Feb.	28	Balance	✔			6 3 7 00	

ACCOUNT Prepaid Insurance   ACCOUNT NO. 160

DATE		ITEM	POST. REF.	DEBIT	CREDIT	BALANCE	
						DEBIT	CREDIT
Feb.	28	Balance	✔			9 0 0 00	

9-1 and 9-2 ON YOUR OWN (continued)

GENERAL LEDGER

ACCOUNT Accounts Payable—Jaeger Repair   ACCOUNT NO. 210

DATE		ITEM	POST. REF.	DEBIT	CREDIT	BALANCE	
						DEBIT	CREDIT
20-- Feb.	28	Balance	✔				7 5 8 00

ACCOUNT Accounts Payable—Dakota Supply   ACCOUNT NO. 220

DATE		ITEM	POST. REF.	DEBIT	CREDIT	BALANCE	
						DEBIT	CREDIT
20-- Feb.	28	Balance	✔				1 2 9 00

ACCOUNT Keith Altobelli, Capital   ACCOUNT NO. 310

DATE		ITEM	POST. REF.	DEBIT	CREDIT	BALANCE	
						DEBIT	CREDIT
20-- Feb.	28	Balance	✔				5 1 6 0 00

ACCOUNT Keith Altobelli, Drawing   ACCOUNT NO. 320

DATE		ITEM	POST. REF.	DEBIT	CREDIT	BALANCE	
						DEBIT	CREDIT
20-- Feb.	28	Balance	✔			1 7 5 0 00	

ACCOUNT Income Summary   ACCOUNT NO. 330

DATE		ITEM	POST. REF.	DEBIT	CREDIT	BALANCE	
						DEBIT	CREDIT

ACCOUNT Sales   ACCOUNT NO. 410

DATE		ITEM	POST. REF.	DEBIT	CREDIT	BALANCE	
						DEBIT	CREDIT
20-- Feb.	28	Balance	✔				6 3 4 7 00

GENERAL LEDGER

ACCOUNT Insurance Expense   ACCOUNT NO. 510

DATE	ITEM	POST. REF.	DEBIT	CREDIT	BALANCE DEBIT	BALANCE CREDIT

ACCOUNT Miscellaneous Expense   ACCOUNT NO. 520

DATE	ITEM	POST. REF.	DEBIT	CREDIT	BALANCE DEBIT	BALANCE CREDIT
Feb. 28	Balance	✔			9 6 2 00	

ACCOUNT Supplies Expense   ACCOUNT NO. 530

DATE	ITEM	POST. REF.	DEBIT	CREDIT	BALANCE DEBIT	BALANCE CREDIT

ACCOUNT Utilities Expense   ACCOUNT NO. 540

DATE	ITEM	POST. REF.	DEBIT	CREDIT	BALANCE DEBIT	BALANCE CREDIT
Feb. 28	Balance	✔			1 4 1 4 00	

ACCOUNT   ACCOUNT NO.

DATE	ITEM	POST. REF.	DEBIT	CREDIT	BALANCE DEBIT	BALANCE CREDIT

ACCOUNT   ACCOUNT NO.

DATE	ITEM	POST. REF.	DEBIT	CREDIT	BALANCE DEBIT	BALANCE CREDIT

9-3 WORK TOGETHER, p. 209

Preparing a post-closing trial balance

_____

_____

ACCOUNT TITLE	DEBIT	CREDIT

Preparing a post-closing trial balance

ACCOUNT TITLE	DEBIT	CREDIT

9-1 and 9-2   APPLICATION PROBLEMS, p. 211

9-1 Journalizing and posting adjusting entries
9-2 Journalizing and posting closing entries

GENERAL JOURNAL   PAGE _____

	DATE		ACCOUNT TITLE	DOC. NO.	POST. REF.	DEBIT	CREDIT	
1								1
2								2
3								3
4								4
5								5
6								6
7								7
8								8
9								9
10								10
11								11
12								12
13								13
14								14
15								15
16								16
17								17
18								18
19								19
20								20
21								21
22								22
23								23
24								24
25								25
26								26
27								27
28								28
29								29
30								30
31								31
32								32

APPLICATION PROBLEMS (continued)

GENERAL LEDGER

ACCOUNT Cash   ACCOUNT NO. 110

DATE		ITEM	POST. REF.	DEBIT	CREDIT	BALANCE	
						DEBIT	CREDIT
20-- Apr.	30	Balance	✔			9 5 0 0 00	

ACCOUNT Petty Cash   ACCOUNT NO. 120

DATE		ITEM	POST. REF.	DEBIT	CREDIT	BALANCE	
						DEBIT	CREDIT
20-- Apr.	30	Balance	✔			1 0 0 00	

ACCOUNT Accounts Receivable—Betsy Russell   ACCOUNT NO. 130

DATE		ITEM	POST. REF.	DEBIT	CREDIT	BALANCE	
						DEBIT	CREDIT
20-- Apr.	30	Balance	✔			1 6 5 0 00	

ACCOUNT Accounts Receivable—Charles Healy   ACCOUNT NO. 140

DATE		ITEM	POST. REF.	DEBIT	CREDIT	BALANCE	
						DEBIT	CREDIT
20-- Apr.	30	Balance	✔			1 4 0 3 00	

ACCOUNT Supplies   ACCOUNT NO. 150

DATE		ITEM	POST. REF.	DEBIT	CREDIT	BALANCE	
						DEBIT	CREDIT
20-- Apr.	30	Balance	✔			4 0 0 00	

ACCOUNT Prepaid Insurance   ACCOUNT NO. 160

DATE		ITEM	POST. REF.	DEBIT	CREDIT	BALANCE	
						DEBIT	CREDIT
20-- Apr.	30	Balance	✔			8 0 0 00	

9-1 and 9-2   APPLICATION PROBLEMS (continued)

GENERAL LEDGER

ACCOUNT Accounts Payable—Lindgren Supply   ACCOUNT NO. 210

DATE		ITEM	POST. REF.	DEBIT	CREDIT	BALANCE	
						DEBIT	CREDIT
Apr.²⁰ ⁻ ⁻	30	Balance	✔				5 4 8 00

ACCOUNT Accounts Payable—Taxes By Thomas   ACCOUNT NO. 220

DATE		ITEM	POST. REF.	DEBIT	CREDIT	BALANCE	
						DEBIT	CREDIT
Apr.²⁰ ⁻ ⁻	30	Balance	✔				1 1 1 00

ACCOUNT Ken Cherniak, Capital   ACCOUNT NO. 310

DATE		ITEM	POST. REF.	DEBIT	CREDIT	BALANCE	
						DEBIT	CREDIT
Apr.²⁰ ⁻ ⁻	30	Balance	✔				11 8 1 0 00

ACCOUNT Ken Cherniak, Drawing   ACCOUNT NO. 320

DATE		ITEM	POST. REF.	DEBIT	CREDIT	BALANCE	
						DEBIT	CREDIT
Apr.²⁰ ⁻ ⁻	30	Balance	✔			8 5 5 00	

ACCOUNT Income Summary   ACCOUNT NO. 330

DATE		ITEM	POST. REF.	DEBIT	CREDIT	BALANCE	
						DEBIT	CREDIT

ACCOUNT Sales   ACCOUNT NO. 410

DATE		ITEM	POST. REF.	DEBIT	CREDIT	BALANCE	
						DEBIT	CREDIT
Apr.²⁰ ⁻ ⁻	30	Balance	✔				4 4 0 0 00

APPLICATION PROBLEMS (concluded)

GENERAL LEDGER

ACCOUNT **Advertising Expense** ACCOUNT NO. 510

DATE		ITEM	POST. REF.	DEBIT	CREDIT	BALANCE	
						DEBIT	CREDIT
Apr. 20--	30	Balance	✔			8 0 0 00	

ACCOUNT **Insurance Expense** ACCOUNT NO. 520

DATE		ITEM	POST. REF.	DEBIT	CREDIT	BALANCE	
						DEBIT	CREDIT

ACCOUNT **Miscellaneous Expense** ACCOUNT NO. 530

DATE		ITEM	POST. REF.	DEBIT	CREDIT	BALANCE	
						DEBIT	CREDIT
Apr. 20--	30	Balance	✔			3 5 1 00	

ACCOUNT **Supplies Expense** ACCOUNT NO. 540

DATE		ITEM	POST. REF.	DEBIT	CREDIT	BALANCE	
						DEBIT	CREDIT

ACCOUNT **Utilities Expense** ACCOUNT NO. 550

DATE		ITEM	POST. REF.	DEBIT	CREDIT	BALANCE	
						DEBIT	CREDIT
Apr. 20--	30	Balance	✔			1 0 1 0 00	

ACCOUNT ACCOUNT NO.

DATE		ITEM	POST. REF.	DEBIT	CREDIT	BALANCE	
						DEBIT	CREDIT

9-3 APPLICATION PROBLEM, p. 212

Preparing a post-closing trial balance

ACCOUNT TITLE	DEBIT	CREDIT

Extra form

ACCOUNT TITLE	DEBIT	CREDIT

9-4 MASTERY PROBLEM, p. 212

Journalizing and posting adjusting and closing entries; preparing a post-closing trial balance

1., 2.

GENERAL JOURNAL   PAGE

	DATE	ACCOUNT TITLE	DOC. NO.	POST. REF.	DEBIT	CREDIT	
1							1
2							2
3							3
4							4
5							5
6							6
7							7
8							8
9							9
10							10
11							11
12							12
13							13
14							14
15							15
16							16
17							17
18							18
19							19
20							20
21							21
22							22
23							23
24							24
25							25
26							26
27							27
28							28
29							29
30							30

MASTERY PROBLEM (continued)

1., 2.   **GENERAL LEDGER**

ACCOUNT Cash   ACCOUNT NO. 110

DATE		ITEM	POST. REF.	DEBIT	CREDIT	BALANCE	
						DEBIT	CREDIT
Oct. 20--	31	Balance	✔			6 4 0 0 00	

ACCOUNT Petty Cash   ACCOUNT NO. 120

DATE		ITEM	POST. REF.	DEBIT	CREDIT	BALANCE	
						DEBIT	CREDIT
Oct. 20--	31	Balance	✔			1 0 0 00	

ACCOUNT Accounts Receivable—Debbie McDonald   ACCOUNT NO. 130

DATE		ITEM	POST. REF.	DEBIT	CREDIT	BALANCE	
						DEBIT	CREDIT
Oct. 20--	31	Balance	✔			6 5 7 00	

ACCOUNT Accounts Receivable—Howard Kikles   ACCOUNT NO. 140

DATE		ITEM	POST. REF.	DEBIT	CREDIT	BALANCE	
						DEBIT	CREDIT
Oct. 20--	31	Balance	✔			5 9 9 00	

ACCOUNT Supplies   ACCOUNT NO. 150

DATE		ITEM	POST. REF.	DEBIT	CREDIT	BALANCE	
						DEBIT	CREDIT
Oct. 20--	31	Balance	✔			2 7 5 00	

ACCOUNT Prepaid Insurance   ACCOUNT NO. 160

DATE		ITEM	POST. REF.	DEBIT	CREDIT	BALANCE	
						DEBIT	CREDIT
Oct. 20--	31	Balance	✔			4 5 0 00	

9-4 MASTERY PROBLEM (continued)

1., 2.
GENERAL LEDGER

ACCOUNT Accounts Payable—Bailey's Supply   ACCOUNT NO. 210

DATE		ITEM	POST. REF.	DEBIT	CREDIT	BALANCE DEBIT	BALANCE CREDIT
Oct. 20--	31	Balance	✔				1 8 7 00

ACCOUNT Accounts Payable—Freida's on Fulton   ACCOUNT NO. 220

DATE		ITEM	POST. REF.	DEBIT	CREDIT	BALANCE DEBIT	BALANCE CREDIT
Oct. 20--	31	Balance	✔				1 2 6 00

ACCOUNT Jane Wisen, Capital   ACCOUNT NO. 310

DATE		ITEM	POST. REF.	DEBIT	CREDIT	BALANCE DEBIT	BALANCE CREDIT
Oct. 20--	31	Balance	✔				6 4 3 0 00

ACCOUNT Jane Wisen, Drawing   ACCOUNT NO. 320

DATE		ITEM	POST. REF.	DEBIT	CREDIT	BALANCE DEBIT	BALANCE CREDIT
Oct. 20--	31	Balance	✔			1 5 0 0 00	

ACCOUNT Income Summary   ACCOUNT NO. 330

DATE		ITEM	POST. REF.	DEBIT	CREDIT	BALANCE DEBIT	BALANCE CREDIT

ACCOUNT Sales   ACCOUNT NO. 410

DATE		ITEM	POST. REF.	DEBIT	CREDIT	BALANCE DEBIT	BALANCE CREDIT
Oct. 20--	31	Balance	✔				4 2 3 8 00

1., 2.   **GENERAL LEDGER**

ACCOUNT Advertising Expense   ACCOUNT NO. 510

DATE		ITEM	POST. REF.	DEBIT	CREDIT	BALANCE	
						DEBIT	CREDIT
20-- Oct.	31	Balance	✔			3 8 2 00	

ACCOUNT Insurance Expense   ACCOUNT NO. 520

DATE		ITEM	POST. REF.	DEBIT	CREDIT	BALANCE	
						DEBIT	CREDIT

ACCOUNT Supplies Expense   ACCOUNT NO. 530

DATE		ITEM	POST. REF.	DEBIT	CREDIT	BALANCE	
						DEBIT	CREDIT

ACCOUNT Utilities Expense   ACCOUNT NO. 540

DATE		ITEM	POST. REF.	DEBIT	CREDIT	BALANCE	
						DEBIT	CREDIT
20-- Oct.	31	Balance	✔			6 1 8 00	

ACCOUNT   ACCOUNT NO.

DATE		ITEM	POST. REF.	DEBIT	CREDIT	BALANCE	
						DEBIT	CREDIT

ACCOUNT   ACCOUNT NO.

DATE		ITEM	POST. REF.	DEBIT	CREDIT	BALANCE	
						DEBIT	CREDIT

9-4 MASTERY PROBLEM (concluded)

3.

ACCOUNT TITLE	DEBIT	CREDIT

Extra form

ACCOUNT TITLE	DEBIT	CREDIT

9-5 CHALLENGE PROBLEM, p. 213

Journalizing and posting adjusting and closing entries with a net loss; preparing a post-closing trial balance

1., 2.

GENERAL JOURNAL   PAGE

	DATE		ACCOUNT TITLE	DOC. NO.	POST. REF.	DEBIT	CREDIT	
1								1
2								2
3								3
4								4
5								5
6								6
7								7
8								8
9								9
10								10
11								11
12								12
13								13
14								14
15								15
16								16
17								17
18								18
19								19
20								20
21								21
22								22
23								23
24								24
25								25
26								26
27								27
28								28
29								29
30								30
31								31

1., 2.   **GENERAL LEDGER**

ACCOUNT Cash   ACCOUNT NO. 110

DATE	ITEM	POST. REF.	DEBIT	CREDIT	BALANCE DEBIT	BALANCE CREDIT
Sept. 30	Balance	✔			7 6 7 8 00	

ACCOUNT Petty Cash   ACCOUNT NO. 120

DATE	ITEM	POST. REF.	DEBIT	CREDIT	BALANCE DEBIT	BALANCE CREDIT
Sept. 30	Balance	✔			1 0 0 00	

ACCOUNT Accounts Receivable—Jennifer Balsa   ACCOUNT NO. 130

DATE	ITEM	POST. REF.	DEBIT	CREDIT	BALANCE DEBIT	BALANCE CREDIT
Sept. 30	Balance	✔			1 6 4 00	

ACCOUNT Supplies   ACCOUNT NO. 140

DATE	ITEM	POST. REF.	DEBIT	CREDIT	BALANCE DEBIT	BALANCE CREDIT
Sept. 30	Balance	✔			2 1 9 0 00	

ACCOUNT Prepaid Insurance   ACCOUNT NO. 150

DATE	ITEM	POST. REF.	DEBIT	CREDIT	BALANCE DEBIT	BALANCE CREDIT
Sept. 30	Balance	✔			8 7 5 00	

ACCOUNT Accounts Payable—Alto Supplies   ACCOUNT NO. 210

DATE	ITEM	POST. REF.	DEBIT	CREDIT	BALANCE DEBIT	BALANCE CREDIT
Sept. 30	Balance	✔				7 3 3 00

9-5 CHALLENGE PROBLEM (continued)

1., 2.   **GENERAL LEDGER**

ACCOUNT Jon Mancini, Capital   ACCOUNT NO. 310

DATE		ITEM	POST. REF.	DEBIT	CREDIT	BALANCE	
						DEBIT	CREDIT
Sept.	30	Balance	✔				9 5 0 0 00

ACCOUNT Jon Mancini, Drawing   ACCOUNT NO. 320

DATE		ITEM	POST. REF.	DEBIT	CREDIT	BALANCE	
						DEBIT	CREDIT
Sept.	30	Balance	✔			5 0 0 00	

ACCOUNT Income Summary   ACCOUNT NO. 330

DATE		ITEM	POST. REF.	DEBIT	CREDIT	BALANCE	
						DEBIT	CREDIT

ACCOUNT Sales   ACCOUNT NO. 410

DATE		ITEM	POST. REF.	DEBIT	CREDIT	BALANCE	
						DEBIT	CREDIT
Sept.	30	Balance	✔				4 5 9 6 00

ACCOUNT Advertising Expense   ACCOUNT NO. 510

DATE		ITEM	POST. REF.	DEBIT	CREDIT	BALANCE	
						DEBIT	CREDIT
Sept.	30	Balance	✔			5 5 0 00	

ACCOUNT Insurance Expense   ACCOUNT NO. 520

DATE		ITEM	POST. REF.	DEBIT	CREDIT	BALANCE	
						DEBIT	CREDIT

1., 2.   **GENERAL LEDGER**

ACCOUNT Miscellaneous Expense   ACCOUNT NO. 530

DATE		ITEM	POST. REF.	DEBIT	CREDIT	BALANCE	
						DEBIT	CREDIT
Sept.	30	Balance	✔			5 8 00	

ACCOUNT Supplies Expense   ACCOUNT NO. 540

DATE		ITEM	POST. REF.	DEBIT	CREDIT	BALANCE	
						DEBIT	CREDIT

ACCOUNT Utilities Expense   ACCOUNT NO. 550

DATE		ITEM	POST. REF.	DEBIT	CREDIT	BALANCE	
						DEBIT	CREDIT
Sept.	30	Balance	✔			2 7 1 4 00	

ACCOUNT   ACCOUNT NO.

DATE		ITEM	POST. REF.	DEBIT	CREDIT	BALANCE	
						DEBIT	CREDIT

ACCOUNT   ACCOUNT NO.

DATE		ITEM	POST. REF.	DEBIT	CREDIT	BALANCE	
						DEBIT	CREDIT

ACCOUNT   ACCOUNT NO.

DATE		ITEM	POST. REF.	DEBIT	CREDIT	BALANCE	
						DEBIT	CREDIT

9-5 **CHALLENGE PROBLEM (continued)**

3.

ACCOUNT TITLE	DEBIT	CREDIT

4.

REINFORCEMENT ACTIVITY 1

PART B, p. 216

An Accounting Cycle for a Proprietorship: End-of-Fiscal-Period Work

The general ledger prepared in Reinforcement Activity 1, Part A, is needed to complete Reinforcement Activity 1, Part B.

8., 9., 10., 11., 12.

ACCOUNT TITLE	TRIAL BALANCE		ADJUSTMENTS		INCOME STATEMENT		BALANCE SHEET	
	DEBIT 1	CREDIT 2	DEBIT 3	CREDIT 4	DEBIT 5	CREDIT 6	DEBIT 7	CREDIT 8
1								
2								
3								
4								
5								
6								
7								
8								
9								
10								
11								
12								
13								
14								
15								
16								
17								
18								
19								
20								
21								
22								
23								
24								

REINFORCEMENT ACTIVITY 1

PART B (continued)

17. Post-Closing Trial Balance

ACCOUNT TITLE	DEBIT	CREDIT

REINFORCEMENT ACTIVITY 1

PART B (continued)

13. Income Statement

					% OF SALES

14. Balance Sheet

REINFORCEMENT ACTIVITY 1

PART B (concluded)

15., 16.

GENERAL JOURNAL

	DATE		ACCOUNT TITLE	DOC. NO.	POST. REF.	DEBIT	CREDIT	
1								1
2								2
3								3
4								4
5								5
6								6
7								7
8								8
9								9
10								10
11								11
12								12
13								13
14								14
15								15
16								16
17								17
18								18
19								19
20								20
21								21
22								22
23								23
24								24
25								25
26								26
27								27
28								28
29								29
30								30
31								31
32								32

10-1 WORK TOGETHER, p. 228

Journalizing purchases using a purchases journal

PURCHASES JOURNAL   PAGE 10

	DATE		ACCOUNT CREDITED	PURCH. NO.	POST. REF.	PURCHASES DR. ACCTS. PAY. CR.	
1							1
2							2
3							3
4							4
5							5
6							6
7							7
8							8
9							9
10							10
11							11
12							12
13							13
14							14
15							15
16							16
17							17
18							18
19							19
20							20
21							21
22							22
23							23
24							24
25							25
26							26
27							27
28							28
29							29
30							30
31							31
32							32
33							33

Journalizing purchases using a purchases journal

PURCHASES JOURNAL   PAGE 11

	DATE	ACCOUNT CREDITED	PURCH. NO.	POST. REF.	PURCHASES DR. ACCTS. PAY. CR.	
1						1
2						2
3						3
4						4
5						5
6						6
7						7
8						8
9						9
10						10
11						11
12						12
13						13
14						14
15						15
16						16
17						17
18						18
19						19
20						20
21						21
22						22
23						23
24						24
25						25
26						26
27						27
28						28
29						29
30						30
31						31
32						32
33						33

10-2 and 10-3 WORK TOGETHER, pp. 233, 239

10-2 Journalizing cash payments using a cash payments journal
10-3 Performing other cash payments journal operations

CASH PAYMENTS JOURNAL

PAGE 10

	DATE	ACCOUNT TITLE	CK. NO.	POST. REF.	GENERAL DEBIT 1	GENERAL CREDIT 2	ACCOUNTS PAYABLE DEBIT 3	CASH CREDIT 4	
1									1
2									2
3									3
4									4
5									5
6									6
7									7
8									8
9									9
10									10
11									11
12									12
13									13
14									14
15									15
16									16

Column Title	Debit Column Totals	Credit Column Totals
General Debit		
General Credit		
Accounts Payable Debit		
Cash Credit		
Totals		

10-2 Journalizing cash payments using a cash payments journal
10-3 Performing other cash payments journal operations

CASH PAYMENTS JOURNAL

PAGE 11

				1	2	3	4	
				GENERAL		ACCOUNTS PAYABLE DEBIT	CASH CREDIT	
DATE	ACCOUNT TITLE	CK. NO.	POST. REF.	DEBIT	CREDIT			
1								1
2								2
3								3
4								4
5								5
6								6
7								7
8								8
9								9
10								10
11								11
12								12
13								13
14								14
15								15
16								16

Column Title	Debit Column Totals	Credit Column Totals
General Debit	_____	
General Credit		_____
Accounts Payable Debit	_____	
Cash Credit		_____
Totals	_____	_____

10-4 **WORK TOGETHER and**
ON YOUR OWN, p. 243

Journalizing other transactions using a general journal

GENERAL JOURNAL   PAGE 8

	DATE	ACCOUNT TITLE	DOC. NO.	POST. REF.	DEBIT	CREDIT	
1							1
2							2
3							3
4							4
5							5
6							6
7							7
8							8
9							9
10							10
11							11
12							12
13							13
14							14
15							15
16							16
17							17
18							18
19							19
20							20
21							21
22							22
23							23
24							24
25							25
26							26
27							27
28							28
29							29
30							30
31							31
32							32
33							33

Extra form

GENERAL JOURNAL

	DATE	ACCOUNT TITLE	DOC. NO.	POST. REF.	DEBIT	CREDIT	
1							1
2							2
3							3
4							4
5							5
6							6
7							7
8							8
9							9
10							10
11							11
12							12
13							13
14							14
15							15
16							16
17							17
18							18
19							19
20							20
21							21
22							22
23							23
24							24
25							25
26							26
27							27
28							28
29							29
30							30
31							31
32							32
33							33

10-1 APPLICATION PROBLEM, p. 245

Journalizing purchases using a purchases journal

PURCHASES JOURNAL   PAGE 9

	DATE		ACCOUNT CREDITED	PURCH. NO.	POST. REF.	PURCHASES DR. ACCTS. PAY. CR.	
1							1
2							2
3							3
4							4
5							5
6							6
7							7
8							8
9							9
10							10
11							11
12							12
13							13
14							14
15							15
16							16
17							17
18							18
19							19
20							20
21							21
22							22
23							23
24							24
25							25
26							26
27							27
28							28
29							29
30							30
31							31
32							32
33							33

Extra form

PURCHASES JOURNAL

PAGE

	DATE		ACCOUNT CREDITED	PURCH. NO.	POST. REF.	PURCHASES DR. ACCTS. PAY. CR.	
1							1
2							2
3							3
4							4
5							5
6							6
7							7
8							8
9							9
10							10
11							11
12							12
13							13
14							14
15							15
16							16
17							17
18							18
19							19
20							20
21							21
22							22
23							23
24							24
25							25
26							26
27							27
28							28
29							29
30							30
31							31
32							32
33							33

Name _____ Date _____ Class _____

10-2 and 10-3 APPLICATION PROBLEMS, pp. 245, 246

10-2 Journalizing cash payments using a cash payments journal
10-3 Performing additional cash payments journal operations

CASH PAYMENTS JOURNAL

PAGE 22

	DATE	ACCOUNT TITLE	CK. NO.	POST. REF.	GENERAL DEBIT 1	GENERAL CREDIT 2	ACCOUNTS PAYABLE DEBIT 3	CASH CREDIT 4	
1									1
2									2
3									3
4									4
5									5
6									6
7									7
8									8
9									9
10									10
11									11
12									12
13									13
14									14
15									15
16									16
17									17
18									18
19									19
20									20
21									21
22									22

(Use the form on the next page to prove the equality of debits and credits.)

APPLICATION PROBLEM (concluded)

Column Title	Debit Column Totals	Credit Column Totals
General Debit	_____	
General Credit		_____
Accounts Payable Debit	_____	
Cash Credit		_____
Totals	==========	==========

Extra form

Column Title	Debit Column Totals	Credit Column Totals
General Debit	_____	
General Credit		_____
Accounts Payable Debit	_____	
Cash Credit		_____
Totals	==========	==========

Name _____ Date _____ Class _____

10-4 APPLICATION PROBLEM, p. 246

Journalizing other transactions using a general journal

GENERAL JOURNAL   PAGE 10

	DATE	ACCOUNT TITLE	DOC. NO.	POST. REF.	DEBIT	CREDIT	
1							1
2							2
3							3
4							4
5							5
6							6
7							7
8							8
9							9
10							10
11							11
12							12
13							13
14							14
15							15
16							16
17							17
18							18
19							19
20							20
21							21
22							22
23							23
24							24
25							25
26							26
27							27
28							28
29							29
30							30
31							31
32							32
33							33

Extra form

GENERAL JOURNAL

PAGE

	DATE	ACCOUNT TITLE	DOC. NO.	POST. REF.	DEBIT	CREDIT	
1							1
2							2
3							3
4							4
5							5
6							6
7							7
8							8
9							9
10							10
11							11
12							12
13							13
14							14
15							15
16							16
17							17
18							18
19							19
20							20
21							21
22							22
23							23
24							24
25							25
26							26
27							27
28							28
29							29
30							30
31							31
32							32
33							33

Name _____ Date _____ Class _____

10-5 MASTERY PROBLEM, p. 246

Journalizing purchases, cash payments, and other transactions

1., 5.

PURCHASES JOURNAL   PAGE 11

	DATE	ACCOUNT CREDITED	PURCH. NO.	POST. REF.	PURCHASES DR. ACCTS. PAY. CR.	
1						1
2						2
3						3
4						4
5						5
6						6
7						7
8						8
9						9
10						10
11						11
12						12
13						13

1.

GENERAL JOURNAL   PAGE 10

	DATE	ACCOUNT TITLE	DOC. NO.	POST. REF.	DEBIT	CREDIT	
1							1
2							2
3							3
4							4
5							5
6							6
7							7
8							8
9							9
10							10
11							11
12							12
13							13

1., 2.

CASH PAYMENTS JOURNAL

PAGE 20

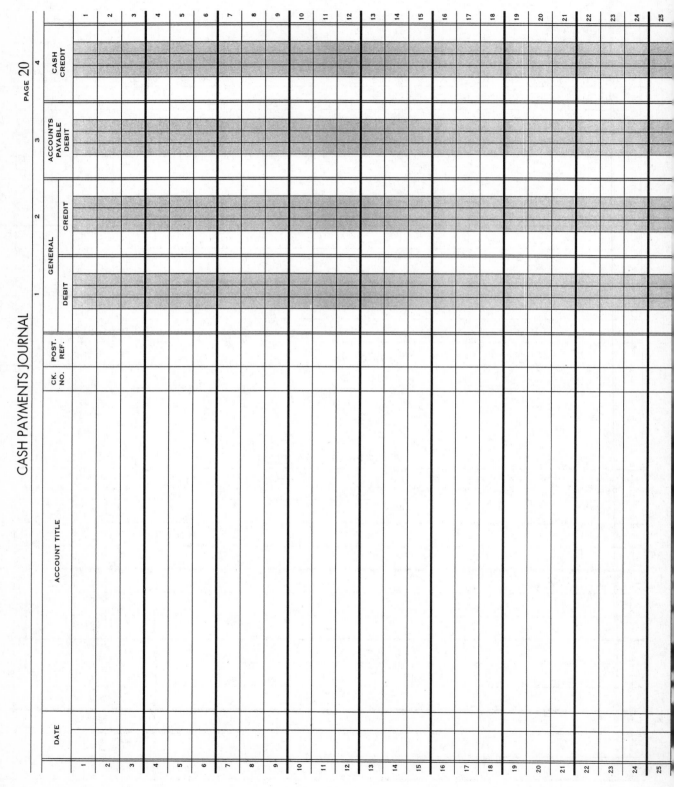

	DATE	ACCOUNT TITLE	CK. NO.	POST. REF.	GENERAL DEBIT	GENERAL CREDIT	ACCOUNTS PAYABLE DEBIT	CASH CREDIT	
1									1
2									2
3									3
4									4
5									5
6									6
7									7
8									8
9									9
10									10
11									11
12									12
13									13
14									14
15									15
16									16
17									17
18									18
19									19
20									20
21									21
22									22
23									23
24									24
25									25

10-5 MASTERY PROBLEM (concluded)

3., 4., 6., 7.

CASH PAYMENTS JOURNAL

PAGE 21

				GENERAL		ACCOUNTS PAYABLE DEBIT	CASH CREDIT
DATE	ACCOUNT TITLE	CK. NO.	POST. REF.	DEBIT (1)	CREDIT (2)	(3)	(4)
1							
2							
3							
4							
5							
6							
7							
8							

2.

Column Title	Debit Column Totals	Credit Column Totals
General Debit		
General Credit		
Accounts Payable Debit		
Cash Credit		
Totals		

3.

Column Title	Debit Column Totals	Credit Column Totals
General Debit		
General Credit		
Accounts Payable Debit		
Cash Credit		
Totals		

6.

Column Title	Debit Column Totals	Credit Column Totals
General Debit		
General Credit		
Accounts Payable Debit		
Cash Credit		
Totals		

Extra form

CASH PAYMENTS JOURNAL

| | | | | GENERAL | | ACCOUNTS PAYABLE DEBIT | CASH CREDIT |
DATE	ACCOUNT TITLE	CK. NO.	POST. REF.	DEBIT	CREDIT		

10-6 CHALLENGE PROBLEM, p. 248

Journalizing purchases, cash payments, and other transactions

1.

PURCHASES JOURNAL

	DATE		ACCOUNT CREDITED	PURCH. NO.	POST. REF.	PURCHASES DR. ACCTS. PAY. CR.	
1							1
2							2
3							3
4							4
5							5
6							6
7							7
8							8
9							9
10							10
11							11
12							12
13							13
14							14
15							15
16							16
17							17
18							18
19							19
20							20
21							21
22							22
23							23
24							24
25							25
26							26
27							27
28							28
29							29
30							30
31							31

1.

CASH PAYMENTS JOURNAL

	DATE	ACCOUNT TITLE	CK. NO.	POST. REF.	GENERAL DEBIT 1	GENERAL CREDIT 2	ACCOUNTS PAYABLE DEBIT 3	CASH CREDIT 4	
1									1
2									2
3									3
4									4
5									5
6									6
7									7
8									8
9									9
10									10
11									11
12									12
13									13
14									14
15									15
16									16
17									17
18									18
19									19
20									20
21									21
22									22
23									23
24									24

10-6 CHALLENGE PROBLEM (continued)

1.

GENERAL JOURNAL   PAGE 11

	DATE	ACCOUNT TITLE	DOC. NO.	POST. REF.	DEBIT	CREDIT	
1							1
2							2
3							3
4							4
5							5
6							6
7							7
8							8
9							9
10							10
11							11
12							12
13							13
14							14
15							15
16							16
17							17
18							18
19							19
20							20
21							21
22							22
23							23
24							24
25							25
26							26
27							27
28							28
29							29
30							30
31							31
32							32

2.

11-1 WORK TOGETHER, p. 258

Journalizing sales on account; proving and ruling a sales journal

5., 6.

SALES JOURNAL   PAGE 9

	DATE		ACCOUNT DEBITED	SALE NO.	POST. REF.	1 ACCOUNTS RECEIVABLE DEBIT	2 SALES CREDIT	3 SALES TAX PAYABLE CREDIT	
1									1
2									2
3									3
4									4
5									5
6									6
7									7
8									8
9									9
10									10
11									11
12									12
13									13
14									14
15									15

6.

Col. No.	Column Title	Debit Totals	Credit Totals
1	Accounts Receivable Debit	_____	
2	Sales Credit		_____
3	Sales Tax Payable Credit		_____
	Totals	=========	=========

Journalizing sales on account; proving and ruling a sales journal

7., 8.

SALES JOURNAL   PAGE 10

	DATE		ACCOUNT DEBITED	SALE NO.	POST. REF.	1 ACCOUNTS RECEIVABLE DEBIT	2 SALES CREDIT	3 SALES TAX PAYABLE CREDIT	
1									1
2									2
3									3
4									4
5									5
6									6
7									7
8									8
9									9
10									10
11									11
12									12
13									13
14									14
15									15

8.

Col. No.	Column Title	Debit Totals	Credit Totals
1	Accounts Receivable Debit		
2	Sales Credit		
3	Sales Tax Payable Credit		
	Totals		

11-2 **WORK TOGETHER, p. 264**

Journalizing cash receipts; proving and ruling a cash receipts journal

4., 5., 7.

CASH RECEIPTS JOURNAL

PAGE 16

					GENERAL		ACCOUNTS RECEIVABLE CREDIT	SALES CREDIT	SALES TAX PAYABLE CREDIT	CASH DEBIT	
DATE	ACCOUNT TITLE	DOC. NO.	POST. REF.	DEBIT	CREDIT						
				1	2	3	4	5	6		
1											1
2											2
3											3
4											4
5											5
6											6
7											7
8											8
9											9
10											10

5.

Col. No.	Column Title	Debit Totals	Credit Totals
1	General Debit..................		
2	General Credit.................		
3	Accounts Receivable Credit.....		
4	Sales Credit...................		
5	Sales Tax Payable Credit.......		
6	Cash Debit....................		
	Totals.......................		

6.

CASH PROOF

Cash on hand at the beginning of the month	
Plus total cash received during the month	
Equals total	
Less total cash paid during the month	
Equals cash balance on hand at end of the month	
Checkbook balance on the next unused check stub	

Journalizing cash receipts; proving and ruling a cash receipts journal

8., 9., 11.

CASH RECEIPTS JOURNAL

PAGE 17

	DATE	ACCOUNT TITLE	DOC. NO.	POST. REF.	GENERAL DEBIT (1)	GENERAL CREDIT (2)	ACCOUNTS RECEIVABLE CREDIT (3)	SALES CREDIT (4)	SALES TAX PAYABLE CREDIT (5)	CASH DEBIT (6)	
1											1
2											2
3											3
4											4
5											5
6											6
7											7
8											8
9											9
10											10

9.

Col. No.	Column Title	Debit Totals	Credit Totals
1	General Debit...............		
2	General Credit..............		
3	Accounts Receivable Credit....		
4	Sales Credit................		
5	Sales Tax Payable Credit......		
6	Cash Debit.................		
	Totals..................		

10.

CASH PROOF

Cash on hand at the beginning of the month.............
Plus total cash received during the month..............
Equals total.....................
Less total cash paid during the month................
Equals cash balance on hand at end of the month.........
Checkbook balance on the next unused check stub..........

11-1 APPLICATION PROBLEM, p. 266

Journalizing sales on account; proving and ruling a sales journal

1., 2.

SALES JOURNAL   PAGE 15

	DATE		ACCOUNT DEBITED	SALE NO.	POST. REF.	ACCOUNTS RECEIVABLE DEBIT (1)	SALES CREDIT (2)	SALES TAX PAYABLE CREDIT (3)	
1									1
2									2
3									3
4									4
5									5
6									6
7									7
8									8
9									9
10									10
11									11
12									12
13									13
14									14
15									15

2.

Col. No.	Column Title	Debit Totals	Credit Totals
1	Accounts Receivable Debit	_____	
2	Sales Credit		_____
3	Sales Tax Payable Credit		_____
	Totals	=========	=========

Extra form

SALES JOURNAL

	DATE		ACCOUNT DEBITED	SALE NO.	POST. REF.	ACCOUNTS RECEIVABLE DEBIT	SALES CREDIT	SALES TAX PAYABLE CREDIT	
						1	2	3	
1									1
2									2
3									3
4									4
5									5
6									6
7									7
8									8
9									9
10									10
11									11
12									12
13									13
14									14
15									15
16									16
17									17
18									18
19									19
20									20
21									21
22									22
23									23
24									24
25									25
26									26
27									27
28									28
29									29
30									30
31									31
32									32
33									33

PAGE

11-2 APPLICATION PROBLEM, p. 266

Journalizing sales and cash receipts; proving and ruling a cash receipts journal

1., 2., 4.

CASH RECEIPTS JOURNAL

PAGE 15

					1	2	3	4	5	6
					GENERAL		ACCOUNTS RECEIVABLE CREDIT	SALES CREDIT	SALES TAX PAYABLE CREDIT	CASH DEBIT
DATE	ACCOUNT TITLE	DOC. NO.	POST. REF.		DEBIT	CREDIT				
				1						
				2						
				3						
				4						
				5						
				6						
				7						
				8						
				9						
				10						
				11						

2.

Col. No.	Column Title	Debit Totals	Credit Totals
1	General Debit.............	_____	
2	General Credit............		_____
3	Accounts Receivable Credit..		_____
4	Sales Credit..............		_____
5	Sales Tax Payable Credit....		_____
6	Cash Debit...............	_____	
	Totals...................	======	======

3.

CASH PROOF

Cash on hand at the beginning of the month . . . . _____

Plus total cash received during the month . . . . _____

Equals total . . . . _____

Less total cash paid during the month . . . . _____

Equals cash balance on hand at end of the month . . . . ======

Checkbook balance on the next unused check stub . . . . ======

Extra form

CASH RECEIPTS JOURNAL

	DATE	ACCOUNT TITLE	DOC. NO.	POST. REF.	GENERAL DEBIT 1	GENERAL CREDIT 2	ACCOUNTS RECEIVABLE CREDIT 3	SALES CREDIT 4	SALES TAX PAYABLE CREDIT 5	CASH DEBIT 6	
1											1
2											2
3											3
4											4
5											5
6											6
7											7
8											8
9											9
10											10
11											11
12											12
13											13
14											14
15											15
16											16
17											17
18											18
19											19
20											20
21											21
22											22
23											23
24											24
25											25

11-3 MASTERY PROBLEM, p. 267

Journalizing sales and cash receipts transactions; proving and ruling journals

1., 2., 3.

SALES JOURNAL   PAGE 19

	DATE	ACCOUNT DEBITED	SALE NO.	POST. REF.	ACCOUNTS RECEIVABLE DEBIT	SALES CREDIT	SALES TAX PAYABLE CREDIT	
1	20-- Oct. 25	Brought Forward		✔	4 0 3 1 04	3 8 7 6 00	1 5 5 04	1
2								2
3								3
4								4
5								5
6								6
7								7
8								8
9								9
10								10
11								11
12								12
13								13
14								14
15								15

2.

Col. No.	Column Title	Debit Totals	Credit Totals
1	Accounts Receivable Debit	_____	
2	Sales Credit		_____
3	Sales Tax Payable Credit		_____
	Totals	_____	_____

1., 4., 6.

CASH RECEIPTS JOURNAL

PAGE 20

	DATE	ACCOUNT TITLE	DOC. NO.	POST. REF.	GENERAL DEBIT	GENERAL CREDIT	ACCOUNTS RECEIVABLE CREDIT	SALES CREDIT	SALES TAX PAYABLE CREDIT	CASH DEBIT	
1	Oct. 25	Brought Forward		✓			3 0 3 7 84	20 7 4 5 00	8 2 9 80	24 6 1 2 64	1
2											2
3											3
4											4
5											5
6											6
7											7
8											8
9											9
10											10

4.

Col. No.	Column Title	Debit Totals	Credit Totals
1	General Debit	_____	
2	General Credit		_____
3	Accounts Receivable Credit		_____
4	Sales Credit		_____
5	Sales Tax Payable Credit		_____
6	Cash Debit	_____	
	Totals	══════	══════

5.

CASH PROOF

Cash on hand at the beginning of the month ....

Plus total cash received during the month ....

Equals total ....

Less total cash paid during the month ....

Equals cash balance on hand at end of the month ....

Checkbook balance on the next unused check stub ....

Name _____ Date _____ Class _____

CHALLENGE PROBLEM, p. 267

Journalizing transactions; proving and ruling special journals

1., 2., 5.

PURCHASES JOURNAL   PAGE 5

	DATE	ACCOUNT CREDITED	PURCH. NO.	POST. REF.	PURCHASES DR. ACCTS. PAY. CR.	
1						1
2						2
3						3
4						4
5						5
6						6

1., 2., 5.

SALES JOURNAL   PAGE 5

	DATE	ACCOUNT DEBITED	SALE NO.	POST. REF.	1 ACCOUNTS RECEIVABLE DEBIT	2 SALES CREDIT	3 SALES TAX PAYABLE CREDIT	
1								1
2								2
3								3
4								4
5								5
6								6
7								7

3. Sales Journal Proof

Col. No.	Column Title	Debit Totals	Credit Totals
1	Accounts Receivable Debit	_____	
2	Sales Credit		_____
3	Sales Tax Payable Credit		_____
	Totals	_____	_____

1.

GENERAL JOURNAL   PAGE 5

	DATE		ACCOUNT TITLE	DOC. NO.	POST. REF.	DEBIT	CREDIT	
1								1
2								2
3								3
4								4
5								5
6								6
7								7
8								8
9								9
10								10
11								11
12								12
13								13
14								14
15								15
16								16
17								17
18								18
19								19
20								20

3. Cash Payments Journal Proof

Column Title	Debit Column Totals	Credit Column Totals
General Debit	_____	
General Credit		_____
Accounts Payable Debit	_____	
Cash Credit		_____
Totals	_____	_____

11-4 CHALLENGE PROBLEM (continued)

1., 2., 5.

CASH PAYMENTS JOURNAL

PAGE 7

					GENERAL		ACCOUNTS PAYABLE DEBIT	CASH CREDIT
DATE	ACCOUNT TITLE	CK. NO.	POST. REF.	DEBIT	CREDIT			
				1	2		3	4

1., 2., 5.

CASH RECEIPTS JOURNAL

PAGE 6

				1	2	3	4	5	6
			GENERAL	ACCOUNTS RECEIVABLE CREDIT	SALES CREDIT	SALES TAX PAYABLE CREDIT	CASH DEBIT	
DATE	ACCOUNT TITLE	DOC. NO.	POST. REF.	DEBIT	CREDIT				

(rows numbered 1–11)

3. Cash Receipts Journal Proof

Col. No.	Column Title	Debit Totals	Credit Totals
1	General Debit...............		
2	General Credit..............		
3	Accounts Receivable Credit.......		
4	Sales Credit...............		
5	Sales Tax Payable Credit........		
6	Cash Debit................		
	Totals................		

4.

CASH PROOF

Cash on hand at the beginning of the month .... _____

Plus total cash received during the month .... _____

Equals total .... _____

Less total cash paid during the month .... _____

Equals cash balance on hand at end of the month .... _____

Checkbook balance on the next unused check stub .... _____

12-1 WORK TOGETHER, p. 277

Posting from a purchases journal to an accounts payable ledger

PURCHASES JOURNAL
PAGE 10

	DATE	ACCOUNT CREDITED	PURCH. NO.	POST. REF.	PURCHASES DR. ACCTS. PAY. CR.	
7	19	Regal Designs	89		1 4 0 3 20	7
14	31	Total			11 8 1 8 40	14
15						15

4., 5.

VENDOR						VENDOR NO.	
DATE		ITEM	POST. REF.	DEBIT	CREDIT	CREDIT BALANCE	

(Note: This purchases journal is used to complete 12-6 WORK TOGETHER.)

12-1 ON YOUR OWN, p. 277

Posting from a purchases journal to an accounts payable ledger

PURCHASES JOURNAL

PAGE 11

	DATE	ACCOUNT CREDITED	PURCH. NO.	POST. REF.	PURCHASES DR. ACCTS. PAY. CR.	
6	17	Can Do Graphics	99		1 5 7 8 60	6
15	30	Total			13 2 9 5 70	15
16						16

6., 7.

VENDOR						VENDOR NO.	
DATE		ITEM	POST. REF.	DEBIT	CREDIT	CREDIT BALANCE	

(Note: This purchases journal is used to complete 12-6 ON YOUR OWN.)

12-2 WORK TOGETHER, p. 282

Additional posting to an accounts payable ledger

CASH PAYMENTS JOURNAL
PAGE 15

DATE	ACCOUNT TITLE	CK. NO.	POST. REF.	GENERAL DEBIT	GENERAL CREDIT	ACCOUNTS PAYABLE DEBIT	CASH CREDIT	
19	Supplies—Office	C290		69 60			69 60	14
20	Electro-Graphics Supply	C291				776 00	776 00	15
31	Totals			11 671 38	1 623 22	8 656 00	18 704 16	24
								25

GENERAL JOURNAL
PAGE 11

DATE	ACCOUNT TITLE	DOC. NO.	POST. REF.	DEBIT	CREDIT	
26	Supplies—Office	M32		2 544 00		12
	Accounts Pay./Electro-Graphics Supply				2 544 00	13

*(Note: This cash payments journal is used to complete 12-5 and 12-6 WORK TOGETHER.
This general journal is used to complete 12-5 WORK TOGETHER.)*

Additional posting to an accounts payable ledger

CASH PAYMENTS JOURNAL

PAGE 16

	DATE	ACCOUNT TITLE	CK. NO.	POST. REF.	GENERAL DEBIT	GENERAL CREDIT	ACCOUNTS PAYABLE DEBIT	CASH CREDIT	
11	16	Supplies—Store	320		78 30			78 30	11
12	17	Art and Things	321				873 00	873 00	12
23	30	Totals			1313 30	1826 12	9738 00	21042 18	23
24									24

GENERAL JOURNAL

PAGE 12

	DATE	ACCOUNT TITLE	DOC. NO.	POST. REF.	DEBIT	CREDIT	
14	27	Supplies—Office	M40		160 00		14
15		Accounts Pay./Electro-Graphics Supply				160 00	15

(Note: This cash payments journal is used to complete 12-5 and 12-6 ON YOUR OWN. This general journal is used to complete 12-5 ON YOUR OWN.)

12-2 WORK TOGETHER (concluded)

3., 4.

VENDOR Electro-Graphics Supply   VENDOR NO. 230

DATE		ITEM	POST. REF.	DEBIT	CREDIT	CREDIT BALANCE
20‑‑ Oct.	1	Balance	✔			7 7 6 00

5.

6., 7.

VENDOR Art and Things   VENDOR NO. 210

DATE		ITEM	POST. REF.	DEBIT	CREDIT	CREDIT BALANCE
20-- Nov.	1	Balance	✔			8 7 3 00
	10		P11		2 8 6 2 00	3 7 3 5 00

VENDOR Electro-Graphics Supply   VENDOR NO. 230

DATE		ITEM	POST. REF.	DEBIT	CREDIT	CREDIT BALANCE
20-- Nov.	1	Balance	✔			2 5 4 4 00
	5		CP16	2 5 4 4 00		—

8.

Name _____ Date _____ Class _____

12-3 WORK TOGETHER, p. 286

Posting from a sales journal to an accounts receivable ledger

SALES JOURNAL   PAGE 10

	DATE	ACCOUNT DEBITED	SALE NO.	POST. REF.	ACCOUNTS RECEIVABLE DEBIT (1)	SALES CREDIT (2)	SALES TAX PAYABLE CREDIT (3)	
5	20	Maria Farrell	84		5 7 6 64	5 4 4 00	3 2 64	5
12	31	Totals			7 3 7 7 60	6 9 6 0 00	4 1 7 60	12
13								13

3., 4.

CUSTOMER _____   CUSTOMER NO. _____

	DATE	ITEM	POST. REF.	DEBIT	CREDIT	DEBIT BALANCE

(Note: This sales journal is used to complete 12-6 WORK TOGETHER.)

ON YOUR OWN, p. 286

Posting from a sales journal to an accounts receivable ledger

SALES JOURNAL   PAGE 11

	DATE	ACCOUNT DEBITED	SALE NO.	POST. REF.	1 ACCOUNTS RECEIVABLE DEBIT	2 SALES CREDIT	3 SALES TAX PAYABLE CREDIT	
8	18	David Bishop	102		6 48 72	6 12 00	3 6 72	8
13	30	Totals			8 2 9 9 80	7 8 3 0 00	4 6 9 80	13
14								14

5., 6.

CUSTOMER   CUSTOMER NO.

	DATE	ITEM	POST. REF.	DEBIT	CREDIT	DEBIT BALANCE	

(Note: This sales journal is used to complete 12-6 ON YOUR OWN.)

12-4 WORK TOGETHER, p. 290

Posting from a cash receipts journal to an accounts receivable ledger

CASH RECEIPTS JOURNAL

PAGE 12

DATE	ACCOUNT TITLE	DOC. NO.	POST. REF.	GENERAL DEBIT (1)	GENERAL CREDIT (2)	ACCOUNTS RECEIVABLE CREDIT (3)	SALES CREDIT (4)	SALES TAX PAYABLE CREDIT (5)	CASH DEBIT (6)	
21	Alfredo Lopez	R104				254 40			254 40	9
31	Totals					6360 00	1832 000	1099 20	25779 20	17
										18

3.

CUSTOMER Alfredo Lopez   CUSTOMER NO. 130

DATE	ITEM	POST. REF.	DEBIT	CREDIT	DEBIT BALANCE
20-- Oct. 1	Balance	✔			254 40
12		S10	1272 00		1526 40

4.

(Note: This cash receipts journal is used to complete 12-6 WORK TOGETHER.)

12-4 ON YOUR OWN p. 290

Posting from a cash receipts journal to an accounts receivable ledger

CASH RECEIPTS JOURNAL

PAGE 13

DATE	ACCOUNT TITLE	DOC. NO.	POST. REF.	GENERAL DEBIT	GENERAL CREDIT	ACCOUNTS RECEIVABLE CREDIT	SALES CREDIT	SALES TAX PAYABLE CREDIT	CASH DEBIT
20	Brandee Sparks	R124				286 20			286 20
30	Totals					7155 00	20 610 00	1236 60	29 001 60

5.

CUSTOMER Brandee Sparks

CUSTOMER NO. 140

DATE	ITEM	POST. REF.	DEBIT	CREDIT	DEBIT BALANCE
20-- Nov. 1	Balance	✔			286 20
12		S11	1431 00		1717 20

6.

(Note: This cash receipts journal is used to complete 12-6 ON YOUR OWN.)

Name _____ Date _____ Class _____

12-5 WORK TOGETHER, p. 295

Posting to a general ledger

3., 4., 5.

ACCOUNT _____ ACCOUNT NO. _____

DATE	ITEM	POST. REF.	DEBIT	CREDIT	BALANCE DEBIT	BALANCE CREDIT

ACCOUNT Accounts Payable   ACCOUNT NO. 2110

DATE	ITEM	POST. REF.	DEBIT	CREDIT	BALANCE DEBIT	BALANCE CREDIT
20-- Oct. 1	Balance	✔				2 5 1 7 80

(Note: This Accounts Payable account form is used to complete 12-6 WORK TOGETHER.)

ON YOUR OWN, p. 295

Posting to a general ledger

6., 7., 8.

ACCOUNT Supplies—Office   ACCOUNT NO. 1145

DATE		ITEM	POST. REF.	DEBIT	CREDIT	BALANCE DEBIT	BALANCE CREDIT
Nov.	1	Balance	✔			6 4 3 7 60	

ACCOUNT   ACCOUNT NO.

DATE		ITEM	POST. REF.	DEBIT	CREDIT	BALANCE DEBIT	BALANCE CREDIT

ACCOUNT Accounts Payable   ACCOUNT NO. 2110

DATE		ITEM	POST. REF.	DEBIT	CREDIT	BALANCE DEBIT	BALANCE CREDIT
Nov.	1	Balance	✔				8 2 2 4 20

(Note: This Accounts Payable account form is used to complete 12-6 ON YOUR OWN.)

12-6 WORK TOGETHER, p. 302

Posting totals to a general ledger

3., 4., 5., 6.

ACCOUNT Cash   ACCOUNT NO. 1110

DATE		ITEM	POST. REF.	DEBIT	CREDIT	BALANCE DEBIT	BALANCE CREDIT
20-- Oct.	1	Balance	✔			13 2 3 5 58	

ACCOUNT Accounts Receivable   ACCOUNT NO. 1130

DATE		ITEM	POST. REF.	DEBIT	CREDIT	BALANCE DEBIT	BALANCE CREDIT
20-- Oct.	1	Balance	✔			1 3 5 5 74	

ACCOUNT Sales Tax Payable   ACCOUNT NO. 2140

DATE		ITEM	POST. REF.	DEBIT	CREDIT	BALANCE DEBIT	BALANCE CREDIT
20-- Oct.	1	Balance	✔				1 4 1 0 00
	15		CP15	1 4 1 0 00		—	—

ACCOUNT Sales   ACCOUNT NO. 4110

DATE		ITEM	POST. REF.	DEBIT	CREDIT	BALANCE DEBIT	BALANCE CREDIT
20-- Oct.	1	Balance	✔				233 3 3 5 00

ACCOUNT Purchases   ACCOUNT NO. 5110

DATE		ITEM	POST. REF.	DEBIT	CREDIT	BALANCE DEBIT	BALANCE CREDIT
20-- Oct.	1	Balance	✔			106 5 5 9 60	

Posting totals to a general ledger

7., 8., 9., 10.

ACCOUNT Cash   ACCOUNT NO. 1110

DATE		ITEM	POST. REF.	DEBIT	CREDIT	BALANCE	
						DEBIT	CREDIT
Nov. 20--	1	Balance	✔			20 3 1 0 62	

ACCOUNT Accounts Receivable   ACCOUNT NO. 1130

DATE		ITEM	POST. REF.	DEBIT	CREDIT	BALANCE	
						DEBIT	CREDIT
Nov. 20--	1	Balance	✔			2 3 7 3 34	

ACCOUNT Sales Tax Payable   ACCOUNT NO. 2140

DATE		ITEM	POST. REF.	DEBIT	CREDIT	BALANCE	
						DEBIT	CREDIT
Nov. 20--	1	Balance	✔				1 5 1 6 80
	15		CP16	1 5 1 6 80		—	—

ACCOUNT Sales   ACCOUNT NO. 4110

DATE		ITEM	POST. REF.	DEBIT	CREDIT	BALANCE	
						DEBIT	CREDIT
Nov. 20--	1	Balance	✔				258 6 1 5 00

ACCOUNT Purchases   ACCOUNT NO. 5110

DATE		ITEM	POST. REF.	DEBIT	CREDIT	BALANCE	
						DEBIT	CREDIT
Nov. 20--	1	Balance	✔			118 3 7 8 00	

12-1 APPLICATION PROBLEM, p. 304

Posting from a purchases journal to an accounts payable ledger

2.

PURCHASES JOURNAL

PAGE 10

	DATE		ACCOUNT CREDITED	PURCH. NO.	POST. REF.	PURCHASES DR. ACCTS. PAY. CR.	
1	20-- Oct.	4	Nutrition Center	78		2 0 1 6 00	1
2		20	Cornucopia, Inc.	79		4 5 8 4 00	2
3		25	Sports Nutrition	80		5 4 0 0 00	3
4		30	Healthy Foods	81		3 3 9 6 00	4

1., 2.   **ACCOUNTS PAYABLE LEDGER**

VENDOR _____   VENDOR NO. _____

DATE	ITEM	POST. REF.	DEBIT	CREDIT	CREDIT BALANCE

VENDOR _____   VENDOR NO. _____

DATE	ITEM	POST. REF.	DEBIT	CREDIT	CREDIT BALANCE

VENDOR _____   VENDOR NO. _____

DATE	ITEM	POST. REF.	DEBIT	CREDIT	CREDIT BALANCE

VENDOR _____   VENDOR NO. _____

DATE	ITEM	POST. REF.	DEBIT	CREDIT	CREDIT BALANCE

VENDOR _____   VENDOR NO. _____

DATE	ITEM	POST. REF.	DEBIT	CREDIT	CREDIT BALANCE

Extra form

	DATE		ACCOUNT CREDITED	PURCH. NO.	POST. REF.	PURCHASES DR. ACCTS. PAY. CR.			
1									1
2									2
3									3
4									4
5									5
6									6
7									7
8									8
9									9
10									10
11									11
12									12
13									13
14									14
15									15
16									16
17									17
18									18
19									19
20									20
21									21
22									22
23									23
24									24
25									25
26									26
27									27
28									28
29									29
30									30
31									31
32									32
33									33

12-2 APPLICATION PROBLEM, p. 304

Posting from other journals to an accounts payable ledger

1.

CASH PAYMENTS JOURNAL

PAGE 10

	DATE	ACCOUNT TITLE	CK. NO.	POST. REF.	GENERAL DEBIT	GENERAL CREDIT	ACCOUNTS PAYABLE DEBIT	CASH CREDIT	
1	Oct. 9	Cornucopia, Inc.	184				3 0 9 0 00	3 0 9 0 00	1
2	11	Healthy Foods	185				5 0 6 4 00	5 0 6 4 00	2
3	15	Sports Nutrition	186				4 5 1 2 00	4 5 1 2 00	3
4	28	Nutrition Center	187				2 0 1 6 00	2 0 1 6 00	4
5									5
6									6
7									7
8									8

GENERAL JOURNAL

PAGE 10

	DATE	ACCOUNT TITLE	DOC. NO.	POST. REF.	DEBIT	CREDIT	
1	Oct. 9	Supplies—Office	M26		9 6 00		1
2		Accounts Payable/Office Center		6		9 6 00	2
3							3
4							4
5							5
6							6

2.

12-3 APPLICATION PROBLEM, p. 304

Posting from a sales journal to an accounts receivable ledger

2.

SALES JOURNAL

PAGE 10

	DATE		ACCOUNT DEBITED	SALE NO.	POST. REF.	1 ACCOUNTS RECEIVABLE DEBIT	2 SALES CREDIT	3 SALES TAX PAYABLE CREDIT	
1	20-- Oct.	6	Southwest Community Club	69		3 0 0 1 92	2 8 3 2 00	1 6 9 92	1
2		9	Children's Center	70		1 7 5 5 36	1 6 5 6 00	9 9 36	2
3		12	Eastman Sports Arena	71		1 1 1 9 36	1 0 5 6 00	6 3 36	3
4		30	Maple Tree Club	72		2 5 4 4 00	2 4 0 0 00	1 4 4 00	4

1., 2.

ACCOUNTS RECEIVABLE LEDGER

CUSTOMER   CUSTOMER NO.

DATE	ITEM	POST. REF.	DEBIT	CREDIT	DEBIT BALANCE

CUSTOMER   CUSTOMER NO.

DATE	ITEM	POST. REF.	DEBIT	CREDIT	DEBIT BALANCE

CUSTOMER   CUSTOMER NO.

DATE	ITEM	POST. REF.	DEBIT	CREDIT	DEBIT BALANCE

CUSTOMER   CUSTOMER NO.

DATE	ITEM	POST. REF.	DEBIT	CREDIT	DEBIT BALANCE

Extra form

SALES JOURNAL

	DATE		ACCOUNT DEBITED	SALE NO.	POST. REF.	ACCOUNTS RECEIVABLE DEBIT	SALES CREDIT	SALES TAX PAYABLE CREDIT	
1									1
2									2
3									3
4									4
5									5
6									6
7									7
8									8
9									9
10									10
11									11
12									12
13									13
14									14
15									15
16									16
17									17
18									18
19									19
20									20
21									21
22									22
23									23
24									24
25									25
26									26
27									27
28									28
29									29
30									30
31									31
32									32
33									33

12-4 **APPLICATION PROBLEM, p. 305**

Posting from a cash receipts journal to an accounts receivable ledger

1.

CASH RECEIPTS JOURNAL

PAGE 10

DATE	ACCOUNT TITLE	DOC. NO.	POST. REF.	GENERAL DEBIT	GENERAL CREDIT	ACCOUNTS RECEIVABLE CREDIT	SALES CREDIT	SALES TAX PAYABLE CREDIT	CASH DEBIT	
20-- Oct. 5	Children's Center	R170				4 4 1 6 00			4 4 1 6 00	1
14	Eastman Sports Arena	R171				2 2 2 0 00			2 2 2 0 00	2
24	Maple Tree Club	R172				3 5 2 8 00			3 5 2 8 00	3
										4
										5
										6
										7
										8
										9
										10
										11
										12
										13
										14
										15
										16
										17
										18
										19
										20
										21
										22
										23

2.

Extra form

CASH PAYMENTS JOURNAL

						PAGE	
		1	**2**		**3**	**4**	
DATE	ACCOUNT TITLE	CK. NO.	POST. REF.	GENERAL		ACCOUNTS PAYABLE DEBIT	CASH CREDIT
				DEBIT	CREDIT		

12-5 APPLICATION PROBLEM, p. 305

Posting to a general ledger

2.

CASH PAYMENTS JOURNAL

PAGE 11

	DATE	ACCOUNT TITLE	CK. NO.	POST. REF.	1 GENERAL DEBIT	2 GENERAL CREDIT	3 ACCOUNTS PAYABLE DEBIT	4 CASH CREDIT	
1	20-- Nov. 1	Rent Expense	202		1 2 0 0 00			1 2 0 0 00	1
2	2	Prepaid Insurance	203		1 4 4 0 00			1 4 4 0 00	2
10	15	Sales Tax Payable	211		1 6 1 5 20			1 6 1 5 20	10
21	30	Totals			6 0 6 1 00	—	1 4 6 8 2 00	2 0 7 4 3 00	21
22									22
23									23

GENERAL JOURNAL

PAGE 11

	DATE	ACCOUNT TITLE	DOC. NO.	POST. REF.	DEBIT	CREDIT	
10	28	Supplies—Office	M31		1 2 5 00		10
11		Accounts Payable/Office Center		240		1 2 5 00	11

12-5 APPLICATION PROBLEM (continued)

1., 2.   **GENERAL LEDGER**

ACCOUNT _____   ACCOUNT NO. _____

DATE	ITEM	POST. REF.	DEBIT	CREDIT	BALANCE	
					DEBIT	CREDIT

ACCOUNT _____   ACCOUNT NO. _____

DATE	ITEM	POST. REF.	DEBIT	CREDIT	BALANCE	
					DEBIT	CREDIT

ACCOUNT _____   ACCOUNT NO. _____

DATE	ITEM	POST. REF.	DEBIT	CREDIT	BALANCE	
					DEBIT	CREDIT

ACCOUNT _____   ACCOUNT NO. _____

DATE	ITEM	POST. REF.	DEBIT	CREDIT	BALANCE	
					DEBIT	CREDIT

1., 2.   **GENERAL LEDGER**

ACCOUNT _____   ACCOUNT NO. _____

DATE	ITEM	POST. REF.	DEBIT	CREDIT	BALANCE	
					DEBIT	CREDIT

ACCOUNT _____   ACCOUNT NO. _____

DATE	ITEM	POST. REF.	DEBIT	CREDIT	BALANCE	
					DEBIT	CREDIT

ACCOUNT _____   ACCOUNT NO. _____

DATE	ITEM	POST. REF.	DEBIT	CREDIT	BALANCE	
					DEBIT	CREDIT

ACCOUNT _____   ACCOUNT NO. _____

DATE	ITEM	POST. REF.	DEBIT	CREDIT	BALANCE	
					DEBIT	CREDIT

ACCOUNT _____   ACCOUNT NO. _____

DATE	ITEM	POST. REF.	DEBIT	CREDIT	BALANCE	
					DEBIT	CREDIT

12-6 APPLICATION PROBLEM, p. 305

Posting totals to a general ledger

SALES JOURNAL
PAGE 11

DATE	ACCOUNT DEBITED	SALE NO.	POST. REF.	1 ACCOUNTS RECEIVABLE DEBIT	2 SALES CREDIT	3 SALES TAX PAYABLE CREDIT
30	Totals			9262 28	8738 00	524 28

PURCHASES JOURNAL
PAGE 11

DATE	ACCOUNT CREDITED	PURCH. NO.	POST. REF.	PURCHASES DR. ACCTS. PAY. CR.
30	Total			16165 80

CASH RECEIPTS JOURNAL
PAGE 11

DATE	ACCOUNT TITLE	DOC. NO.	POST. REF.	1 GENERAL DEBIT	2 GENERAL CREDIT	3 ACCOUNTS RECEIVABLE CREDIT	4 SALES CREDIT	5 SALES TAX PAYABLE CREDIT	6 CASH DEBIT
30	Totals					8420 64	20520 00	1231 20	30171 84

Extra form

CASH RECEIPTS JOURNAL

PAGE

DATE	ACCOUNT TITLE	DOC. NO.	POST. REF.	GENERAL DEBIT 1	GENERAL CREDIT 2	ACCOUNTS RECEIVABLE CREDIT 3	SALES CREDIT 4	SALES TAX PAYABLE CREDIT 5	CASH DEBIT 6

12-7 MASTERY PROBLEM, p. 306

Posting to general and subsidiary ledgers

1., 2.

SALES JOURNAL   PAGE 11

	DATE	ACCOUNT DEBITED	SALE NO.	POST. REF.	ACCOUNTS RECEIVABLE DEBIT (1)	SALES CREDIT (2)	SALES TAX PAYABLE CREDIT (3)	
1	20-- Nov. 6	John Falk	72		9 15 84	8 64 00	5 1 84	1
2	17	Allen Stewart	73		8 64 96	8 16 00	4 8 96	2
3	30	Linda Karagin	74		7 56 84	7 14 00	4 2 84	3
4								4
5								5

1., 3.

PURCHASES JOURNAL   PAGE 11

	DATE	ACCOUNT CREDITED	PURCH. NO.	POST. REF.	PURCHASES DR. ACCTS. PAY. CR.	
1	20-- Nov. 3	Aquacare	73		1 36 3 20	1
2	14	Sun-Brite Pool Supplies	74		3 22 8 00	2
3	21	Malibu Pools	75		4 46 4 00	3
4	27	Custom Pool Supply	76		3 51 6 00	4
5						5
6						6

1.

GENERAL JOURNAL   PAGE 11

	DATE	ACCOUNT TITLE	DOC. NO.	POST. REF.	DEBIT	CREDIT	
1	20-- Nov. 24	Karl Jantzen, Drawing	M38		1 65 60		1
2		Purchases				1 65 60	2

2. Sales Journal Proof

Col. No.	Column Title	Debit Totals	Credit Totals
1	Accounts Receivable Debit	_____	
2	Sales Credit		_____
3	Sales Tax Payable Credit		_____
	Totals	═══════	═══════

1., 4.

CASH RECEIPTS JOURNAL

PAGE 11

	DATE	ACCOUNT TITLE	DOC. NO.	POST. REF.	GENERAL DEBIT	GENERAL CREDIT	ACCOUNTS RECEIVABLE CREDIT	SALES CREDIT	SALES TAX PAYABLE CREDIT	CASH DEBIT	
1	Nov. 5	Cheryl Blackman	R96				546 96			546 96	1
2	7		T7	✓				4368 00	262 08	4630 08	2
3	10	Linda Karagin	R97				1068 48			1068 48	3
4	14		T14	✓				4956 00	297 36	5253 36	4
5	21		T21	✓				4752 00	285 12	5037 12	5
6	23	John Falk	R98				1723 56			1723 56	6
7	28		T28	✓				5136 00	308 16	5444 16	7
8	30		T30	✓				1008 00	60 48	1068 48	8
9											9
10											10
11											11

4. Cash Receipts Journal Proof

Col. No.	Column Title	Debit Totals	Credit Totals
1	General Debit	_____	
2	General Credit		_____
3	Accounts Receivable Credit		_____
4	Sales Credit		_____
5	Sales Tax Payable Credit		_____
6	Cash Debit	_____	
	Totals	_____	_____

12-7 MASTERY PROBLEM (continued)

1., 5.

CASH PAYMENTS JOURNAL

PAGE 15

	DATE	ACCOUNT TITLE	CK. NO.	POST. REF.	GENERAL DEBIT	GENERAL CREDIT	ACCOUNTS PAYABLE DEBIT	CASH CREDIT	
1	20-- Nov. 2	Rent Expense	231		1500 00			1500 00	1
2	2	Utilities Expense	232		207 60			207 60	2
3	4	Custom Pool Supply	233				2382 00	2382 00	3
4	6	Aquacare	234				3816 00	3816 00	4
5	9	Malibu Pools	235				3468 00	3468 00	5
6	13	Sun-Brite Pool Supplies	236				2832 00	2832 00	6
7	13	Aquacare	237				1363 20	1363 20	7
8	16	Karl Jantzen, Drawing	238		1200 00			1200 00	8
9	16	Jeff Rutherford, Drawing	239		1200 00			1200 00	9
10	17	Miscellaneous Expense	240		96 00			96 00	10
11	20	Advertising Expense	241		320 40			320 40	11
12	26	Supplies—Office	242		99 60			99 60	12
13	28	Supplies—Store	243		127 20			127 20	13
14									14
15									15

5. Cash Payments Journal Proof

Column Title	Debit Column Totals	Credit Column Totals
General Debit	_____	
General Credit		_____
Accounts Payable Debit	_____	
Cash Credit		_____
Totals	_____	_____

6.

12-7 **MASTERY PROBLEM (continued)**

1., 2., 3., 4., 5.   **GENERAL LEDGER**

ACCOUNT Cash   ACCOUNT NO. 1110

DATE	ITEM	POST. REF.	DEBIT	CREDIT	BALANCE DEBIT	BALANCE CREDIT
20-- Nov. 1	Balance	✔			20 3 1 6 00	

ACCOUNT Accounts Receivable   ACCOUNT NO. 1130

DATE	ITEM	POST. REF.	DEBIT	CREDIT	BALANCE DEBIT	BALANCE CREDIT
20-- Nov. 1	Balance	✔			3 3 3 9 00	

ACCOUNT Supplies—Office   ACCOUNT NO. 1150

DATE	ITEM	POST. REF.	DEBIT	CREDIT	BALANCE DEBIT	BALANCE CREDIT
20-- Nov. 1	Balance	✔			3 5 5 2 00	

ACCOUNT Supplies—Store   ACCOUNT NO. 1160

DATE	ITEM	POST. REF.	DEBIT	CREDIT	BALANCE DEBIT	BALANCE CREDIT
20-- Nov. 1	Balance	✔			4 1 0 4 00	

ACCOUNT Accounts Payable   ACCOUNT NO. 2110

DATE	ITEM	POST. REF.	DEBIT	CREDIT	BALANCE DEBIT	BALANCE CREDIT
20-- Nov. 1	Balance	✔				12 4 9 8 00

ACCOUNT Sales Tax Payable   ACCOUNT NO. 2120

DATE	ITEM	POST. REF.	DEBIT	CREDIT	BALANCE DEBIT	BALANCE CREDIT
20-- Nov. 1	Balance	✔				1 3 3 2 00

1., 2., 3., 4., 5.   **GENERAL LEDGER**

ACCOUNT Karl Jantzen, Drawing   ACCOUNT NO. 3120

| DATE | | ITEM | POST. REF. | DEBIT | CREDIT | BALANCE | |
						DEBIT	CREDIT
20-- Nov.	1	Balance	✔			15 2 8 8 00	

ACCOUNT Jeff Rutherford, Drawing   ACCOUNT NO. 3140

| DATE | | ITEM | POST. REF. | DEBIT | CREDIT | BALANCE | |
						DEBIT	CREDIT
20-- Nov.	1	Balance	✔			14 8 3 2 00	

ACCOUNT Sales   ACCOUNT NO. 4110

| DATE | | ITEM | POST. REF. | DEBIT | CREDIT | BALANCE | |
						DEBIT	CREDIT
20-- Nov.	1	Balance	✔				220 5 1 2 00

ACCOUNT Purchases   ACCOUNT NO. 5110

| DATE | | ITEM | POST. REF. | DEBIT | CREDIT | BALANCE | |
						DEBIT	CREDIT
20-- Nov.	1	Balance	✔			113 7 9 6 00	

ACCOUNT Advertising Expense   ACCOUNT NO. 6110

| DATE | | ITEM | POST. REF. | DEBIT | CREDIT | BALANCE | |
						DEBIT	CREDIT
20-- Nov.	1	Balance	✔			2 3 5 8 00	

ACCOUNT Miscellaneous Expense   ACCOUNT NO. 6140

| DATE | | ITEM | POST. REF. | DEBIT | CREDIT | BALANCE | |
						DEBIT	CREDIT
20-- Nov.	1	Balance	✔			1 3 6 5 60	

12-7 MASTERY PROBLEM (continued)

1., 2., 3., 4., 5.   **GENERAL LEDGER**

ACCOUNT Rent Expense   ACCOUNT NO. 6160

DATE	ITEM	POST. REF.	DEBIT	CREDIT	BALANCE DEBIT	BALANCE CREDIT
20-- Nov. 1	Balance	✔			15 0 0 0 00	

ACCOUNT Utilities Expense   ACCOUNT NO. 6190

DATE	ITEM	POST. REF.	DEBIT	CREDIT	BALANCE DEBIT	BALANCE CREDIT
20-- Nov. 1	Balance	✔			2 0 7 6 00	

1.   **ACCOUNTS PAYABLE LEDGER**

VENDOR Aquacare   VENDOR NO. 210

DATE	ITEM	POST. REF.	DEBIT	CREDIT	CREDIT BALANCE
20-- Nov. 1	Balance	✔			3 8 1 6 00

VENDOR Custom Pool Supply   VENDOR NO. 220

DATE	ITEM	POST. REF.	DEBIT	CREDIT	CREDIT BALANCE
20-- Nov. 1	Balance	✔			2 3 8 2 00

VENDOR Malibu Pools   VENDOR NO. 230

DATE	ITEM	POST. REF.	DEBIT	CREDIT	CREDIT BALANCE
20-- Nov. 1	Balance	✔			3 4 6 8 00

VENDOR Sun-Brite Pool Supplies   VENDOR NO. 240

DATE	ITEM	POST. REF.	DEBIT	CREDIT	CREDIT BALANCE
20-- Nov. 1	Balance	✔			2 8 3 2 00

1.

ACCOUNTS RECEIVABLE LEDGER

CUSTOMER Cheryl Blackman   CUSTOMER NO. 110

DATE		ITEM	POST. REF.	DEBIT	CREDIT	DEBIT BALANCE
20-- Nov.	1	Balance	✔			5 4 6 96

CUSTOMER John Falk   CUSTOMER NO. 120

DATE		ITEM	POST. REF.	DEBIT	CREDIT	DEBIT BALANCE
20-- Nov.	1	Balance	✔			1 7 2 3 56

CUSTOMER Linda Karagin   CUSTOMER NO. 130

DATE		ITEM	POST. REF.	DEBIT	CREDIT	DEBIT BALANCE
20-- Nov.	1	Balance	✔			1 0 6 8 48

CUSTOMER Allen Stewart   CUSTOMER NO. 140

DATE	ITEM	POST. REF.	DEBIT	CREDIT	DEBIT BALANCE

12-8 CHALLENGE PROBLEM, p. 306

Journalizing and posting business transactions

1., 2.

SALES JOURNAL   PAGE

	DATE		ACCOUNT DEBITED	SALE NO.	POST. REF.	1 ACCOUNTS RECEIVABLE DEBIT	2 SALES CREDIT	3 SALES TAX PAYABLE CREDIT	
1									1
2									2
3									3
4									4
5									5

1., 3.

PURCHASES JOURNAL   PAGE

	DATE		ACCOUNT CREDITED	PURCH. NO.	POST. REF.	PURCHASES DR. ACCTS. PAY. CR.	
1							1
2							2
3							3
4							4
5							5

1.

GENERAL JOURNAL   PAGE

	DATE		ACCOUNT TITLE	DOC. NO.	POST. REF.	DEBIT	CREDIT	
1								1
2								2
3								3
4								4

2. Sales Journal Proof

Col. No.	Column Title	Debit Totals	Credit Totals
1	Accounts Receivable Debit	_____	
2	Sales Credit		_____
3	Sales Tax Payable Credit		_____
	Totals	_____	_____

1., 4., 6.

CASH RECEIPTS JOURNAL

PAGE

	DATE	ACCOUNT TITLE	DOC. NO.	POST. REF.	GENERAL DEBIT	GENERAL CREDIT	ACCOUNTS RECEIVABLE CREDIT	SALES CREDIT	SALES TAX PAYABLE CREDIT	CASH DEBIT	
1											1
2											2
3											3
4											4
5											5
6											6
7											7
8											8
9											9
10											10

4. Cash Receipts Journal Proof

Col. No.	Column Title	Debit Totals	Credit Totals
1	General Debit		
2	General Credit		
3	Accounts Receivable Credit		
4	Sales Credit		
5	Sales Tax Payable Credit		
6	Cash Debit		
	Totals		

12-8 CHALLENGE PROBLEM (continued)

1., 4., 7.

CASH PAYMENTS JOURNAL

PAGE ____

| | | | | | | GENERAL | | ACCOUNTS PAYABLE | CASH |
| | | | | | | 1 | 2 | 3 | 4 |
DATE	ACCOUNT TITLE	CK. NO.	POST. REF.		DEBIT	CREDIT	DEBIT	CREDIT
				1				
				2				
				3				
				4				
				5				
				6				
				7				
				8				
				9				
				10				
				11				
				12				
				13				
				14				

4. Cash Payments Journal Proof

Column Title	Debit Column Totals	Credit Column Totals
General Debit		
General Credit		
Accounts Payable Debit		
Cash Credit		
Totals		

5.

CASH PROOF

Cash on hand at the beginning of the month . . . .   ————

Plus total cash received during the month . . . .   ————

Equals total . . . .   ————

Less total cash paid during the month . . . .   ————

Equals cash balance on hand at end of the month . . . .   ————

Checkbook balance on the next unused check stub . . . .   ————

8.

12-8 CHALLENGE PROBLEM (continued)

1., 2., 3., 6., 7.   **GENERAL LEDGER**

ACCOUNT Cash   ACCOUNT NO. 1110

DATE		ITEM	POST. REF.	DEBIT	CREDIT	BALANCE	
						DEBIT	CREDIT
20-- Oct.	1	Balance	✔			20 2 2 0 00	

ACCOUNT Accounts Receivable   ACCOUNT NO. 1130

DATE		ITEM	POST. REF.	DEBIT	CREDIT	BALANCE	
						DEBIT	CREDIT
20-- Oct.	1	Balance	✔			3 4 7 9 40	

ACCOUNT Supplies—Office   ACCOUNT NO. 1150

DATE		ITEM	POST. REF.	DEBIT	CREDIT	BALANCE	
						DEBIT	CREDIT
20-- Oct.	1	Balance	✔			3 1 6 2 00	

ACCOUNT Supplies—Store   ACCOUNT NO. 1160

DATE		ITEM	POST. REF.	DEBIT	CREDIT	BALANCE	
						DEBIT	CREDIT
20-- Oct.	1	Balance	✔			2 5 9 2 00	

ACCOUNT Accounts Payable   ACCOUNT NO. 2110

DATE		ITEM	POST. REF.	DEBIT	CREDIT	BALANCE	
						DEBIT	CREDIT
20-- Oct.	1	Balance	✔				9 6 2 7 60

ACCOUNT Sales Tax Payable   ACCOUNT NO. 2120

DATE		ITEM	POST. REF.	DEBIT	CREDIT	BALANCE	
						DEBIT	CREDIT
20-- Oct.	1	Balance	✔				1 5 7 4 40

1., 2., 3., 6., 7. **GENERAL LEDGER**

ACCOUNT Julie Freed, Drawing ACCOUNT NO. 3120

DATE		ITEM	POST. REF.	DEBIT	CREDIT	BALANCE DEBIT	BALANCE CREDIT
20-- Oct.	1	Balance	✔			14 300 00	

ACCOUNT Troy Nordstrom, Drawing ACCOUNT NO. 3140

DATE		ITEM	POST. REF.	DEBIT	CREDIT	BALANCE DEBIT	BALANCE CREDIT
20-- Oct.	1	Balance	✔			14 040 00	

ACCOUNT Sales ACCOUNT NO. 4110

DATE		ITEM	POST. REF.	DEBIT	CREDIT	BALANCE DEBIT	BALANCE CREDIT
20-- Oct.	1	Balance	✔				262 498 80

ACCOUNT Purchases ACCOUNT NO. 5110

DATE		ITEM	POST. REF.	DEBIT	CREDIT	BALANCE DEBIT	BALANCE CREDIT
20-- Oct.	1	Balance	✔			135 000 00	

ACCOUNT Advertising Expense ACCOUNT NO. 6110

DATE		ITEM	POST. REF.	DEBIT	CREDIT	BALANCE DEBIT	BALANCE CREDIT
20-- Oct.	1	Balance	✔			3 528 00	

ACCOUNT Miscellaneous Expense ACCOUNT NO. 6140

DATE		ITEM	POST. REF.	DEBIT	CREDIT	BALANCE DEBIT	BALANCE CREDIT
20-- Oct.	1	Balance	✔			1 692 00	

12-8 **CHALLENGE PROBLEM (continued)**

1., 2., 3., 6., 7.   **GENERAL LEDGER**

ACCOUNT Rent Expense   ACCOUNT NO. 6160

DATE	ITEM	POST. REF.	DEBIT	CREDIT	BALANCE DEBIT	BALANCE CREDIT
20-- Oct. 1	Balance	✔			10 3 5 0 00	

ACCOUNT Utilities Expense   ACCOUNT NO. 6190

DATE	ITEM	POST. REF.	DEBIT	CREDIT	BALANCE DEBIT	BALANCE CREDIT
20-- Oct. 1	Balance	✔			2 1 4 2 00	

1.   **ACCOUNTS PAYABLE LEDGER**

VENDOR Design Golf   VENDOR NO. 210

DATE	ITEM	POST. REF.	DEBIT	CREDIT	CREDIT BALANCE
20-- Oct. 1	Balance	✔			2 9 1 6 00

VENDOR Eagle Golf Equipment   VENDOR NO. 220

DATE	ITEM	POST. REF.	DEBIT	CREDIT	CREDIT BALANCE
20-- Oct. 1	Balance	✔			2 3 5 8 00

VENDOR Golf Source   VENDOR NO. 230

DATE	ITEM	POST. REF.	DEBIT	CREDIT	CREDIT BALANCE

VENDOR Pro Golf Supply   VENDOR NO. 240

DATE	ITEM	POST. REF.	DEBIT	CREDIT	CREDIT BALANCE
20-- Oct. 1	Balance	✔			1 1 3 7 60

1.

ACCOUNTS PAYABLE LEDGER

VENDOR Vista Golf Co.   VENDOR NO. 250

DATE	ITEM	POST. REF.	DEBIT	CREDIT	CREDIT BALANCE
20-- Oct. 1	Balance	✔			3 2 1 6 00

ACCOUNTS RECEIVABLE LEDGER

CUSTOMER David Bench   CUSTOMER NO. 110

DATE	ITEM	POST. REF.	DEBIT	CREDIT	DEBIT BALANCE
20-- Oct. 1	Balance	✔			9 7 2 00

CUSTOMER Viola Davis   CUSTOMER NO. 120

DATE	ITEM	POST. REF.	DEBIT	CREDIT	DEBIT BALANCE
20-- Oct. 1	Balance	✔			8 2 9 44

CUSTOMER Barry Fuller   CUSTOMER NO. 130

DATE	ITEM	POST. REF.	DEBIT	CREDIT	DEBIT BALANCE

CUSTOMER Doris McCarley   CUSTOMER NO. 140

DATE	ITEM	POST. REF.	DEBIT	CREDIT	DEBIT BALANCE
20-- Oct. 1	Balance	✔			1 3 9 2 84

CUSTOMER Leona Silva   CUSTOMER NO. 150

DATE	ITEM	POST. REF.	DEBIT	CREDIT	DEBIT BALANCE
20-- Oct. 1	Balance	✔			2 8 5 12

12-8 CHALLENGE PROBLEM (concluded)

9. Approaches to Collecting and Paying Sales Taxes

_____

_____

_____

_____

_____

_____

_____

_____

_____

_____

_____

_____

_____

_____

_____

_____

_____

_____

_____

_____

_____

_____

_____

_____

_____

_____

_____

_____

_____

_____

_____

Extra forms

ACCOUNT _____   ACCOUNT NO. _____

DATE		ITEM	POST. REF.	DEBIT	CREDIT	BALANCE	
						DEBIT	CREDIT

ACCOUNT _____   ACCOUNT NO. _____

DATE		ITEM	POST. REF.	DEBIT	CREDIT	BALANCE	
						DEBIT	CREDIT

VENDOR _____   VENDOR NO. _____

DATE		ITEM	POST. REF.	DEBIT	CREDIT	CREDIT BALANCE

VENDOR _____   VENDOR NO. _____

DATE		ITEM	POST. REF.	DEBIT	CREDIT	CREDIT BALANCE

CUSTOMER _____   CUSTOMER NO. _____

DATE		ITEM	POST. REF.	DEBIT	CREDIT	DEBIT BALANCE

CUSTOMER _____   CUSTOMER NO. _____

DATE		ITEM	POST. REF.	DEBIT	CREDIT	DEBIT BALANCE

Name _____ Date _____ Class _____

13-1 WORK TOGETHER, p. 315

Preparing payroll time cards

| Employee Number | Hours Worked | | Regular Rate | Earnings | | Total Earnings |
	Regular	Overtime		Regular	Overtime	
1	40	5	$ 9.00	_____	_____	_____
2	40	3	12.50	_____	_____	_____
3	30	0	9.75	_____	_____	_____
4	40	2	11.00	_____	_____	_____

Extra form

| Employee Number | Hours Worked | | Regular Rate | Earnings | | Total Earnings |
	Regular	Overtime		Regular	Overtime	

Preparing payroll time cards

Employee Number	Hours Worked		Regular Rate	Earnings		Total Earnings
	Regular	Overtime		Regular	Overtime	
1	40	6	$ 9.80	_____	_____	_____
2	25	0	7.00	_____	_____	_____
3	40	4	12.00	_____	_____	_____
4	40	3	10.50	_____	_____	_____

Extra form

Employee Number	Hours Worked		Regular Rate	Earnings		Total Earnings
	Regular	Overtime		Regular	Overtime	

13-2 WORK TOGETHER, p. 321

Determining payroll tax withholding

No.	Employee Name	Marital Status	Number of Withholding Allowances	Total Earnings	Federal Income Tax Withholding	Social Security Tax Withholding	Medicare Tax Withholding
3	Bates, Eric C.	M	2	$1,090.00	____	____	____
4	Cohen, Jason K.	S	1	840.00	____	____	____
1	Grimes, Christi L.	M	3	1,020.00	____	____	____
6	Key, Sharon C.	S	2	980.00	____	____	____

Extra form

No.	Employee Name	Marital Status	Number of Withholding Allowances	Total Earnings	Federal Income Tax Withholding	Social Security Tax Withholding	Medicare Tax Withholding

Determining payroll tax withholding

No.	Name	Marital Status	Number of Withholding Allowances	Total Earnings	Federal Income Tax Withholding	Social Security Tax Withholding	Medicare Tax Withholding
2	Marquez, Lola S.	S	1	$ 925.00	___	___	___
5	Norris, John F.	M	4	1,250.00	___	___	___
7	Rice, James H.	S	2	1,000.00	___	___	___
9	Vale, Ann M.	M	0	1,050.00	___	___	___

Extra form

No.	Name	Marital Status	Number of Withholding Allowances	Total Earnings	Federal Income Tax Withholding	Social Security Tax Withholding	Medicare Tax Withholding

13-3 WORK TOGETHER, p. 326

Preparing payroll records

4., 5.

PAYROLL REGISTER

SEMIMONTHLY PERIOD ENDED _____   DATE OF PAYMENT _____

EMPL. NO.	EMPLOYEE'S NAME	MARI-TAL STATUS	NO. OF ALLOW-ANCES	EARNINGS REGULAR	EARNINGS OVERTIME	TOTAL	DEDUCTIONS FEDERAL INCOME TAX	SOC. SEC. TAX	MEDICARE TAX	HEALTH INSURANCE	OTHER	TOTAL	NET PAY	CHECK NO.
				1	2	3	4	5	6	7	8	9	10	
1	5	Hensley, Judy	M	2	1 040 00	39 00									1
2	9	McCune, Mike	S	1	920 00	51 75									2
3															3
22															22

OTHER DEDUCTIONS: B—U.S. SAVINGS BONDS; UW—UNITED WAY

6.

EARNINGS RECORD FOR QUARTER ENDED _____

EMPLOYEE NO. _____   LAST NAME _____   FIRST _____   MIDDLE INITIAL _____   MARITAL STATUS _____   WITHHOLDING ALLOWANCES _____

RATE OF PAY _____ PER HR. _____   SOCIAL SECURITY NO. _____   POSITION _____

PAY PERIOD NO.	ENDED	EARNINGS REGULAR	EARNINGS OVERTIME	TOTAL	DEDUCTIONS FEDERAL INCOME TAX	SOC. SEC. TAX	MEDICARE TAX	HEALTH INSURANCE	OTHER	TOTAL	NET PAY	ACCUMULATED EARNINGS
		1	2	3	4	5	6	7	8	9	10	11
1												
7	QUARTERLY TOTALS											

OTHER DEDUCTIONS: B—U.S. SAVINGS BONDS; UW—UNITED WAY

Preparing payroll records

7., 8.

PAYROLL REGISTER

SEMIMONTHLY PERIOD ENDED July 15, 20 --   DATE OF PAYMENT July 15, 20 --

EMPL. NO.	EMPLOYEE'S NAME	MARI-TAL STATUS	NO. OF ALLOW-ANCES	EARNINGS REGULAR	EARNINGS OVERTIME	EARNINGS TOTAL	DEDUCTIONS FEDERAL INCOME TAX	DEDUCTIONS SOC. SEC. TAX	DEDUCTIONS MEDICARE TAX	DEDUCTIONS HEALTH INSURANCE	DEDUCTIONS OTHER	DEDUCTIONS TOTAL	NET PAY	CHECK NO.
				1	2	3	4	5	6	7	8	9	10	
8	Eubanks, Gary	M	3	1024 00	76 80									1
15	Park, Ellen	S	2	920 00	138 00									2
														3
														22

OTHER DEDUCTIONS: B—U.S. SAVINGS BONDS; UW—UNITED WAY

EARNINGS RECORD FOR QUARTER ENDED

EMPLOYEE NO. _____

LAST NAME _____   FIRST _____   MIDDLE INITIAL _____   MARITAL STATUS _____

RATE OF PAY _____   PER HR. _____   SOCIAL SECURITY NO. _____   POSITION _____   WITHHOLDING ALLOWANCES _____

PAY PERIOD NO.	PAY PERIOD ENDED	EARNINGS REGULAR	EARNINGS OVERTIME	EARNINGS TOTAL	DEDUCTIONS FEDERAL INCOME TAX	DEDUCTIONS SOC. SEC. TAX	DEDUCTIONS MEDICARE TAX	DEDUCTIONS HEALTH INSURANCE	DEDUCTIONS OTHER	DEDUCTIONS TOTAL	NET PAY	ACCUMULATED EARNINGS
		1	2	3	4	5	6	7	8	9	10	11
1												
7	QUARTERLY TOTALS											

9.

OTHER DEDUCTIONS: B—U.S. SAVINGS BONDS; UW—UNITED WAY

13-4 WORK TOGETHER, p. 329

Preparing payroll checks

4., 5.

NO. **599**

Date: _____ 20___ $_____

To: _____

For: _____

_____

BAL. BRO'T. FOR'D			
AMT. DEPOSITED			
TOTAL			
AMT. THIS CHECK			
BAL. CAR'D. FOR'D			

GENERAL ACCOUNT   NO. **599**   66-877/530

ANTIQUE SHOP

_____ 20 _____

PAY TO THE ORDER OF _____ $ _____

_____ DOLLARS

For Classroom Use Only

Peoples Bank and Trust
Charlotte, NC 28206-8444

⑆053008774⑆ 196‴2236‴4 2⑈

CHECK NO. **186**

PERIOD ENDING			
EARNINGS	$		
REG.	$		
O.T.	$		
DEDUCTIONS	$		
INC. TAX	$		
SOC. SEC. TAX	$		
MED. TAX	$		
HEALTH INS.	$		
OTHER	$		
NET PAY	$		

PAYROLL ACCOUNT   66-877/530

_____ 20 _____

NO. **186**

PAY TO THE ORDER OF _____ $ _____

_____ DOLLARS

For Classroom Use Only   ANTIQUE SHOP

Peoples Bank and Trust
Charlotte, NC 28206-8444

⑆053008774⑆ 196‴2236‴44⑈

CHECK NO. **187**

PERIOD ENDING			
EARNINGS	$		
REG.	$		
O.T.	$		
DEDUCTIONS	$		
INC. TAX	$		
SOC. SEC. TAX	$		
MED. TAX	$		
HEALTH INS.	$		
OTHER	$		
NET PAY	$		

PAYROLL ACCOUNT   66-877/530

_____ 20 _____

NO. **187**

PAY TO THE ORDER OF _____ $ _____

_____ DOLLARS

For Classroom Use Only   ANTIQUE SHOP

Peoples Bank and Trust
Charlotte, NC 28206-8444

⑆053008774⑆ 196‴2236‴44⑈

Preparing payroll checks

6., 7.

NO. **651**

Date: _____ 20___ $_____

To: _____

_____

For: _____

_____

BAL. BRO'T. FOR'D			
AMT. DEPOSITED			
TOTAL			
AMT. THIS CHECK			
BAL. CAR'D. FOR'D			

GENERAL ACCOUNT   NO. **651**   66-877 / 530

THE SIGN SHOP

_____ 20 _____

PAY TO THE ORDER OF _____ $ _____

_____ DOLLARS

For Classroom Use Only

Peoples Bank and Trust

Charlotte, NC 28206-8444

⑈053008774⑈ 196⑈2236⑈42⑈

CHECK NO. **211**

PERIOD ENDING			
EARNINGS	$		
REG.	$		
O.T.	$		
DEDUCTIONS	$		
INC. TAX	$		
SOC. SEC. TAX	$		
MED. TAX	$		
HEALTH INS.	$		
OTHER	$		
NET PAY	$		

PAYROLL ACCOUNT   66-877 / 530

_____ 20 _____

NO. **211**

PAY TO THE ORDER OF _____ $ _____

_____ DOLLARS

For Classroom Use Only

Peoples Bank and Trust

Charlotte, NC 28206-8444

THE SIGN SHOP

⑈053008774⑈ 196⑈2236⑈44⑈

CHECK NO. **212**

PERIOD ENDING			
EARNINGS	$		
REG.	$		
O.T.	$		
DEDUCTIONS	$		
INC. TAX	$		
SOC. SEC. TAX	$		
MED. TAX	$		
HEALTH INS.	$		
OTHER	$		
NET PAY	$		

PAYROLL ACCOUNT   66-877 / 530

_____ 20 _____

NO. **212**

PAY TO THE ORDER OF _____ $ _____

_____ DOLLARS

For Classroom Use Only

Peoples Bank and Trust

Charlotte, NC 28206-8444

THE SIGN SHOP

⑈053008774⑈ 196⑈2236⑈44⑈

13-1 APPLICATION PROBLEM, p. 331

Preparing payroll time cards

1., 2.

EMPLOYEE NO. 16
NAME Sylvia A. Rodriguez
PERIOD ENDING April 15, 20 – –

	MORNING IN	MORNING OUT	AFTERNOON IN	AFTERNOON OUT	OVERTIME IN	OVERTIME OUT	HOURS REG	HOURS OT	AMOUNT
2	758	1202	1259	503					
3	757	1203	100	500	702	832			
4	800	1200	1259	500					
5	759	1201	1258	504					
6	759	1202	1255	503					
9	758	1201	1256	502					
10	756	1200	1257	501					
11	757	1202	1257	458					
12	758	1200	1259	501					
13	759	1204	1259	500					

	HOURS	RATE	AMOUNT
REGULAR		9.20	
OVERTIME			
TOTAL HOURS		TOTAL EARNINGS	

EMPLOYEE NO. 11
NAME Henry F. Miller
PERIOD ENDING April 15, 20 – –

	MORNING IN	MORNING OUT	AFTERNOON IN	AFTERNOON OUT	OVERTIME IN	OVERTIME OUT	HOURS REG	HOURS OT	AMOUNT
2	757	1201	1259	502					
3	757	1202	1258	501					
4	756	1204	100	501	556	659			
5	757	1205	1259	500					
6	759	1205	100	502					
9	757	1204	1259	505					
10	758	1205	1256	504	600	731			
11	756	1202	1257	502					
12	756	1201	1259	501	700	932			
13	757	1200	101	500					

	HOURS	RATE	AMOUNT
REGULAR		9.80	
OVERTIME			
TOTAL HOURS		TOTAL EARNINGS	

EMPLOYEE NO. 14
NAME Marie L. Kerns
PERIOD ENDING April 15, 20 – –

	MORNING IN	MORNING OUT	AFTERNOON IN	AFTERNOON OUT	OVERTIME IN	OVERTIME OUT	HOURS REG	HOURS OT	AMOUNT
2	759	1201	1256	501					
3	757	1202	1257	502					
4	756	1201	1258	504	701	802			
5	802	1204	101	506					
6	756	1203	1259	500					
9	759	1200	1259	459	559	731			
10	800	1200	1258	501					
11	759	1202	1257	506					
12	756	1159	1256	502	558	732			
13	757	1203	1257	501					

	HOURS	RATE	AMOUNT
REGULAR		11.80	
OVERTIME			
TOTAL HOURS		TOTAL EARNINGS	

Extra forms

EMPLOYEE NO.

NAME

PERIOD ENDING

MORNING		AFTERNOON		OVERTIME		HOURS	
IN	OUT	IN	OUT	IN	OUT	REG	OT

	HOURS	RATE	AMOUNT
REGULAR			
OVERTIME			
TOTAL HOURS		TOTAL EARNINGS	

EMPLOYEE NO.

NAME

PERIOD ENDING

MORNING		AFTERNOON		OVERTIME		HOURS	
IN	OUT	IN	OUT	IN	OUT	REG	OT

	HOURS	RATE	AMOUNT
REGULAR			
OVERTIME			
TOTAL HOURS		TOTAL EARNINGS	

EMPLOYEE NO.

NAME

PERIOD ENDING

MORNING		AFTERNOON		OVERTIME		HOURS	
IN	OUT	IN	OUT	IN	OUT	REG	OT

	HOURS	RATE	AMOUNT
REGULAR			
OVERTIME			
TOTAL HOURS		TOTAL EARNINGS	

13-2 APPLICATION PROBLEM, p. 331

Determining payroll tax withholding

1., 2.

Employee		Marital Status	Number of Withholding Allowances	Total Earnings	Federal Income Tax Withholding	Social Security Tax Withholding	Medicare Tax Withholding
No.	Name						
2	Baird, Tony W.	M	2	$1,220.00	_____	_____	____
6	Delgado, Rudy C.	M	3	1,090.00	_____	_____	____
3	Garza, Kay H.	S	1	940.00	_____	_____	____
1	Hess, Monica T.	M	5	1,060.00	_____	_____	____
8	Levy, Irving S.	S	1	910.00	_____	_____	____
7	Minick, Esther A.	S	2	990.00	_____	_____	____
4	Pharr, Angela S.	S	1	900.00	_____	_____	____
5	Reiner, Greg R.	M	3	1,250.00	_____	_____	____

Extra form

Employee		Marital Status	Number of Withholding Allowances	Total Earnings	Federal Income Tax Withholding	Social Security Tax Withholding	Medicare Tax Withholding
No.	Name						

Extra forms

Employee		Marital Status	Number of Withholding Allowances	Total Earnings	Federal Income Tax Withholding	Social Security Tax Withholding	Medicare Tax Withholding
No.	Name						

Employee		Marital Status	Number of Withholding Allowances	Total Earnings	Federal Income Tax Withholding	Social Security Tax Withholding	Medicare Tax Withholding
No.	Name						

13-3   APPLICATION PROBLEM, p. 331

Preparing a payroll register

PAYROLL REGISTER

SEMIMONTHLY PERIOD ENDED _____   DATE OF PAYMENT _____

EMPL. NO.	EMPLOYEE'S NAME	MARITAL STATUS	NO. OF ALLOWANCES	EARNINGS REGULAR	EARNINGS OVERTIME	EARNINGS TOTAL	DEDUCTIONS FEDERAL INCOME TAX	DEDUCTIONS SOC. SEC. TAX	DEDUCTIONS MEDICARE TAX	DEDUCTIONS HEALTH INSURANCE	DEDUCTIONS OTHER	TOTAL	NET PAY	CHECK NO.
2	Askew, Celia R.	S	1	984 00	18 45					40 00 B	20 00			
10	Bates, James C.	M	3	704 00						65 00				
9	Cates, Paula M.	M	2	744 00	83 70					50 00 B	10 00			
3	Day, Stacy L.	M	2	784 00						50 00 B	10 00			
6	Fox, Lisa M.	S	1	680 00	51 00					40 00				
11	Jantz, Glen F.	S	1	824 00						40 00				
1	Miller, Martin L.	S	2	1056 00	99 00					50 00				
5	Picard, Angela S.	M	4	1120 00						65 00 B	50 00			
4	Sanchez, Juan M.	M	3	960 00	36 00					65 00				
7	Todd, Jennifer N.	S	1	1120 00	63 00					40 00 B	20 00			
8	Vargas, Frank M.	M	2	840 00						50 00				
12	Wyatt, Scott A.	S	1	800 00	30 00					40 00 B	10 00			

OTHER DEDUCTIONS: B—U.S. SAVINGS BONDS; UW—UNITED WAY

Extra form

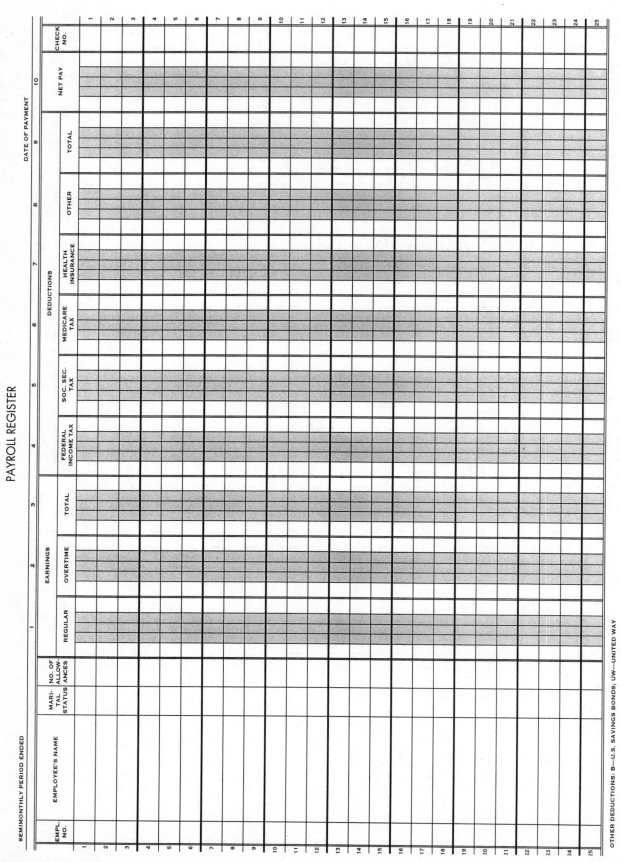

PAYROLL REGISTER

13-4 APPLICATION PROBLEM, p. 332

Preparing an employee earnings record
1., 2., 3., 4.

EARNINGS RECORD FOR QUARTER ENDED _____

EMPLOYEE NO. _____

LAST NAME _____ FIRST _____ MIDDLE INITIAL _____ MARITAL STATUS _____

SOCIAL SECURITY NO. _____ POSITION _____

RATE OF PAY _____ PER HR. _____ WITHHOLDING ALLOWANCES _____

PAY PERIOD		EARNINGS			DEDUCTIONS						NET PAY	ACCUMULATED EARNINGS
NO.	ENDED	REGULAR	OVERTIME	TOTAL	FEDERAL INCOME TAX	SOC. SEC. TAX	MEDICARE TAX	HEALTH INSURANCE	OTHER	TOTAL		
		1	2	3	4	5	6	7	8	9	10	11
1	7/15	1320 00	135 00	1455 00	144 00	94 58	21 83	60 00	B 10 00	330 41	1124 59	
2	7/31	1200 00	90 00	1290 00	120 00	83 85	19 35	60 00	B 10 00	293 20	996 80	
3	8/15	1320 00		1320 00	126 00	85 80	19 80	60 00	B 10 00	301 60	1018 40	
4	8/31	1020 00		1020 00	81 00	66 30	15 30	60 00	B 10 00	232 60	787 40	
5	9/15	1320 00	135 00	1455 00								
6	9/30	1200 00		1200 00								
7	QUARTERLY TOTALS											

OTHER DEDUCTIONS: B—U.S. SAVINGS BONDS; UW—UNITED WAY

EARNINGS RECORD FOR QUARTER ENDED

EMPLOYEE NO.

RATE OF PAY _____ PER HR.

LAST NAME _____ FIRST _____ MIDDLE INITIAL _____ MARITAL STATUS _____ WITHHOLDING ALLOWANCES _____

SOCIAL SECURITY NO. _____ POSITION _____

PAY PERIOD		EARNINGS			DEDUCTIONS						NET PAY	ACCUMULATED EARNINGS
NO.	ENDED	REGULAR	OVERTIME	TOTAL	FEDERAL INCOME TAX	SOC. SEC. TAX	MEDICARE TAX	HEALTH INSURANCE	OTHER	TOTAL		
		1	2	3	4	5	6	7	8	9	10	11
1												
2												
3												
4												
5												
6												
7												
QUARTERLY TOTALS												

OTHER DEDUCTIONS: B—U.S. SAVINGS BONDS; UW—UNITED WAY

13-5 APPLICATION PROBLEM, p. 332

Preparing payroll checks

1., 2.

NO. **630**	
Date: _____ 20___ $_____	GENERAL ACCOUNT NO. **630** 66-877 / 530
To: _____	ROYAL APPLIANCES _____ 20 _____
_____	PAY TO THE ORDER OF _____ $ _____
For: _____	_____ DOLLARS
BAL. BRO'T. FOR'D	For Classroom Use Only
AMT. DEPOSITED	**Peoples Bank and Trust**
TOTAL	Charlotte, NC 28206-8444
AMT. THIS CHECK	⑆053008774⑆ 196⑈2236⑈42⑈
BAL. CAR'D. FOR'D	

CHECK NO. **823**	
PERIOD ENDING	PAYROLL ACCOUNT 66-877 / 530
EARNINGS $	_____ 20 _____ NO. **823**
REG. $	PAY TO THE ORDER OF _____ $ _____
O.T. $	_____ DOLLARS
DEDUCTIONS $	For Classroom Use Only ROYAL APPLIANCES
INC. TAX $	**Peoples Bank and Trust**
SOC. SEC. TAX $	Charlotte, NC 28206-8444
MEDICARE TAX $	⑆053008774⑆ 196⑈2236⑈44⑈
HEALTH INS. $	
OTHER $	
NET PAY $	

CHECK NO. **827**	
PERIOD ENDING	PAYROLL ACCOUNT 66-877 / 530
EARNINGS $	_____ 20 _____ NO. **827**
REG. $	PAY TO THE ORDER OF _____ $ _____
O.T. $	_____ DOLLARS
DEDUCTIONS $	For Classroom Use Only ROYAL APPLIANCES
INC. TAX $	**Peoples Bank and Trust**
SOC. SEC. TAX $	Charlotte, NC 28206-8444
MEDICARE TAX $	⑆053008774⑆ 196⑈2236⑈44⑈
HEALTH INS. $	
OTHER $	
NET PAY $	

Extra forms

NO.				
Date: ____ 20___ $ _____				
To: _____				
For: _____				
BAL. BRO'T. FOR'D				
AMT. DEPOSITED				
TOTAL				
AMT. THIS CHECK				
BAL. CAR'D. FOR'D				

GENERAL ACCOUNT   NO. _____   66-877 / 530

_____ 20 _____

PAY TO THE ORDER OF _____ $ _____

_____ DOLLARS

For Classroom Use Only

Peoples Bank and Trust
Charlotte, NC 28206-8444

⑆053008774⑆ 196⑈2236⑈42⑉

CHECK NO.				
PERIOD ENDING				
EARNINGS	$			
REG.	$			
O.T.	$			
DEDUCTIONS	$			
INC TAX	$			
SOC. SEC TAX	$			
MED. TAX	$			
HEALTH INS.	$			
OTHER	$			
NET PAY	$			

PAYROLL ACCOUNT   66-877 / 530

_____ 20 _____   NO.

PAY TO THE ORDER OF _____ $ _____

_____ DOLLARS

For Classroom Use Only

Peoples Bank and Trust
Charlotte, NC 28206-8444

⑆053008774⑆ 196⑈2236⑈44⑉

CHECK NO.				
PERIOD ENDING				
EARNINGS	$			
REG.	$			
O.T.	$			
DEDUCTIONS	$			
INC TAX	$			
SOC. SEC TAX	$			
MED. TAX	$			
HEALTH INS.	$			
OTHER	$			
NET PAY	$			

PAYROLL ACCOUNT   66-877 / 530

_____ 20 _____   NO.

PAY TO THE ORDER OF _____ $ _____

_____ DOLLARS

For Classroom Use Only

Peoples Bank and Trust
Charlotte, NC 28206-8444

⑆053008774⑆ 196⑈2236⑈44⑉

13-6 MASTERY PROBLEM, p. 333

Preparing a semimonthly payroll

1.

PAYROLL REGISTER

SEMIMONTHLY PERIOD ENDED

DATE OF PAYMENT

EMPL. NO.	EMPLOYEE'S NAME	MARI-TAL STATUS	NO. OF ALLOW-ANCES	EARNINGS			DEDUCTIONS							NET PAY	CHECK NO.
				REGULAR	OVERTIME	TOTAL	FEDERAL INCOME TAX	SOC. SEC. TAX	MEDICARE TAX	HEALTH INSURANCE	OTHER	TOTAL			
				1	2	3	4	5	6	7	8	9		10	
1															1
2															2
3															3
4															4
5															5
6															6
7															7
8															8
9															9
10															10
11															11
12															12
13															13
14															14
15															15
16															16
17															17
18															18
19															19
20															20
21															21
22															22
23															23
24															24
25															25

OTHER DEDUCTIONS: B—U.S. SAVINGS BONDS; UW—UNITED WAY

Extra form

PAYROLL REGISTER

SEMIMONTHLY PERIOD ENDED

DATE OF PAYMENT

EMPL. NO.	EMPLOYEE'S NAME	MARI-TAL STATUS	NO. OF ALLOW-ANCES	EARNINGS			DEDUCTIONS						NET PAY	CHECK NO.
				REGULAR	OVERTIME	TOTAL	FEDERAL INCOME TAX	SOC. SEC. TAX	MEDICARE TAX	HEALTH INSURANCE	OTHER	TOTAL		
				1	2	3	4	5	6	7	8	9	10	
1														1
2														2
3														3
4														4
5														5
6														6
7														7
8														8
9														9
10														10
11														11
12														12
13														13
14														14
15														15
16														16
17														17
18														18
19														19
20														20
21														21
22														22
23														23
24														24
25														25

OTHER DEDUCTIONS: B—U.S. SAVINGS BONDS; UW—UNITED WAY

13-6 MASTERY PROBLEM (concluded)

2., 3.

NO. 872	**GENERAL ACCOUNT** NO. **872** 8-8335 / 430
Date: _____ 20___ $_____	RAINBO COMPANY _____ 20 ___
To: _____	PAY TO THE ORDER OF _____ $ _____
For: _____	_____ DOLLARS
BAL. BRO'T. FOR'D	*For Classroom Use Only*
AMT. DEPOSITED	**First Security Bank of Pittsburgh**
TOTAL	Pittsburgh, PA 15210-3402
AMT. THIS CHECK	
BAL. CAR'D. FOR'D	⑆043083356⑆ 005972164⑆

CHECK NO. 528	**PAYROLL ACCOUNT** 8-8335 / 430
PERIOD ENDING	_____ 20 ___
EARNINGS $	NO. **528**
REG. $	PAY TO THE ORDER OF _____ $ _____
O.T. $	_____ DOLLARS
DEDUCTIONS $	*For Classroom Use Only* RAINBO COMPANY
INC. TAX $	**First Security Bank of Pittsburgh**
SOC. SEC. TAX $	Pittsburgh, PA 15210-3402
MED. TAX $	
HEALTH INS. $	⑆043083356⑆ 005972165⑆
OTHER $	
NET PAY $	

CHECK NO. 533	**PAYROLL ACCOUNT** 8-8335 / 430
PERIOD ENDING	_____ 20 ___
EARNINGS $	NO. **533**
REG. $	PAY TO THE ORDER OF _____ $ _____
O.T. $	_____ DOLLARS
DEDUCTIONS $	*For Classroom Use Only* RAINBO COMPANY
INC. TAX $	**First Security Bank of Pittsburgh**
SOC. SEC. TAX $	Pittsburgh, PA 15210-3402
MED. TAX $	
HEALTH INS. $	⑆043083356⑆ 005972165⑆
OTHER $	
NET PAY $	

Extra forms

NO.

Date: _____ 20___ $_____

To: _____

For: _____

BAL. BRO'T. FOR'D		
AMT. DEPOSITED		
TOTAL		
AMT. THIS CHECK		
BAL. CAR'D. FOR'D		

GENERAL ACCOUNT　　　NO. _____　　　8-8335/430

_____ 20 ___

PAY TO THE ORDER OF _____ $ _____

_____ DOLLARS

For Classroom Use Only

First Security Bank of Pittsburgh
Pittsburgh, PA 15210-3402

⑆043083356⑆ 005972164⑊

CHECK NO.

PERIOD ENDING		
EARNINGS	$	
REG.	$	
O.T.	$	
DEDUCTIONS	$	
INC. TAX	$	
SOC. SEC. TAX	$	
MED. TAX	$	
HEALTH INS.	$	
OTHER	$	
NET PAY	$	

PAYROLL ACCOUNT　　　8-8335/430

_____ 20 ___

NO.

PAY TO THE ORDER OF _____ $ _____

_____ DOLLARS

For Classroom Use Only

First Security Bank of Pittsburgh
Pittsburgh, PA 15210-3402

⑆043083356⑆ 005972165⑊

CHECK NO.

PERIOD ENDING		
EARNINGS	$	
REG.	$	
O.T.	$	
DEDUCTIONS	$	
INC. TAX	$	
SOC. SEC. TAX	$	
MED. TAX	$	
HEALTH INS.	$	
OTHER	$	
NET PAY	$	

PAYROLL ACCOUNT　　　8-8335/430

_____ 20 ___

NO.

PAY TO THE ORDER OF _____ $ _____

_____ DOLLARS

For Classroom Use Only

First Security Bank of Pittsburgh
Pittsburgh, PA 15210-3402

⑆043083356⑆ 005972165⑊

13-7 CHALLENGE PROBLEM, p. 334

Calculating piecework wages

PAYROLL REGISTER

SEMIMONTHLY PERIOD ENDED _____ DATE OF PAYMENT _____

| EMPL. NO. | EMPLOYEE'S NAME | MARI-TAL STATUS | NO. OF ALLOW-ANCES | EARNINGS | | | DEDUCTIONS | | | | | | NET PAY | CHECK NO. |
| | | | | REGULAR | INCENTIVE | TOTAL | FEDERAL INCOME TAX | SOC. SEC. TAX | MEDICARE TAX | HEALTH INSURANCE | OTHER | TOTAL | | |
				1	2	3	4	5	6	7	8	9	10	
1	C2	Martinez, Luis L.	S	1											
2	C4	Price, Nancy C.	M	1											
3	C8	King, Debra S.	M	2											
4	A1	Heath, Scott R.	S	1											
5	A6	Nowlin, Daniel W.	M	3											
6	A7	Scofield, Martha A.	S	1											
7	F5	Isaacs, Julie M.	M	2											
8	F3	Stewart, Gary W.	M	2											
9															
10															
11															
12															
13															
14															
15															
16															
17															
18															
19															
20															
21															
22															
23															
24															
25															

OTHER DEDUCTIONS: B—U.S. SAVINGS BONDS; UW—UNITED WAY

Extra form

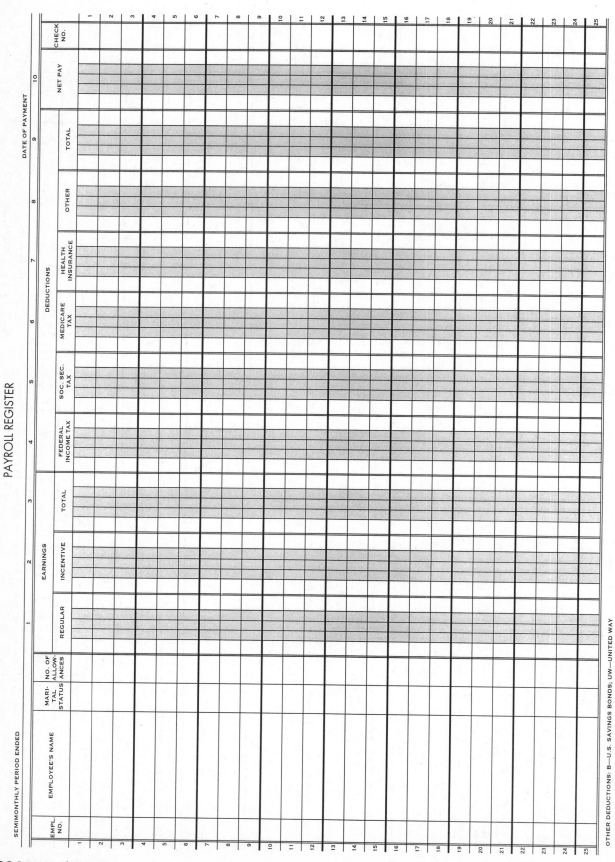

PAYROLL REGISTER

SEMIMONTHLY PERIOD ENDED _____ DATE OF PAYMENT _____

EMPL. NO.	EMPLOYEE'S NAME	MARITAL STATUS	NO. OF ALLOWANCES	EARNINGS			DEDUCTIONS						NET PAY	CHECK NO.
				REGULAR 1	INCENTIVE 2	TOTAL 3	FEDERAL INCOME TAX 4	SOC. SEC. TAX 5	MEDICARE TAX 6	HEALTH INSURANCE 7	OTHER 8	TOTAL 9	NET PAY 10	
1														1
2														2
3														3
4														4
5														5
6														6
7														7
8														8
9														9
10														10
11														11
12														12
13														13
14														14
15														15
16														16
17														17
18														18
19														19
20														20
21														21
22														22
23														23
24														24
25														25

OTHER DEDUCTIONS: B—U.S. SAVINGS BONDS; UW—UNITED WAY

14-1 **WORK TOGETHER, p. 343**

Recording a payroll

5.

Cash

Employee Income Tax Payable

Social Security Tax Payable

Medicare Tax Payable

Salary Expense

Extra forms

6.

CASH PAYMENTS JOURNAL

PAGE 4

			GENERAL		ACCOUNTS PAYABLE DEBIT	CASH CREDIT
DATE	ACCOUNT TITLE	CK. NO.	POST. REF.	DEBIT	CREDIT		

Recording a payroll

7.

Cash
_____

Employee Income Tax Payable
_____

Social Security Tax Payable
_____

Medicare Tax Payable
_____

Salary Expense
_____

Extra forms

_____   _____   _____   _____   _____

8.

CASH PAYMENTS JOURNAL

PAGE 4

| | | | CK. NO. | POST. REF. | GENERAL | | ACCOUNTS PAYABLE DEBIT | CASH CREDIT |
ACCOUNT TITLE	DATE				DEBIT 1	CREDIT 2	3	4
								1
								2
								3
								4
								5
								6
								7
								8
								9

14-2 WORK TOGETHER, p. 348

Recording employer payroll taxes

3., 4.

Employee Name	Accumulated Earnings, April 30	Total Earnings for May 1–15 Pay Period	Unemployment Taxable Earnings
Beltran, Tamela C.	$5,100.00	$637.50	_____
Cintron, Irma V.	7,350.00	920.00	_____
Totals		_____	_____

Social Security Tax Payable	_____
Medicare Tax Payable	_____
Unemployment Tax Payable—Federal	_____
Unemployment Tax Payable—State	_____
Total Payroll Taxes	_____

5.

GENERAL JOURNAL

PAGE

	DATE	ACCOUNT TITLE	DOC. NO.	POST. REF.	DEBIT	CREDIT	
1							1
2							2
3							3
4							4
5							5
6							6
7							7
8							8
9							9
10							10

Recording employer payroll taxes

6., 7.

Employee Name	Accumulated Earnings, May 31	Total Earnings for June 1–15 Pay Period	Unemployment Taxable Earnings
Cowaski, Renee Y.	$ 5,730.00	$ 720.00	————
LeCrone, Mark J.	10,500.00	1,320.00	————
	Totals	————	————

Social Security Tax Payable	————
Medicare Tax Payable	————
Unemployment Tax Payable—Federal	————
Unemployment Tax Payable—State	————
Total Payroll Taxes	————

8.

GENERAL JOURNAL

PAGE

	DATE	ACCOUNT TITLE	DOC. NO.	POST. REF.	DEBIT	CREDIT	
1							1
2							2
3							3
4							4
5							5
6							6
7							7
8							8
9							9
10							10

Name _____ Date _____ Class _____

Reporting withholding and payroll taxes

Form **941**

Department of the Treasury
Internal Revenue Service

Employer's Quarterly Federal Tax Return

▶ See separate instructions for information on completing this return.
Please type or print.

Enter state code for state in which deposits were made ONLY if different from state in address to the right ▶ ☐

Name (as distinguished from trade name)

Trade name, if any

Address (number and street)

Date quarter ended

Employer identification number

City, state, and ZIP code

OMB No. 1545-0029

T	
FF	
FD	
FP	
I	
T	

If address is different from prior return, check here ▶ ☐

IRS Use

1 1 1 1 1 1 1 1 1 1   2   3 3 3 3 3 3 3   4 4 4   5 5 5

6   7   8 8 8 8 8 8 8   9 9 9 9 9   10 10 10 10 10 10 10 10 10 10

If you do not have to file returns in the future, check here ▶ ☐ and enter date final wages paid ▶
If you are a seasonal employer, see **Seasonal employers** on page 1 of the instructions and check here ▶ ☐

1	Number of employees in the pay period that includes March 12th . ▶	1			
2	Total wages and tips, plus other compensation		**2**	
3	Total income tax withheld from wages, tips, and sick pay . . .		**3**	
4	Adjustment of withheld income tax for preceding quarters of calendar year		**4**	
5	Adjusted total of income tax withheld (line 3 as adjusted by line 4—see instructions)		**5**	

6	Taxable social security wages	**6a**		× 13% (.13) =	**6b**	
	Taxable social security tips	**6c**		× 13% (.13) =	**6d**	
7	Taxable Medicare wages and tips . . .	**7a**		× 3% (.03) =	**7b**	

8	Total social security and Medicare taxes (add lines 6b, 6d, and 7b). Check here if wages are not subject to social security and/or Medicare tax . . . . ▶ ☐	**8**	
9	Adjustment of social security and Medicare taxes (see instructions for required explanation) Sick Pay $ _____ ± Fractions of Cents $ _____ ± Other $ _____ =	**9**	
10	Adjusted total of social security and Medicare taxes (line 8 as adjusted by line 9—see instructions)	**10**	
11	**Total taxes** (add lines 5 and 10)	**11**	
12	Advance earned income credit (EIC) payments made to employees . . .	**12**	
13	Net taxes (subtract line 12 from line 11). **This should equal line 17, column (d) below (or line D of Schedule B (Form 941))**	**13**	
14	Total deposits for quarter, including overpayment applied from a prior quarter . . .	**14**	
15	**Balance due** (subtract line 14 from line 13). See instructions	**15**	
16	**Overpayment,** if line 14 is more than line 13, enter excess here ▶ $ _____ and check if to be: ☐ Applied to next return **OR** ☐ Refunded.		

  • **All filers:** If line 13 is less than $500, you need not complete line 17 or Schedule B (Form 941).
  • **Semiweekly schedule depositors:** Complete Schedule B (Form 941) and check here . . . . ▶ ☐
  • **Monthly schedule depositors:** Complete line 17, columns (a) through (d), and check here . . . . ▶ ☐

17	**Monthly Summary of Federal Tax Liability.** Do not complete if you were a semiweekly schedule depositor.			
	(a) First month liability	**(b)** Second month liability	**(c)** Third month liability	**(d)** Total liability for quarter

Sign Here

Under penalties of perjury, I declare that I have examined this return, including accompanying schedules and statements, and to the best of my knowledge and belief, it is true, correct, and complete.

Signature ▶   Print Your Name and Title ▶   Date ▶

For Privacy Act and Paperwork Reduction Act Notice, see page 4 of separate instructions.   Cat. No. 17001Z   Form **941**

Reporting withholding and payroll taxes

Form **941**

Department of the Treasury
Internal Revenue Service

Employer's Quarterly Federal Tax Return

▶ See separate instructions for information on completing this return.
Please type or print.

Enter state code for state in which deposits were made ONLY if different from state in address to the right ▶ (see page 3 of instructions).

Name (as distinguished from trade name)

Trade name, if any

Address (number and street)

Date quarter ended

Employer identification number

City, state, and ZIP code

OMB No. 1545-0029

T	
FF	
FD	
FP	
I	
T	

If address is different from prior return, check here ▶

IRS Use

| 1 | 1 | 1 | 1 | 1 | 1 | 1 | 1 | 1 | 1 | | 2 | 3 | 3 | 3 | 3 | 3 | 3 | 3 | | 4 | 4 | 4 | 4 | 4 | | 5 | 5 | 5 |

6   7   8   8   8   8   8   8   8   9   9   9   9   10 10 10 10 10 10 10 10 10

If you do not have to file returns in the future, check here ▶ ☐   and enter date final wages paid ▶
If you are a seasonal employer, see **Seasonal employers** on page 1 of the instructions and check here ▶ ☐

1	Number of employees in the pay period that includes March 12th . ▶	**1**	
2	Total wages and tips, plus other compensation	**2**	
3	Total income tax withheld from wages, tips, and sick pay . . .	**3**	
4	Adjustment of withheld income tax for preceding quarters of calendar year	**4**	
5	Adjusted total of income tax withheld (line 3 as adjusted by line 4—see instructions) . . .	**5**	

6	Taxable social security wages	**6a**		× 13% (.13) =	**6b**	
	Taxable social security tips	**6c**		× 13% (.13) =	**6d**	
7	Taxable Medicare wages and tips . . .	**7a**		× 3% (.03) =	**7b**	

8	Total social security and Medicare taxes (add lines 6b, 6d, and 7b). Check here if wages are not subject to social security and/or Medicare tax . . . . ▶ ☐	**8**	
9	Adjustment of social security and Medicare taxes (see instructions for required explanation) Sick Pay $ _____ ± Fractions of Cents $ _____ ± Other $ _____ =	**9**	
10	Adjusted total of social security and Medicare taxes (line 8 as adjusted by line 9—see instructions) . . .	**10**	
11	**Total taxes** (add lines 5 and 10)	**11**	
12	Advance earned income credit (EIC) payments made to employees	**12**	
13	Net taxes (subtract line 12 from line 11). **This should equal line 17, column (d) below (or line D of Schedule B (Form 941))**	**13**	
14	Total deposits for quarter, including overpayment applied from a prior quarter . .	**14**	
15	**Balance due** (subtract line 14 from line 13). See instructions	**15**	

16 Overpayment, if line 14 is more than line 13, enter excess here ▶ $ _____
and check if to be: ☐ Applied to next return **OR** ☐ Refunded.

- **All filers:** If line 13 is less than $500, you need not complete line 17 or Schedule B (Form 941).
- **Semiweekly schedule depositors:** Complete Schedule B (Form 941) and check here . . . . ▶ ☐
- **Monthly schedule depositors:** Complete line 17, columns (a) through (d), and check here . . . . ▶ ☐

17	**Monthly Summary of Federal Tax Liability.** Do not complete if you were a semiweekly schedule depositor.		
(a) First month liability	**(b)** Second month liability	**(c)** Third month liability	**(d)** Total liability for quarter

Sign Here

Under penalties of perjury, I declare that I have examined this return, including accompanying schedules and statements, and to the best of my knowledge and belief, it is true, correct, and complete.

Signature ▶

Print Your Name and Title ▶

Date ▶

For Privacy Act and Paperwork Reduction Act Notice, see page 4 of separate instructions.   Cat. No. 17001Z   Form **941**

14-4 WORK TOGETHER, p. 359

Paying withholding and payroll taxes

3., 4.

CASH PAYMENTS JOURNAL

			GENERAL		ACCOUNTS PAYABLE DEBIT	CASH CREDIT
DATE	ACCOUNT TITLE	CK. NO.	POST. REF.	DEBIT	CREDIT		

				1	2	3	4	PAGE

Paying withholding and payroll taxes

5., 6.

CASH PAYMENTS JOURNAL

PAGE

	DATE	ACCOUNT TITLE	CK. NO.	POST. REF.	GENERAL DEBIT 1	GENERAL CREDIT 2	ACCOUNTS PAYABLE DEBIT 3	CASH CREDIT 4	
1									1
2									2
3									3
4									4
5									5
6									6
7									7
8									8
9									9
10									10
11									11
12									12
13									13
14									14
15									15
16									16
17									17
18									18
19									19
20									20
21									21
22									22

14-1 **APPLICATION PROBLEM, p. 361**

Recording a payroll

CASH PAYMENTS JOURNAL

						GENERAL		ACCOUNTS PAYABLE DEBIT	CASH CREDIT
						1 DEBIT	2 CREDIT	3	4
DATE	ACCOUNT TITLE	CK. NO.	POST. REF.						
1									
2									
3									
4									
5									
6									
7									
8									
9									
10									
11									
12									
13									
14									
15									
16									
17									
18									
19									
20									
21									
22									
23									

Extra form

CASH PAYMENTS JOURNAL

PAGE

				1	2	3	4	5	6	7	8	9	10	11	12	13	14	15	16	17	18	19	20	21	22	23	24	

14-2 APPLICATION PROBLEM, p. 361

Recording employer payroll taxes

1., 2., 4.

Employee Name	Accumulated Earnings, March 31	Total Earnings for April 1–15 Pay Period	Unemployment Taxable Earnings, April 15	Accumulated Earnings, April 15	Total Earnings for April 16–30 Pay Period	Unemployment Taxable Earnings, April 30
Bolser, Frank T.	$4,860.00	$ 810.00	_____	_____	$ 795.00	_____
Denham, Beth R.	5,670.00	945.00	_____	_____	980.00	_____
Harjo, Teresa S.	7,500.00	1,250.00	_____	_____	1,250.00	_____
Knutzen, John L.	3,720.00	620.00	_____	_____	635.00	_____
Prescott, Laura F.	4,560.00	760.00	_____	_____	740.00	_____
Schmidt, Ian T.	6,900.00	1,150.00	_____	_____	1,125.00	_____
	Totals	_____	_____	Totals	_____	_____

Social Security Tax Payable	_____		Social Security Tax Payable	_____
Medicare Tax Payable	_____		Medicare Tax Payable	_____
Unemployment Tax Payable—Federal	_____		Unemployment Tax Payable—Federal	_____
Unemployment Tax Payable—State	_____		Unemployment Tax Payable—State	_____

3., 5.

GENERAL JOURNAL   PAGE

	DATE	ACCOUNT TITLE	DOC. NO.	POST. REF.	DEBIT	CREDIT	
1							1
2							2
3							3
4							4
5							5
6							6
7							7
8							8
9							9
10							10
11							11
12							12
13							13

Extra form

GENERAL JOURNAL

PAGE

	DATE	ACCOUNT TITLE	DOC. NO.	POST. REF.	DEBIT	CREDIT	
1							1
2							2
3							3
4							4
5							5
6							6
7							7
8							8
9							9
10							10
11							11
12							12
13							13
14							14
15							15
16							16
17							17
18							18
19							19
20							20
21							21
22							22
23							23
24							24
25							25
26							26
27							27
28							28
29							29
30							30
31							31
32							32

Name _____ Date _____ Class _____

14-3 APPLICATION PROBLEM, p. 362

Reporting withholding and payroll taxes

Form **941**

Department of the Treasury
Internal Revenue Service

Employer's Quarterly Federal Tax Return
▶ See separate instructions for information on completing this return.
Please type or print.

Enter state code for state in which deposits were made ONLY if different from state in address to the right ▶ [:]
(see page 3 of instructions).

Name (as distinguished from trade name)	Date quarter ended
Trade name, if any	Employer identification number
Address (number and street)	City, state, and ZIP code

OMB No. 1545-0029

| T |
| FF |
| FD |
| FP |
| I |
| T |

If address is different from prior return, check here ▶ [ ]

IRS Use

| 1 1 1 1 1 1 1 1 1 1 1 | 2 | 3 3 3 3 3 3 3 3 | 4 4 4 | 5 5 5 |
| 6 | 7 | 8 8 8 8 8 8 8 | 9 9 9 9 9 | 10 10 10 10 10 10 10 10 10 |

If you do not have to file returns in the future, check here ▶ [ ] and enter date final wages paid ▶
If you are a seasonal employer, see **Seasonal employers** on page 1 of the instructions and check here ▶ [ ]

1	Number of employees in the pay period that includes March 12th . ▶	1		
2	Total wages and tips, plus other compensation	**2**	
3	Total income tax withheld from wages, tips, and sick pay	**3**	
4	Adjustment of withheld income tax for preceding quarters of calendar year	**4**	
5	Adjusted total of income tax withheld (line 3 as adjusted by line 4—see instructions) . . .	**5**	
6	Taxable social security wages	**6a**	$\times$ 13% (.13) =	**6b**	
	Taxable social security tips	**6c**	$\times$ 13% (.13) =	**6d**	
7	Taxable Medicare wages and tips . . .	**7a**	$\times$ 3% (.03) =	**7b**	
8	Total social security and Medicare taxes (add lines 6b, 6d, and 7b). Check here if wages are not subject to social security and/or Medicare tax . . . . ▶ [ ]	**8**	
9	Adjustment of social security and Medicare taxes (see instructions for required explanation) Sick Pay $ _____ ± Fractions of Cents $ _____ ± Other $ _____ =	**9**	
10	Adjusted total of social security and Medicare taxes (line 8 as adjusted by line 9—see instructions)	**10**	
11	**Total taxes** (add lines 5 and 10)	**11**	
12	Advance earned income credit (EIC) payments made to employees	**12**	
13	Net taxes (subtract line 12 from line 11). **This should equal line 17, column (d) below (or line D of Schedule B (Form 941))**	**13**	
14	Total deposits for quarter, including overpayment applied from a prior quarter	**14**	
15	**Balance due** (subtract line 14 from line 13). See instructions	**15**	
16	**Overpayment,** if line 14 is more than line 13, enter excess here ▶ $ _____		

and check if to be: [ ] Applied to next return **OR** [ ] Refunded.

- **All filers:** If line 13 is less than $500, you need not complete line 17 or Schedule B (Form 941).
- **Semiweekly schedule depositors:** Complete Schedule B (Form 941) and check here . . . . ▶ [ ]
- **Monthly schedule depositors:** Complete line 17, columns (a) through (d), and check here . . . . ▶ [ ]

17	**Monthly Summary of Federal Tax Liability.** Do not complete if you were a semiweekly schedule depositor.		
(a) First month liability	**(b)** Second month liability	**(c)** Third month liability	**(d)** Total liability for quarter

Sign Here

Under penalties of perjury, I declare that I have examined this return, including accompanying schedules and statements, and to the best of my knowledge and belief, it is true, correct, and complete.

Signature ▶ _____ Print Your Name and Title ▶ _____ Date ▶ _____

For Privacy Act and Paperwork Reduction Act Notice, see page 4 of separate instructions.   Cat. No. 17001Z   Form **941**

Extra form

Form **941**

Department of the Treasury
Internal Revenue Service

Employer's Quarterly Federal Tax Return

▶ See separate instructions for information on completing this return.

Please type or print.

Enter state code for state in which deposits were made ONLY if different from state in address to the right ▶ ☐ ⋮ (see page 3 of instructions).

Name (as distinguished from trade name)	Date quarter ended
Trade name, if any	Employer identification number
Address (number and street)	City, state, and ZIP code

OMB No. 1545-0029

| T |
| FF |
| FD |
| FP |
| I |
| T |

If address is different from prior return, check here ▶ ☐

IRS Use

| 1 1 1 1 | 1 1 1 1 1 1 | 2 | 3 3 3 3 3 3 3 | 4 4 4 | 5 5 5 |
| 6 | 7 | 8 8 8 8 8 8 8 | 9 9 9 9 9 | 10 10 10 10 10 10 10 10 |

If you do not have to file returns in the future, check here ▶ ☐ and enter date final wages paid ▶

If you are a seasonal employer, see **Seasonal employers** on page 1 of the instructions and check here ▶ ☐

1	Number of employees in the pay period that includes March 12th . ▶	1		
2	Total wages and tips, plus other compensation		**2**	
3	Total income tax withheld from wages, tips, and sick pay		**3**	
4	Adjustment of withheld income tax for preceding quarters of calendar year		**4**	
5	Adjusted total of income tax withheld (line 3 as adjusted by line 4—see instructions) . . .		**5**	
6	Taxable social security wages	6a	× 13% (.13) =	**6b**	
	Taxable social security tips	6c	× 13% (.13) =	**6d**	
7	Taxable Medicare wages and tips . . .	7a	× 3% (.03) =	**7b**	
8	Total social security and Medicare taxes (add lines 6b, 6d, and 7b). Check here if wages are not subject to social security and/or Medicare tax . . . . ▶ ☐		**8**	
9	Adjustment of social security and Medicare taxes (see instructions for required explanation) Sick Pay $ _____ ± Fractions of Cents $ _____ ± Other $ _____ =		**9**	
10	Adjusted total of social security and Medicare taxes (line 8 as adjusted by line 9—see instructions)		**10**	
11	**Total taxes** (add lines 5 and 10)		**11**	
12	Advance earned income credit (EIC) payments made to employees		**12**	
13	Net taxes (subtract line 12 from line 11). **This should equal line 17, column (d) below (or line D of Schedule B (Form 941))**		**13**	
14	Total deposits for quarter, including overpayment applied from a prior quarter		**14**	
15	**Balance due** (subtract line 14 from line 13). See instructions		**15**	
16	**Overpayment,** if line 14 is more than line 13, enter excess here ▶ $ _____ and check if to be: ☐ Applied to next return **OR** ☐ Refunded.			

- **All filers:** If line 13 is less than $500, you need not complete line 17 or Schedule B (Form 941).
- **Semiweekly schedule depositors:** Complete Schedule B (Form 941) and check here . . . . ▶ ☐
- **Monthly schedule depositors:** Complete line 17, columns (a) through (d), and check here . . . . ▶ ☐

17	**Monthly Summary of Federal Tax Liability.** Do not complete if you were a semiweekly schedule depositor.			
	(a) First month liability	**(b)** Second month liability	**(c)** Third month liability	**(d)** Total liability for quarter

Sign Here

Under penalties of perjury, I declare that I have examined this return, including accompanying schedules and statements, and to the best of my knowledge and belief, it is true, correct, and complete.

Signature ▶ _____ Print Your Name and Title ▶ _____ Date ▶ _____

For Privacy Act and Paperwork Reduction Act Notice, see page 4 of separate instructions.   Cat. No. 17001Z   Form **941**

14-4 APPLICATION PROBLEM, p. 362

Paying withholding and payroll taxes

1., 2., 3.

CASH PAYMENTS JOURNAL

PAGE

| | | | | GENERAL | | ACCOUNTS PAYABLE | CASH |
DATE	ACCOUNT TITLE	CK. NO.	POST. REF.	DEBIT	CREDIT	DEBIT	CREDIT
				1	2	3	4
1							
2							
3							
4							
5							
6							
7							
8							
9							
10							
11							
12							
13							
14							
15							
16							
17							
18							
19							
20							
21							
22							

Extra form

CASH PAYMENTS JOURNAL

PAGE _____

DATE	ACCOUNT TITLE	CK. NO.	POST. REF.	GENERAL DEBIT 1	GENERAL CREDIT 2	ACCOUNTS PAYABLE DEBIT 3	CASH CREDIT 4
1							
2							
3							
4							
5							
6							
7							
8							
9							
10							
11							
12							
13							
14							
15							
16							
17							
18							
19							
20							
21							
22							
23							
24							

14-5 MASTERY PROBLEM, p. 362

Journalizing payroll transactions

1., 2.

CASH PAYMENTS JOURNAL

PAGE

	DATE	ACCOUNT TITLE	CK. NO.	POST. REF.	GENERAL DEBIT 1	GENERAL CREDIT 2	ACCOUNTS PAYABLE DEBIT 3	CASH CREDIT 4	
1									1
2									2
3									3
4									4
5									5
6									6
7									7
8									8
9									9
10									10
11									11
12									12
13									13
14									14
15									15
16									16
17									17
18									18
19									19
20									20
21									21
22									22
23									23
24									24
25									25

1.

GENERAL JOURNAL

PAGE

	DATE		ACCOUNT TITLE	DOC. NO.	POST. REF.	DEBIT	CREDIT	
1								1
2								2
3								3
4								4
5								5
6								6
7								7
8								8
9								9
10								10
11								11
12								12
13								13
14								14
15								15
16								16
17								17
18								18
19								19
20								20
21								21
22								22
23								23
24								24
25								25
26								26
27								27
28								28
29								29
30								30
31								31
32								32
33								33

Extra form

CASH PAYMENTS JOURNAL

PAGE

				GENERAL		ACCOUNTS PAYABLE DEBIT	CASH CREDIT
DATE	ACCOUNT TITLE	CK. NO.	POST. REF.	DEBIT	CREDIT		

Journalizing and posting payroll transactions

1., 2.

CASH PAYMENTS JOURNAL

PAGE

| | | | GENERAL | | ACCOUNTS PAYABLE | CASH |
| | | | 1 | 2 | 3 | 4 |
DATE	ACCOUNT TITLE	CK. NO.	POST. REF.	DEBIT	CREDIT	DEBIT	CREDIT
1								1
2								2
3								3
4								4
5								5
6								6
7								7
8								8
9								9
10								10
11								11
12								12
13								13
14								14
15								15
16								16
17								17
18								18
19								19
20								20

14-6 CHALLENGE PROBLEM (continued)

2., 3., 4.

CASH PAYMENTS JOURNAL

PAGE

			GENERAL		ACCOUNTS PAYABLE	CASH
DATE	ACCOUNT TITLE	CK. NO.	POST. REF.	DEBIT	CREDIT	DEBIT	CREDIT
				1	2	3	4
1							
2							
3							
4							
5							
6							
7							
8							
9							
10							
11							
12							
13							
14							
15							
16							
17							
18							
19							
20							

1.

GENERAL JOURNAL

PAGE

	DATE	ACCOUNT TITLE	DOC. NO.	POST. REF.	DEBIT	CREDIT	
1							1
2							2
3							3
4							4
5							5
6							6
7							7
8							8
9							9
10							10
11							11
12							12
13							13
14							14
15							15
16							16
17							17
18							18
19							19
20							20
21							21
22							22
23							23
24							24
25							25
26							26
27							27
28							28
29							29
30							30
31							31
32							32
33							33

14-6 CHALLENGE PROBLEM (continued)

1., 3.

ACCOUNT Employee Income Tax Payable   ACCOUNT NO. 2120

DATE		ITEM	POST. REF.	DEBIT	CREDIT	BALANCE DEBIT	BALANCE CREDIT
20-- Jan.	1	Balance	✔				1 2 9 2 00

ACCOUNT Social Security Tax Payable   ACCOUNT NO. 2130

DATE		ITEM	POST. REF.	DEBIT	CREDIT	BALANCE DEBIT	BALANCE CREDIT
20-- Jan.	1	Balance	✔				1 5 2 7 50

ACCOUNT Medicare Tax Payable   ACCOUNT NO. 2140

DATE		ITEM	POST. REF.	DEBIT	CREDIT	BALANCE DEBIT	BALANCE CREDIT
20-- Jan.	1	Balance	✔				1 7 6 25

1., 3.

ACCOUNT Unemployment Tax Payable—Federal   ACCOUNT NO. 2150

DATE		ITEM	POST. REF.	DEBIT	CREDIT	BALANCE	
						DEBIT	CREDIT
20-- Jan.	1	Balance	✔				2 6 4 00

ACCOUNT Unemployment Tax Payable—State   ACCOUNT NO. 2160

DATE		ITEM	POST. REF.	DEBIT	CREDIT	BALANCE	
						DEBIT	CREDIT
20-- Jan.	1	Balance	✔				1 7 8 2 00

ACCOUNT U.S. Savings Bonds Payable   ACCOUNT NO. 2180

DATE		ITEM	POST. REF.	DEBIT	CREDIT	BALANCE	
						DEBIT	CREDIT
20-- Jan.	1	Balance	✔				3 0 0 00

ACCOUNT Payroll Taxes Expense   ACCOUNT NO. 6150

DATE		ITEM	POST. REF.	DEBIT	CREDIT	BALANCE	
						DEBIT	CREDIT

ACCOUNT Salary Expense   ACCOUNT NO. 6170

DATE		ITEM	POST. REF.	DEBIT	CREDIT	BALANCE	
						DEBIT	CREDIT

REINFORCEMENT ACTIVITY 2 PART A, p. 368

An Accounting Cycle for a Partnership: Journalizing and Posting Transactions

1., 5.

SALES JOURNAL   PAGE 12

	DATE	ACCOUNT DEBITED	SALE NO.	POST. REF.	ACCOUNTS RECEIVABLE DEBIT (1)	SALES CREDIT (2)	SALES TAX PAYABLE CREDIT (3)	
1								1
2								2
3								3
4								4
5								5
6								6
7								7
8								8
9								9
10								10
11								11
12								12

1., 4., 6.

PURCHASES JOURNAL   PAGE 12

	DATE	ACCOUNT CREDITED	PURCH. NO.	POST. REF.	PURCHASES DR. ACCTS. PAY. CR.	
1						1
2						2
3						3
4						4
5						5
6						6
7						7
8						8
9						9
10						10
11						11
12						12

1., 4.

GENERAL JOURNAL   PAGE 12

	DATE	ACCOUNT TITLE	DOC. NO.	POST. REF.	DEBIT	CREDIT	
1							1
2							2
3							3
4							4
5							5
6							6
7							7
8							8
9							9
10							10
11							11
12							12
13							13
14							14
15							15
16							16
17							17
18							18
19							19
20							20
21							21
22							22
23							23
24							24
25							25
26							26
27							27
28							28
29							29
30							30
31							31
32							32
33							33
34							34
35							35

REINFORCEMENT ACTIVITY 2 PART A (continued)

1., 4., 7., 9.

CASH RECEIPTS JOURNAL

PAGE 12

DATE	ACCOUNT TITLE	DOC. NO.	POST. REF.	GENERAL DEBIT (1)	GENERAL CREDIT (2)	ACCOUNTS RECEIVABLE CREDIT (3)	SALES CREDIT (4)	SALES TAX PAYABLE CREDIT (5)	CASH DEBIT (6)

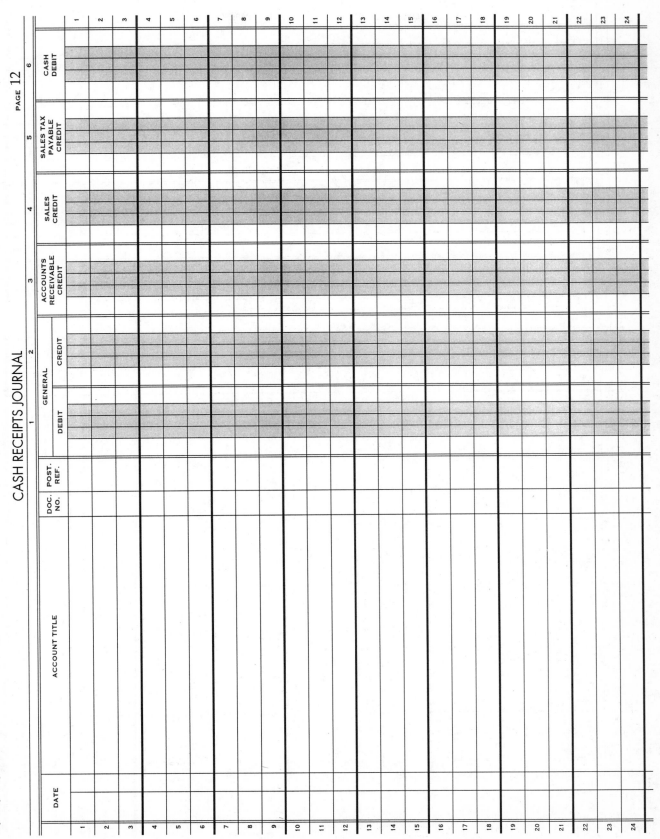

1., 2.

CASH PAYMENTS JOURNAL

PAGE 23

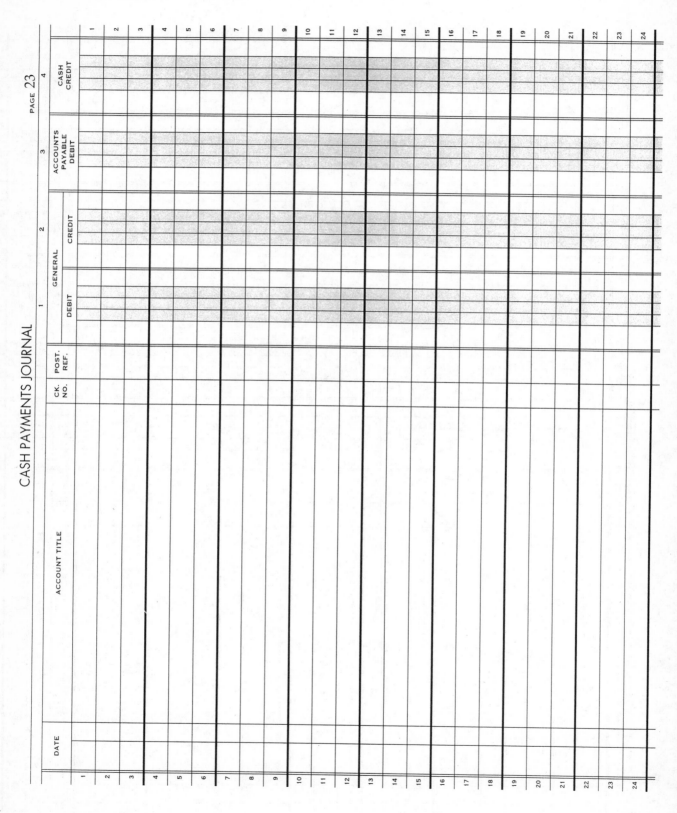

REINFORCEMENT ACTIVITY 2 PART A (continued)

3., 4., 7., 10.

CASH PAYMENTS JOURNAL

PAGE 24

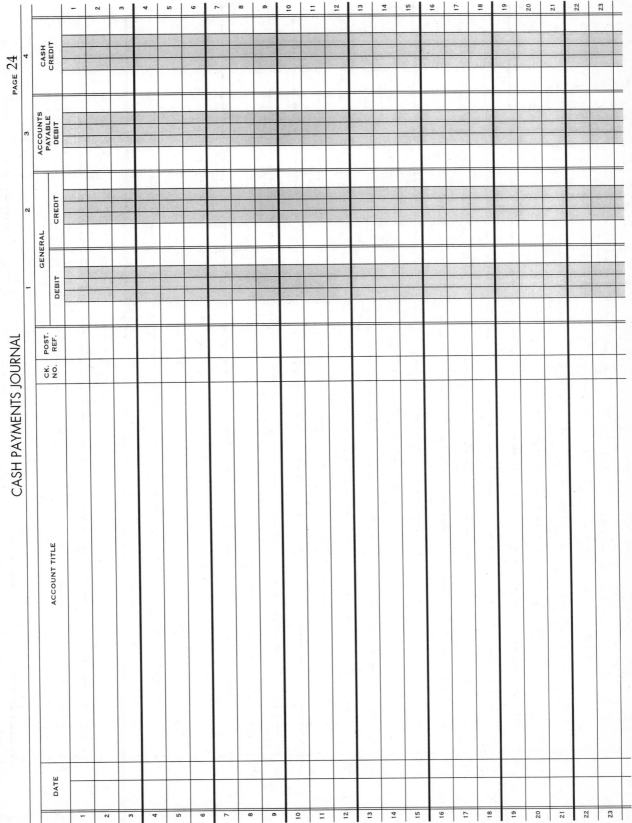

Extra form

CASH PAYMENTS JOURNAL

PAGE

| | | | GENERAL | | ACCOUNTS PAYABLE DEBIT | CASH CREDIT |
DATE	ACCOUNT TITLE	CK. NO.	POST. REF.	DEBIT	CREDIT		
				1	2	3	4
1							
2							
3							
4							
5							
6							
7							
8							
9							
10							
11							
12							
13							
14							
15							
16							
17							
18							
19							
20							
21							
22							
23							
24							

REINFORCEMENT ACTIVITY 2 PART A (continued)

The general ledger used in Reinforcement Activity 2, Part A, will be needed to complete Part B.

1., 4., 5., 6., 9., 10., 12., 18., 19., 20.   **GENERAL LEDGER**

ACCOUNT Cash   ACCOUNT NO. 1110

DATE		ITEM	POST. REF.	DEBIT	CREDIT	BALANCE DEBIT	BALANCE CREDIT
20-- Dec.	1	Balance	✔			23 340 00	

ACCOUNT Petty Cash   ACCOUNT NO. 1120

DATE		ITEM	POST. REF.	DEBIT	CREDIT	BALANCE DEBIT	BALANCE CREDIT
20-- Jan.	1	Balance	✔			500 00	

ACCOUNT Accounts Receivable   ACCOUNT NO. 1130

DATE		ITEM	POST. REF.	DEBIT	CREDIT	BALANCE DEBIT	BALANCE CREDIT
20-- Dec.	1	Balance	✔			1 667 38	

ACCOUNT Merchandise Inventory   ACCOUNT NO. 1140

DATE		ITEM	POST. REF.	DEBIT	CREDIT	BALANCE DEBIT	BALANCE CREDIT
20-- Jan.	1	Balance	✔			258 700 00	

ACCOUNT Supplies—Office   ACCOUNT NO. 1145

DATE		ITEM	POST. REF.	DEBIT	CREDIT	BALANCE DEBIT	BALANCE CREDIT
20-- Dec.	1	Balance	✔			4 430 00	

ACCOUNT Supplies—Store   ACCOUNT NO. 1150

DATE		ITEM	POST. REF.	DEBIT	CREDIT	BALANCE DEBIT	BALANCE CREDIT
20-- Dec.	1	Balance	✔			5 260 00	

1., 4., 5., 6., 9., 10., 12., 18., 19., 20.   GENERAL LEDGER

ACCOUNT Prepaid Insurance   ACCOUNT NO. 1160

DATE		ITEM	POST. REF.	DEBIT	CREDIT	BALANCE DEBIT	BALANCE CREDIT
20-- Dec.	1	Balance	✔			2 1 8 0 00	

ACCOUNT Accounts Payable   ACCOUNT NO. 2110

DATE		ITEM	POST. REF.	DEBIT	CREDIT	BALANCE DEBIT	BALANCE CREDIT
20-- Dec.	1	Balance	✔				5 2 2 2 00

ACCOUNT Employee Income Tax Payable   ACCOUNT NO. 2120

DATE		ITEM	POST. REF.	DEBIT	CREDIT	BALANCE DEBIT	BALANCE CREDIT
20-- Dec.	1	Balance	✔				3 4 2 00

ACCOUNT Social Security Tax Payable   ACCOUNT NO. 2130

DATE		ITEM	POST. REF.	DEBIT	CREDIT	BALANCE DEBIT	BALANCE CREDIT
20-- Dec.	1	Balance	✔				7 6 7 00

ACCOUNT Medicare Tax Payable   ACCOUNT NO. 2135

DATE		ITEM	POST. REF.	DEBIT	CREDIT	BALANCE DEBIT	BALANCE CREDIT
20-- Dec.	1	Balance	✔				1 7 7 00

REINFORCEMENT ACTIVITY 2   PART A (continued)

1., 4., 5., 6., 9., 10., 12., 18., 19., 20.   GENERAL LEDGER

ACCOUNT Sales Tax Payable   ACCOUNT NO. 2140

DATE	ITEM	POST. REF.	DEBIT	CREDIT	BALANCE DEBIT	BALANCE CREDIT
20-- Dec. 1	Balance	✔				1 9 4 5 00

ACCOUNT Unemployment Tax Payable—Federal   ACCOUNT NO. 2150

DATE	ITEM	POST. REF.	DEBIT	CREDIT	BALANCE DEBIT	BALANCE CREDIT
20-- Dec. 1	Balance	✔				1 1 60

ACCOUNT Unemployment Tax Payable—State   ACCOUNT NO. 2160

DATE	ITEM	POST. REF.	DEBIT	CREDIT	BALANCE DEBIT	BALANCE CREDIT
20-- Dec. 1	Balance	✔				7 8 30

ACCOUNT Health Insurance Premiums Payable   ACCOUNT NO. 2170

DATE	ITEM	POST. REF.	DEBIT	CREDIT	BALANCE DEBIT	BALANCE CREDIT
20-- Dec. 1	Balance	✔				3 4 0 00

ACCOUNT U.S. Savings Bonds Payable   ACCOUNT NO. 2180

DATE	ITEM	POST. REF.	DEBIT	CREDIT	BALANCE DEBIT	BALANCE CREDIT
20-- Dec. 1	Balance	✔				6 0 00

ACCOUNT United Way Donations Payable   ACCOUNT NO. 2190

DATE	ITEM	POST. REF.	DEBIT	CREDIT	BALANCE DEBIT	BALANCE CREDIT
20-- Dec. 1	Balance	✔				1 2 0 00

ACCOUNT Ester Burks, Capital   ACCOUNT NO. 3110

DATE	ITEM	POST. REF.	DEBIT	CREDIT	BALANCE DEBIT	BALANCE CREDIT
20-- Jan. 1	Balance	✔				112 5 8 5 50

1., 4., 5., 6., 9., 10., 12., 18., 19., 20.   **GENERAL LEDGER**

ACCOUNT Ester Burks, Drawing   ACCOUNT NO. 3120

DATE		ITEM	POST. REF.	DEBIT	CREDIT	BALANCE	
						DEBIT	CREDIT
20-- Dec.	1	Balance	✔			16 5 0 0 00	

ACCOUNT Juan Ortiz, Capital   ACCOUNT NO. 3130

DATE		ITEM	POST. REF.	DEBIT	CREDIT	BALANCE	
						DEBIT	CREDIT
20-- Jan.	1	Balance	✔				111 7 0 3 58

ACCOUNT Juan Ortiz, Drawing   ACCOUNT NO. 3140

DATE		ITEM	POST. REF.	DEBIT	CREDIT	BALANCE	
						DEBIT	CREDIT
20-- Dec.	1	Balance	✔			16 5 0 0 00	

ACCOUNT Income Summary   ACCOUNT NO. 3150

DATE		ITEM	POST. REF.	DEBIT	CREDIT	BALANCE	
						DEBIT	CREDIT

ACCOUNT Sales   ACCOUNT NO. 4110

DATE		ITEM	POST. REF.	DEBIT	CREDIT	BALANCE	
						DEBIT	CREDIT
20-- Dec.	1	Balance	✔				330 7 0 0 00

ACCOUNT Purchases   ACCOUNT NO. 5110

DATE		ITEM	POST. REF.	DEBIT	CREDIT	BALANCE	
						DEBIT	CREDIT
20-- Dec.	1	Balance	✔			138 9 1 0 00	

Name _____ Date _____ Class _____

REINFORCEMENT ACTIVITY 2   PART A (continued)

1., 4., 5., 6., 9., 10., 12., 18., 19., 20.   **GENERAL LEDGER**

ACCOUNT Advertising Expense   ACCOUNT NO. 6110

DATE		ITEM	POST. REF.	DEBIT	CREDIT	BALANCE DEBIT	BALANCE CREDIT
20-- Dec.	1	Balance	✔			5 0 7 5 00	

ACCOUNT Credit Card Fee Expense   ACCOUNT NO. 6120

DATE		ITEM	POST. REF.	DEBIT	CREDIT	BALANCE DEBIT	BALANCE CREDIT
20-- Dec.	1	Balance	✔			3 4 9 0 00	

ACCOUNT Insurance Expense   ACCOUNT NO. 6130

DATE		ITEM	POST. REF.	DEBIT	CREDIT	BALANCE DEBIT	BALANCE CREDIT

ACCOUNT Miscellaneous Expense   ACCOUNT NO. 6140

DATE		ITEM	POST. REF.	DEBIT	CREDIT	BALANCE DEBIT	BALANCE CREDIT
20-- Dec.	1	Balance	✔			2 0 2 0 00	

ACCOUNT Payroll Taxes Expense   ACCOUNT NO. 6150

DATE		ITEM	POST. REF.	DEBIT	CREDIT	BALANCE DEBIT	BALANCE CREDIT
20-- Dec.	1	Balance	✔			6 8 1 9 60	

1., 4., 5., 6., 9., 10., 12., 18., 19., 20.   **GENERAL LEDGER**

ACCOUNT Rent Expense   ACCOUNT NO. 6160

DATE		ITEM	POST. REF.	DEBIT	CREDIT	BALANCE	
						DEBIT	CREDIT
20-- Dec.	1	Balance	✔			13 2 0 0 00	

ACCOUNT Salary Expense   ACCOUNT NO. 6170

DATE		ITEM	POST. REF.	DEBIT	CREDIT	BALANCE	
						DEBIT	CREDIT
20-- Dec.	1	Balance	✔			62 1 5 0 00	

ACCOUNT Supplies Expense—Office   ACCOUNT NO. 6175

DATE		ITEM	POST. REF.	DEBIT	CREDIT	BALANCE	
						DEBIT	CREDIT

ACCOUNT Supplies Expense—Store   ACCOUNT NO. 6180

DATE		ITEM	POST. REF.	DEBIT	CREDIT	BALANCE	
						DEBIT	CREDIT

ACCOUNT Utilities Expense   ACCOUNT NO. 6190

DATE		ITEM	POST. REF.	DEBIT	CREDIT	BALANCE	
						DEBIT	CREDIT
20-- Dec.	1	Balance	✔			3 3 1 0 00	

REINFORCEMENT ACTIVITY 2   PART A (continued)

1., 4.   **ACCOUNTS PAYABLE LEDGER**

VENDOR ABC Optical Co.   VENDOR NO. 210

DATE		ITEM	POST. REF.	DEBIT	CREDIT	CREDIT BALANCE
20-- Dec.	1	Balance	✔			1 2 7 2 00

VENDOR Central Office Supply   VENDOR NO. 220

DATE		ITEM	POST. REF.	DEBIT	CREDIT	CREDIT BALANCE

VENDOR Eyecare Optical   VENDOR NO. 230

DATE		ITEM	POST. REF.	DEBIT	CREDIT	CREDIT BALANCE
20-- Dec.	1	Balance	✔			1 1 7 0 00

VENDOR Optical Mart   VENDOR NO. 240

DATE		ITEM	POST. REF.	DEBIT	CREDIT	CREDIT BALANCE
20-- Dec.	1	Balance	✔			2 2 0 0 00

VENDOR Solar Optical   VENDOR NO. 250

DATE		ITEM	POST. REF.	DEBIT	CREDIT	CREDIT BALANCE
20-- Dec.	1	Balance	✔			5 8 0 00

VENDOR Zen Supply   VENDOR NO. 260

DATE		ITEM	POST. REF.	DEBIT	CREDIT	CREDIT BALANCE

1.

ACCOUNTS RECEIVABLE LEDGER

customer Doritha Busch   customer no. 110

DATE	ITEM	POST. REF.	DEBIT	CREDIT	DEBIT BALANCE

customer Linda Cortez   customer no. 120

DATE		ITEM	POST. REF.	DEBIT	CREDIT	DEBIT BALANCE
Dec.	1	Balance	✔			4 1 3 40

customer Dallas Giles   customer no. 130

DATE	ITEM	POST. REF.	DEBIT	CREDIT	DEBIT BALANCE

customer Kristin Jung   customer no. 140

DATE		ITEM	POST. REF.	DEBIT	CREDIT	DEBIT BALANCE
Dec.	1	Balance	✔			8 2 1 50

customer Jack O'Brien   customer no. 150

DATE	ITEM	POST. REF.	DEBIT	CREDIT	DEBIT BALANCE

customer Don Teal   customer no. 160

DATE		ITEM	POST. REF.	DEBIT	CREDIT	DEBIT BALANCE
Dec.	1	Balance	✔			4 3 2 48

REINFORCEMENT ACTIVITY 2 — PART A (concluded)

11.

Extra form

15-1, 15-2, and 15-3 WORK TOGETHER, pp. 379, 385, 392

15-1 Beginning an 8-column work sheet, 15-2 Analyzing and recording adjustments on a work sheet, 15-3 Completing an 8-column work sheet

Paradise Company

Work Sheet

For Year Ended December 31, 20 - -

| | TRIAL BALANCE | | ADJUSTMENTS | | INCOME STATEMENT | | BALANCE SHEET | |
ACCOUNT TITLE	DEBIT	CREDIT	DEBIT	CREDIT	DEBIT	CREDIT	DEBIT	CREDIT
	1	2	3	4	5	6	7	8
1 Cash								
2 Petty Cash								
3 Accounts Receivable								
4 Merchandise Inventory								
5 Supplies—Office								
6 Supplies—Store								
7 Prepaid Insurance								
8 Accounts Payable								
9 Sales Tax Payable								
10 Jean Brower, Capital								
11 Jean Brower, Drawing								
12 Dale Edson, Capital								
13 Dale Edson, Drawing								
14 Income Summary								
15 Sales								
16 Purchases								
17 Advertising Expense								
18 Credit Card Fee Expense								
19 Insurance Expense								
20 Miscellaneous Expense								
21 Rent Expense								
22 Supplies Expense—Office								
23 Supplies Expense—Store								
24 Utilities Expense								
25								
26								
27								

15-1 Beginning an 8-column work sheet, 15-2 Analyzing and recording adjustments on a work sheet, 15-3 Completing an 8-column work sheet

Mueller Company

Work Sheet

For Year Ended December 31, 20 – –

	ACCOUNT TITLE	TRIAL BALANCE		ADJUSTMENTS		INCOME STATEMENT		BALANCE SHEET	
		DEBIT	CREDIT	DEBIT	CREDIT	DEBIT	CREDIT	DEBIT	CREDIT
1	Cash								
2	Petty Cash								
3	Accounts Receivable								
4	Merchandise Inventory								
5	Supplies—Office								
6	Supplies—Store								
7	Prepaid Insurance								
8	Accounts Payable								
9	Sales Tax Payable								
10	Harry Glover, Capital								
11	Harry Glover, Drawing								
12	Laura Montez, Capital								
13	Laura Montez, Drawing								
14	Income Summary								
15	Sales								
16	Purchases								
17	Advertising Expense								
18	Credit Card Fee Expense								
19	Insurance Expense								
20	Miscellaneous Expense								
21	Rent Expense								
22	Supplies Expense—Office								
23	Supplies Expense—Store								
24	Utilities Expense								
25									
26									
27									

15-1 and 15-2 WORK TOGETHER (concluded)

ANALYSIS FOR ADJUSTMENTS

1. What is the balance of Merchandise Inventory? _____

2. What should the balance be for this account? _____

3. What must be done to correct the account balance? _____

   _____   _____

4. What adjustment is made? _____

   _____   _____

   _____   _____

1. What is the balance of Supplies—Office? _____

2. What should the balance be for this account? _____

3. What must be done to correct the account balance? _____

   _____   _____

4. What adjustment is made? _____

   _____   _____

   _____   _____

1. What is the balance of Supplies—Store? _____

2. What should the balance be for this account? _____

3. What must be done to correct the account balance? _____

   _____   _____

4. What adjustment is made? _____

   _____   _____

   _____   _____

1. What is the balance of Prepaid Insurance? _____

2. What should the balance be for this account? _____

3. What must be done to correct the account balance? _____

   _____   _____

4. What adjustment is made? _____

   _____   _____

   _____   _____

ANALYSIS FOR ADJUSTMENTS

1. What is the balance of Merchandise Inventory? _____

2. What should the balance be for this account? _____

3. What must be done to correct the account balance?

    _____ _____

4. What adjustment is made?

    _____ _____

    _____ _____

1. What is the balance of Supplies—Office? _____

2. What should the balance be for this account? _____

3. What must be done to correct the account balance?

    _____ _____

4. What adjustment is made?

    _____ _____

    _____ _____

1. What is the balance of Supplies—Store? _____

2. What should the balance be for this account? _____

3. What must be done to correct the account balance?

    _____ _____

4. What adjustment is made?

    _____ _____

    _____ _____

1. What is the balance of Prepaid Insurance? _____

2. What should the balance be for this account? _____

3. What must be done to correct the account balance?

    _____ _____

4. What adjustment is made?

    _____ _____

    _____ _____

15-1 APPLICATION PROBLEM, p. 394

Beginning an 8-column work sheet for a merchandising business

1., 2., 3.

Drake Park Supply Company

Work Sheet

For Year Ended December 31, 20 – –

ACCOUNT TITLE	TRIAL BALANCE		ADJUSTMENTS		INCOME STATEMENT		BALANCE SHEET	
	DEBIT	CREDIT	DEBIT	CREDIT	DEBIT	CREDIT	DEBIT	CREDIT
1								
2								
3								
4								
5								
6								
7								
8								
9								
10								
11								
12								
13								
14								
15								
16								
17								
18								
19								
20								
21								
22								
23								
24								
25								

Extra form

ACCOUNT TITLE	TRIAL BALANCE		ADJUSTMENTS		INCOME STATEMENT		BALANCE SHEET	
	1 DEBIT	2 CREDIT	3 DEBIT	4 CREDIT	5 DEBIT	6 CREDIT	7 DEBIT	8 CREDIT
1								
2								
3								
4								
5								
6								
7								
8								
9								
10								
11								
12								
13								
14								
15								
16								
17								
18								
19								
20								
21								
22								
23								
24								
25								

Name _____ Date _____ Class _____

15-2 APPLICATION PROBLEM, p. 394

Analyzing and recording adjustments on a work sheet

1	2	3	4	5
Business	Adjustment Number	Accounts Affected	Adjustment Column Debit	Adjustment Column Credit
A	1.	Income Summary	$16,800.00	
		Merchandise Inventory		$16,800.00
	2.			
	3.			
	4.			
B	1.			
	2.			
	3.			
	4.			
C	1.			
	2.			
	3.			
	4.			

Extra form

1	2	3	4	5
			Adjustment Column	
Business	Adjustment Number	Accounts Affected	Debit	Credit

15-3 APPLICATION PROBLEM, p. 395

Completing an 8-column work sheet for a merchandising business

1., 2., 3., 4., 5., 6.

Lotus Gallery

Work Sheet

For Year Ended December 31, 20 - -

	TRIAL BALANCE		ADJUSTMENTS		INCOME STATEMENT		BALANCE SHEET	
ACCOUNT TITLE	DEBIT	CREDIT	DEBIT	CREDIT	DEBIT	CREDIT	DEBIT	CREDIT
1 Cash	26320 00							
2 Petty Cash	300 00							
3 Accounts Receivable	10690 00							
4 Merchandise Inventory	254245 00			(a) 14890 00				
5 Supplies—Office	6091 00			(b) 4445 00				
6 Supplies—Store	6516 00			(c) 3678 00				
7 Prepaid Insurance	5540 00			(d) 3020 00				
8 Accounts Payable		10740 00						
9 Sales Tax Payable		1985 00						
10 Debbie Craig, Capital		117880 00						
11 Debbie Craig, Drawing	20530 00							
12 Kara Lee, Capital		118520 00						
13 Kara Lee, Drawing	20980 00							
14 Income Summary			(a) 14890 00					
15 Sales		316440 00						
16 Purchases	178560 00							
17 Advertising Expense	6204 00							
18 Credit Card Fee Expense	3264 00							
19 Insurance Expense			(d) 3020 00					
20 Miscellaneous Expense	2577 00							
21 Rent Expense	20160 00							
22 Supplies Expense—Office			(b) 4445 00					
23 Supplies Expense—Store			(c) 3678 00					
24 Utilities Expense	3588 00							
25	565565 00	565565 00	26033 00	26033 00				
26								
27								

Extra form

ACCOUNT TITLE	TRIAL BALANCE		ADJUSTMENTS		INCOME STATEMENT		BALANCE SHEET	
	DEBIT	CREDIT	DEBIT	CREDIT	DEBIT	CREDIT	DEBIT	CREDIT
	1	2	3	4	5	6	7	8
1								
2								
3								
4								
5								
6								
7								
8								
9								
10								
11								
12								
13								
14								
15								
16								
17								
18								
19								
20								
21								
22								
23								
24								
25								
26								
27								

Extra form

ACCOUNT TITLE	TRIAL BALANCE		ADJUSTMENTS		INCOME STATEMENT		BALANCE SHEET	
	1 DEBIT	2 CREDIT	3 DEBIT	4 CREDIT	5 DEBIT	6 CREDIT	7 DEBIT	8 CREDIT
25								
26								
27								
28								
29								
30								
31								
32								
33								
34								
35								
36								
37								
38								
39								
40								
41								
42								
43								
44								
45								
46								
47								
48								
49								
50								

15-4 MASTERY PROBLEM, p. 395

(Note: This Work Sheet is concluded on page 359.)

Preparing an 8-column work sheet for a merchandising business

1., 2.

Seidler Supply

Work Sheet

For Year Ended December 31, 20 - -

	ACCOUNT TITLE	TRIAL BALANCE DEBIT	TRIAL BALANCE CREDIT	ADJUSTMENTS DEBIT	ADJUSTMENTS CREDIT	INCOME STATEMENT DEBIT	INCOME STATEMENT CREDIT	BALANCE SHEET DEBIT	BALANCE SHEET CREDIT
1	Cash	28488 00							
2	Petty Cash	600 00							
3	Accounts Receivable	12240 00							
4	Merchandise Inventory	222360 00							
5	Supplies—Office	6702 00							
6	Supplies—Store	6882 00							
7	Prepaid Insurance	5130 00							
8	Accounts Payable		11616 00						
9	Employ. Inc. Tax Payable		572 00						
10	Social Security Tax Payable		676 00						
11	Medicare Tax Payable		156 00						
12	Sales Tax Payable		1651 00						
13	Unemploy. Tax Pay.—Fed.		128 00						
14	Unemploy. Tax Pay.—State		864 00						
15	Health Ins. Prem. Payable		1000 00						
16	U.S. Savings Bonds Payable		100 00						
17	United Way Don. Payable		75 00						
18	Rex Flanery, Capital		128990 00						
19	Rex Flanery, Drawing	22000 00							
20	David Stein, Capital		129850 00						
21	David Stein, Drawing	22300 00							
22	Income Summary								
23	Sales		350360 00						
24	Purchases	193550 00							

Seidler Supply

Work Sheet (continued)

For Year Ended December 31, 20 – –

	ACCOUNT TITLE	TRIAL BALANCE DEBIT	TRIAL BALANCE CREDIT	ADJUSTMENTS DEBIT	ADJUSTMENTS CREDIT	INCOME STATEMENT DEBIT	INCOME STATEMENT CREDIT	BALANCE SHEET DEBIT	BALANCE SHEET CREDIT
25	Advertising Expense	7 1 0 0 00							
26	Credit Card Fee Expense	3 2 8 2 00							
27	Insurance Expense								
28	Miscellaneous Expense	2 8 0 6 00							
29	Payroll Taxes Expense	6 2 9 4 00							
30	Rent Expense	20 1 6 0 00							
31	Salary Expense	62 4 0 0 00							
32	Supplies Expense—Office								
33	Supplies Expense—Store								
34	Utilities Expense	3 7 4 4 00							
35		626 0 3 8 00	626 0 3 8 00						
36									
37									
38									
39									
40									
41									
42									
43									
44									
45									
46									
47									
48									
49									
50									

Extra form

ACCOUNT TITLE	TRIAL BALANCE		ADJUSTMENTS		INCOME STATEMENT		BALANCE SHEET	
	DEBIT	CREDIT	DEBIT	CREDIT	DEBIT	CREDIT	DEBIT	CREDIT
	1	2	3	4	5	6	7	8
1								
2								
3								
4								
5								
6								
7								
8								
9								
10								
11								
12								
13								
14								
15								
16								
17								
18								
19								
20								
21								
22								
23								
24								

Extra form

Forms	Advantages	Disadvantages
8-column work sheet		
10-column work sheet		

15-5 CHALLENGE PROBLEM, p. 396

Preparing a 10-column work sheet for a merchandising business

1.

K. B. Cycle Shop
Work Sheet
For Year Ended December 31, 20 – –

	ACCOUNT TITLE	TRIAL BALANCE DEBIT	TRIAL BALANCE CREDIT	ADJUSTMENTS DEBIT	ADJUSTMENTS CREDIT	
1	Cash	38 0 1 0 00				1
2	Petty Cash	5 0 0 00				2
3	Accounts Receivable	14 2 3 0 00				3
4	Merchandise Inventory	323 8 0 5 00				4
5	Supplies—Office	7 6 9 5 00				5
6	Supplies—Store	8 0 0 0 00				6
7	Prepaid Insurance	5 9 4 0 00				7
8	Accounts Payable		15 4 8 0 00			8
9	Sales Tax Payable		1 2 1 5 00			9
10	Kevin Bolin, Capital		170 1 6 0 00			10
11	Kevin Bolin, Drawing	24 0 0 0 00				11
12	Barbara May, Capital		170 0 0 0 00			12
13	Barbara May, Drawing	24 8 0 0 00				13
14	Income Summary					14
15	Sales		269 3 3 0 00			15
16	Purchases	129 8 5 5 00				16
17	Advertising Expense	9 2 1 0 00				17
18	Credit Card Fee Expense	3 5 7 5 00				18
19	Insurance Expense					19
20	Miscellaneous Expense	3 7 9 5 00				20
21	Rent Expense	27 9 0 0 00				21
22	Supplies Expense—Office					22
23	Supplies Expense—Store					23
24	Utilities Expense	4 8 7 0 00				24
25		626 1 8 5 00	626 1 8 5 00			25
26						26
27						27
28						28
29						29

15-5 **CHALLENGE PROBLEM (continued)**

1.

	5	6	7	8	9	10	
	ADJUSTED TRIAL BALANCE		INCOME STATEMENT		BALANCE SHEET		
	DEBIT	CREDIT	DEBIT	CREDIT	DEBIT	CREDIT	
1							1
2							2
3							3
4							4
5							5
6							6
7							7
8							8
9							9
10							10
11							11
12							12
13							13
14							14
15							15
16							16
17							17
18							18
19							19
20							20
21							21
22							22
23							23
24							24
25							25
26							26
27							27
28							28
29							29

2.

Forms	Advantages	Disadvantages
8-column work sheet		
10-column work sheet		

16-1 WORK TOGETHER, p. 404

Preparing an income statement for a merchandising business

A to Z Auto Parts
Work Sheet
For Year Ended December 31, 20--

ACCOUNT TITLE	TRIAL BALANCE DEBIT	TRIAL BALANCE CREDIT	ADJUSTMENTS DEBIT	ADJUSTMENTS CREDIT	INCOME STATEMENT DEBIT	INCOME STATEMENT CREDIT	BALANCE SHEET DEBIT	BALANCE SHEET CREDIT
Cash	23 780 00						23 780 00	
Petty Cash	300 00						300 00	
Accounts Receivable	9 624 00						9 624 00	
Merchandise Inventory	228 820 00			(a) 13 400 00			215 420 00	
Supplies—Office	5 480 00			(b) 4 000 00			1 480 00	
Supplies—Store	5 864 00			(c) 3 310 00			2 554 00	
Prepaid Insurance	4 986 00			(d) 2 700 00			2 286 00	
Accounts Payable		9 666 00						9 666 00
Sales Tax Payable		1 786 00						1 786 00
Mack Cruz, Capital		106 100 00						106 100 00
Mack Cruz, Drawing	18 450 00						18 450 00	
Rose Hurst, Capital		106 700 00						106 700 00
Rose Hurst, Drawing	18 900 00						18 900 00	
Income Summary			(a) 13 400 00		13 400 00			
Sales		284 800 00				284 800 00		
Purchases	160 700 00				160 700 00			
Advertising Expense	5 580 00				5 580 00			
Credit Card Fee Expense	2 940 00				2 940 00			
Insurance Expense			(d) 2 700 00		2 700 00			
Miscellaneous Expense	2 398 00				2 398 00			
Rent Expense	18 000 00				18 000 00			
Supplies Expense—Office			(b) 4 000 00		4 000 00			
Supplies Expense—Store			(c) 3 310 00		3 310 00			
Utilities Expense	3 230 00				3 230 00			
	509 052 00	509 052 00	23 410 00	23 410 00	216 258 00	284 800 00	292 794 00	224 252 00
Net Income					68 542 00			68 542 00
					284 800 00	284 800 00	292 794 00	292 794 00

Preparing an income statement for a merchandising business

Electron Games

Work Sheet

For Year Ended December 31, 20 – –

	TRIAL BALANCE		ADJUSTMENTS		INCOME STATEMENT		BALANCE SHEET	
ACCOUNT TITLE	DEBIT	CREDIT	DEBIT	CREDIT	DEBIT	CREDIT	DEBIT	CREDIT
1 Cash	24 490 00						24 490 00	
2 Petty Cash	5 00 00						5 00 00	
3 Accounts Receivable	11 230 00						11 230 00	
4 Merchandise Inventory	266 960 00			(a)15 640 00			251 320 00	
5 Supplies—Office	6 390 00			(b)4 670 00			1 720 00	
6 Supplies—Store	6 840 00			(c)3 860 00			2 980 00	
7 Prepaid Insurance	5 830 00			(d)3 190 00			2 640 00	
8 Accounts Payable		11 280 00						11 280 00
9 Sales Tax Payable		2 080 00						2 080 00
10 Caren Grant, Capital		121 110 00						121 110 00
11 Caren Grant, Drawing	21 550 00						21 550 00	
12 Craig Payne, Capital		124 440 00						124 440 00
13 Craig Payne, Drawing	22 000 00						22 000 00	
14 Income Summary			(a)15 640 00		15 640 00			
15 Sales		332 260 00				332 260 00		
16 Purchases	187 500 00				187 500 00			
17 Advertising Expense	6 520 00				6 520 00			
18 Credit Card Fee Expense	3 430 00				3 430 00			
19 Insurance Expense			(d)3 190 00		3 190 00			
20 Miscellaneous Expense	2 550 00				2 550 00			
21 Rent Expense	21 600 00				21 600 00			
22 Supplies Expense—Office			(b)4 670 00		4 670 00			
23 Supplies Expense—Store			(c)3 860 00		3 860 00			
24 Utilities Expense	3 770 00				3 770 00			
25	591 160 00	591 160 00	27 360 00	27 360 00	252 730 00	332 260 00	338 430 00	258 900 00
26 Net Income					79 530 00			79 530 00
27					332 260 00	332 260 00	338 430 00	338 430 00

16-1 WORK TOGETHER (concluded)

4., 5.

									% OF SALES

6., 7.

										% OF SALES

16-2 WORK TOGETHER, p. 409

Analyzing component percentages

4., 5.

Component	Acceptable Percentage	Actual Percentage	Acceptable Result		Recommended Action If Needed
			Yes	No	
Cost of merchandise sold	No more than 63.0%				
Gross profit on sales	No less than 37.0%				

Extra form

Component	Acceptable Percentage	Actual Percentage	Acceptable Result		Recommended Action If Needed
			Yes	No	

Analyzing component percentages

6., 7.

Component	Acceptable Percentage	Actual Percentage	Acceptable Result		Recommended Action If Needed
			Yes	No	
Total expenses	No more than 13.0%				
Net income	No less than 25.0%				

Extra form

Component	Acceptable Percentage	Actual Percentage	Acceptable Result		Recommended Action If Needed
			Yes	No	

16-3 WORK TOGETHER, p. 415

Preparing distribution of net income and owners' equity statements

4.

5.

Preparing distribution of net income and owners' equity statements

6.

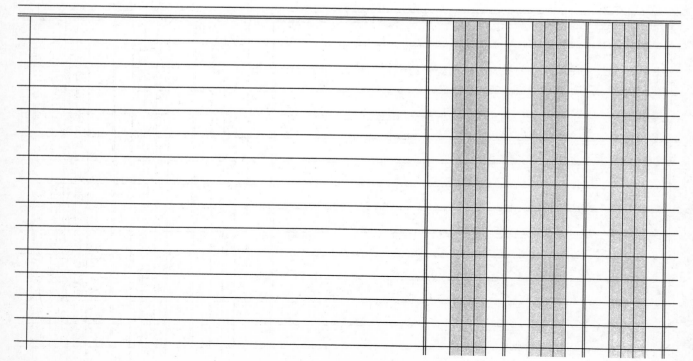

7.

16-4 WORK TOGETHER, p. 420

Preparing a balance sheet for a partnership

Preparing a balance sheet for a partnership

Preparing an income statement for a merchandising business

16-1 APPLICATION PROBLEM, p. 422

Flower Mart

Work Sheet

For Year Ended December 31, 20 - -

	ACCOUNT TITLE	TRIAL BALANCE DEBIT	TRIAL BALANCE CREDIT	ADJUSTMENTS DEBIT	ADJUSTMENTS CREDIT	INCOME STATEMENT DEBIT	INCOME STATEMENT CREDIT	BALANCE SHEET DEBIT	BALANCE SHEET CREDIT	
4	Merchandise Inventory	179900 00			(a) 6820 00			173080 00		4
15	Sales		162300 00				162300 00			15
16	Purchases	73000 00				73000 00				16
17	Advertising Expense	4130 00				4130 00				17
18	Credit Card Fee Expense	1640 00				1640 00				18
19	Insurance Expense			(d) 2160 00		2160 00				19
20	Miscellaneous Expense	1990 00				1990 00				20
21	Rent Expense	12480 00				12480 00				21
22	Supplies Expense—Office			(b) 2490 00		2490 00				22
23	Supplies Expense—Store			(c) 2180 00		2180 00				23
24	Utilities Expense	2140 00				2140 00				24
25		333510 00	333510 00	13650 00	13650 00	109030 00	162300 00	224700 00	171430 00	25
26	Net Income					53270 00			53270 00	26
27						162300 00	162300 00	224700 00	224700 00	27
28										28
29										29
30										30
31										31
32										32

Extra form

					% OF SALES

16-1 APPLICATION PROBLEM (concluded)

1., 2.

			% OF SALES

Extra form

										% OF SALES

16-2 APPLICATION PROBLEM, p. 422

Analyzing component percentages

Historic Door Supply Co.

Income Statement

For Year Ended December 31, 20 – –

			% OF SALES
Revenue:			
Sales		352 6 0 0 00	100.0
Cost of Merchandise Sold:			
Merchandise Inventory, January 1, 20 – –	225 4 0 0 00		
Purchases	158 3 0 0 00		
Total Cost of Merchandise Available for Sale	383 7 0 0 00		
Less Merchandise Inventory, December 31, 20 – –	212 2 0 0 00		
Cost of Merchandise Sold		171 5 0 0 00	48.6
Gross Profit on Sales		181 1 0 0 00	51.4
Expenses:			
Advertising Expense	5 5 0 0 00		
Credit Card Fee Expense	2 8 9 0 00		
Insurance Expense	2 6 4 0 00		
Miscellaneous Expense	2 1 8 2 15		
Payroll Taxes Expense	7 2 9 9 75		
Rent Expense	18 0 0 0 00		
Salary Expense	60 1 5 3 00		
Supplies Expense—Office	3 9 4 0 00		
Supplies Expense—Store	3 2 6 0 00		
Utilities Expense	3 1 8 0 00		
Total Expenses		109 0 4 4 90	30.9
Net Income		72 0 5 5 10	20.4

Extra form

					% OF SALES

16-2 APPLICATION PROBLEM (concluded)

1., 2., 3., 4.

Component	Acceptable Percentage	Actual Percentage	Acceptable Result Yes	Acceptable Result No	Recommended Action If Needed
Cost of merchandise sold	No more than 47.5%				
Gross profit on sales	No less than 52.5%				
Total expenses	No more than 29.0%				
Net income	No less than 23.5%				

Extra form

Component	Acceptable Percentage	Actual Percentage	Acceptable Result Yes	Acceptable Result No	Recommended Action If Needed

16-3 APPLICATION PROBLEM, p. 423

Preparing distribution of net income and owners' equity statements (net income)

1.

2.

16-4 APPLICATION PROBLEM, p. 423

Preparing an owners' equity statement (net loss)

Extra form

16-5 APPLICATION PROBLEM, p. 423

Preparing a balance sheet for a partnership

Athletic Supply

Work Sheet

For Year Ended December 31, 20 – –

	ACCOUNT TITLE	TRIAL BALANCE DEBIT	TRIAL BALANCE CREDIT	ADJUSTMENTS DEBIT	ADJUSTMENTS CREDIT	INCOME STATEMENT DEBIT	INCOME STATEMENT CREDIT	BALANCE SHEET DEBIT	BALANCE SHEET CREDIT	
1	Cash	22738 00						22738 00		1
2	Petty Cash	350 00						350 00		2
3	Accounts Receivable	11622 00						11622 00		3
4	Merchandise Inventory	269832 00			(a) 10236 00			259596 00		4
5	Supplies—Office	5922 00			(b) 3732 00			2190 00		5
6	Supplies—Store	6252 00			(c) 3288 00			2964 00		6
7	Prepaid Insurance	5130 00			(d) 3240 00			1890 00		7
8	Accounts Payable		10596 00						10596 00	8
9	Sales Tax Payable		1014 00						1014 00	9
10										10
11										11
12										12
13										13
14										14
15										15
16										16
17										17
18										18
19										19
20										20
21										21

Extra form

16-5 **APPLICATION PROBLEM (concluded)**

Extra form

16-6 MASTERY PROBLEM, p. 424

Preparing financial statements

1.

		% OF SALES

2.

16-6 MASTERY PROBLEM (continued)

3.

4.

16-7 CHALLENGE PROBLEM, p. 425

Preparing financial statements (unequal distribution of net income; additional investment)

1.

2.

Extra form

17-1 WORK TOGETHER, p. 433

Journalizing adjusting entries

GENERAL JOURNAL   PAGE 12

	DATE		ACCOUNT TITLE	DOC. NO.	POST. REF.	DEBIT	CREDIT	
1								1
2								2
3								3
4								4
5								5
6								6
7								7
8								8
9								9
10								10
11								11
12								12
13								13
14								14
15								15
16								16
17								17
18								18
19								19
20								20
21								21
22								22
23								23
24								24
25								25
26								26
27								27
28								28
29								29
30								30
31								31
32								32
33								33

ON YOUR OWN, p. 433

Journalizing adjusting entries

GENERAL JOURNAL

PAGE 15

	DATE		ACCOUNT TITLE	DOC. NO.	POST. REF.	DEBIT	CREDIT	
1								1
2								2
3								3
4								4
5								5
6								6
7								7
8								8
9								9
10								10
11								11
12								12
13								13
14								14
15								15
16								16
17								17
18								18
19								19
20								20
21								21
22								22
23								23
24								24
25								25
26								26
27								27
28								28
29								29
30								30
31								31
32								32
33								33

17-2 and 17-3 WORK TOGETHER, pp. 438, 442

17-2 Journalizing closing entries for income statement accounts
17-3 Journalizing additional closing entries

GENERAL JOURNAL

PAGE 12

	DATE	ACCOUNT TITLE	DOC. NO.	POST. REF.	DEBIT	CREDIT	
1							1
2							2
3							3
4							4
5							5
6							6
7							7
8							8
9							9
10							10
11							11
12							12
13							13
14							14
15							15
16							16
17							17
18							18
19							19
20							20
21							21
22							22
23							23
24							24
25							25
26							26
27							27
28							28
29							29
30							30
31							31
32							32

17-2 Journalizing closing entries for income statement accounts
17-3 Journalizing additional closing entries

GENERAL JOURNAL   PAGE 15

	DATE	ACCOUNT TITLE	DOC. NO.	POST. REF.	DEBIT	CREDIT	
1							1
2							2
3							3
4							4
5							5
6							6
7							7
8							8
9							9
10							10
11							11
12							12
13							13
14							14
15							15
16							16
17							17
18							18
19							19
20							20
21							21
22							22
23							23
24							24
25							25
26							26
27							27
28							28
29							29
30							30
31							31
32							32

17-2 and 17-3   WORK TOGETHER (concluded)

	ACCOUNT TITLE	INCOME STATEMENT		BALANCE SHEET		
		5 DEBIT	6 CREDIT	7 DEBIT	8 CREDIT	
11	Beth Fairbanks, Drawing			31 0 0 0 00		11
13	Chris Gilder, Drawing			29 9 0 0 00		13
15	Sales		260 0 0 0 00			15
16	Purchases	118 0 0 0 00				16
17	Advertising Expense	4 0 6 0 00				17
18	Credit Card Fee Expense	2 6 7 0 00				18
19	Insurance Expense	3 1 5 0 00				19
20	Miscellaneous Expense	1 7 2 0 00				20
21	Rent Expense	18 0 0 0 00				21
22	Supplies Expense—Office	3 7 3 0 00				22
23	Supplies Expense—Store	3 9 0 0 00				23
24	Utilities Expense	3 6 7 0 00				24
25						25
26						26
27						27
28						28

Fairbanks Auto Supply

Distribution of Net Income Statement

For the Year Ended December 31, 20 – –

Beth Fairbanks	
50% of Net Income	43 0 5 0 00
Chris Gilder	
50% of Net Income	43 0 5 0 00
Net Income	86 1 0 0 00

	ACCOUNT TITLE	INCOME STATEMENT DEBIT (5)	INCOME STATEMENT CREDIT (6)	BALANCE SHEET DEBIT (7)	BALANCE SHEET CREDIT (8)	
11	Orrin Harrod, Drawing			28 0 0 0 00		11
13	Lisa Klaus, Drawing			28 7 0 0 00		13
15	Sales		271 4 0 0 00			15
16	Purchases	132 1 6 0 00				16
17	Advertising Expense	4 5 5 0 00				17
18	Credit Card Fee Expense	2 9 8 0 00				18
19	Insurance Expense	3 5 3 0 00				19
20	Miscellaneous Expense	1 9 3 0 00				20
21	Rent Expense	20 1 6 0 00				21
22	Supplies Expense—Office	4 1 7 0 00				22
23	Supplies Expense—Store	4 3 7 0 00				23
24	Utilities Expense	4 1 2 0 00				24
25						25
26						26
27						27
28						28

Custom Aquarium

Distribution of Net Income Statement

For Year Ended December 31, 20 – –

Orrin Harrod	
50% of Net Income	38 3 1 5 00
Lisa Klaus	
50% of Net Income	38 3 1 5 00
Net Income	76 6 3 0 00

17-4 WORK TOGETHER, p. 447

Preparing a post-closing trial balance

ACCOUNT TITLE	DEBIT	CREDIT

Preparing a post-closing trial balance

ACCOUNT TITLE	DEBIT	CREDIT

17-1 APPLICATION PROBLEM, p. 449

Journalizing adjusting entries

GENERAL JOURNAL

PAGE 12

	DATE	ACCOUNT TITLE	DOC. NO.	POST. REF.	DEBIT	CREDIT	
1							1
2							2
3							3
4							4
5							5
6							6
7							7
8							8
9							9
10							10
11							11
12							12
13							13
14							14
15							15
16							16
17							17
18							18
19							19
20							20
21							21
22							22
23							23
24							24
25							25
26							26
27							27
28							28
29							29
30							30
31							31
32							32
33							33

Extra form

GENERAL JOURNAL

	DATE	ACCOUNT TITLE	DOC. NO.	POST. REF.	DEBIT	CREDIT	
1							1
2							2
3							3
4							4
5							5
6							6
7							7
8							8
9							9
10							10
11							11
12							12
13							13
14							14
15							15
16							16
17							17
18							18
19							19
20							20
21							21
22							22
23							23
24							24
25							25
26							26
27							27
28							28
29							29
30							30
31							31
32							32
33							33

17-2 and 17-3 APPLICATION PROBLEMS, pp. 449, 450

17-2 Journalizing closing entries for income statement accounts
17-3 Journalizing additional closing entries

GENERAL JOURNAL

PAGE 14

	DATE		ACCOUNT TITLE	DOC. NO.	POST. REF.	DEBIT	CREDIT	
1								1
2								2
3								3
4								4
5								5
6								6
7								7
8								8
9								9
10								10
11								11
12								12
13								13
14								14
15								15
16								16
17								17
18								18
19								19
20								20
21								21
22								22
23								23
24								24
25								25
26								26
27								27
28								28
29								29
30								30
31								31
32								32

Extra form

GENERAL JOURNAL

	DATE		ACCOUNT TITLE	DOC. NO.	POST. REF.	DEBIT	CREDIT	
1								1
2								2
3								3
4								4
5								5
6								6
7								7
8								8
9								9
10								10
11								11
12								12
13								13
14								14
15								15
16								16
17								17
18								18
19								19
20								20
21								21
22								22
23								23
24								24
25								25
26								26
27								27
28								28
29								29
30								30
31								31
32								32
33								33

17-4 APPLICATION PROBLEM, p. 450

Preparing a post-closing trial balance

ACCOUNT TITLE	DEBIT	CREDIT

Extra form

ACCOUNT TITLE	DEBIT	CREDIT

410 • Working Papers

17-5 APPLICATION PROBLEM, p. 451

Journalizing and posting adjusting and closing entries; preparing a post-closing trial balance

1., 2., 3., 4.

GENERAL JOURNAL   PAGE 24

	DATE	ACCOUNT TITLE	DOC. NO.	POST. REF.	DEBIT	CREDIT	
1							1
2							2
3							3
4							4
5							5
6							6
7							7
8							8
9							9
10							10
11							11
12							12
13							13
14							14
15							15
16							16
17							17
18							18
19							19
20							20
21							21
22							22
23							23
24							24
25							25
26							26
27							27
28							28
29							29
30							30
31							31
32							32

5.

ACCOUNT TITLE	DEBIT	CREDIT

17-5 **APPLICATION PROBLEM (continued)**

2., 4., 5. **GENERAL LEDGER**

ACCOUNT Cash   ACCOUNT NO. 1110

DATE		ITEM	POST. REF.	DEBIT	CREDIT	BALANCE	
						DEBIT	CREDIT
20-- Dec.	31	Balance	✔			22 3 7 9 00	

ACCOUNT Petty Cash   ACCOUNT NO. 1120

DATE		ITEM	POST. REF.	DEBIT	CREDIT	BALANCE	
						DEBIT	CREDIT
20-- Dec.	31	Balance	✔			4 0 0 00	

ACCOUNT Accounts Receivable   ACCOUNT NO. 1130

DATE		ITEM	POST. REF.	DEBIT	CREDIT	BALANCE	
						DEBIT	CREDIT
20-- Dec.	31	Balance	✔			10 1 8 9 00	

ACCOUNT Merchandise Inventory   ACCOUNT NO. 1140

DATE		ITEM	POST. REF.	DEBIT	CREDIT	BALANCE	
						DEBIT	CREDIT
20-- Jan.	1	Balance	✔			253 0 1 4 00	

ACCOUNT Supplies—Office   ACCOUNT NO. 1145

DATE		ITEM	POST. REF.	DEBIT	CREDIT	BALANCE	
						DEBIT	CREDIT
20-- Dec.	31	Balance	✔			5 4 1 6 00	

ACCOUNT Supplies—Store   ACCOUNT NO. 1150

DATE		ITEM	POST. REF.	DEBIT	CREDIT	BALANCE	
						DEBIT	CREDIT
20-- Dec.	31	Balance	✔			5 2 6 7 00	

ACCOUNT Prepaid Insurance   ACCOUNT NO. 1160

DATE		ITEM	POST. REF.	DEBIT	CREDIT	BALANCE	
						DEBIT	CREDIT
20-- Dec.	31	Balance	✔			4 3 0 0 00	

ACCOUNT Accounts Payable   ACCOUNT NO. 2110

DATE		ITEM	POST. REF.	DEBIT	CREDIT	BALANCE	
						DEBIT	CREDIT
20-- Dec.	31	Balance	✔				10 6 1 5 00

2., 4., 5.   **GENERAL LEDGER**

ACCOUNT Employee Income Tax Payable   ACCOUNT NO. 2120

DATE	ITEM	POST. REF.	DEBIT	CREDIT	BALANCE DEBIT	BALANCE CREDIT
20-- Dec. 31	Balance	✔				4 5 4 00

ACCOUNT Social Security Tax Payable   ACCOUNT NO. 2130

DATE	ITEM	POST. REF.	DEBIT	CREDIT	BALANCE DEBIT	BALANCE CREDIT
20-- Dec. 31	Balance	✔				7 0 4 20

ACCOUNT Medicare Tax Payable   ACCOUNT NO. 2135

DATE	ITEM	POST. REF.	DEBIT	CREDIT	BALANCE DEBIT	BALANCE CREDIT
20-- Dec. 31	Balance	✔				1 6 4 70

ACCOUNT Sales Tax Payable   ACCOUNT NO. 2140

DATE	ITEM	POST. REF.	DEBIT	CREDIT	BALANCE DEBIT	BALANCE CREDIT
20-- Dec. 31	Balance	✔				1 8 1 7 00

ACCOUNT Unemployment Tax Payable—Federal   ACCOUNT NO. 2150

DATE	ITEM	POST. REF.	DEBIT	CREDIT	BALANCE DEBIT	BALANCE CREDIT
20-- Dec. 31	Balance	✔				1 3 60

ACCOUNT Unemployment Tax Payable—State   ACCOUNT NO. 2160

DATE	ITEM	POST. REF.	DEBIT	CREDIT	BALANCE DEBIT	BALANCE CREDIT
20-- Dec. 31	Balance	✔				9 1 80

ACCOUNT Emma Bose, Capital   ACCOUNT NO. 3110

DATE	ITEM	POST. REF.	DEBIT	CREDIT	BALANCE DEBIT	BALANCE CREDIT
20-- Dec. 31	Balance	✔				156 2 6 7 00

ACCOUNT Emma Bose, Drawing   ACCOUNT NO. 3120

DATE	ITEM	POST. REF.	DEBIT	CREDIT	BALANCE DEBIT	BALANCE CREDIT
20-- Dec. 31	Balance	✔			18 2 2 5 00	

17-5 **APPLICATION PROBLEM** (continued)

2., 4., 5. **GENERAL LEDGER**

ACCOUNT Kris Manuel, Capital ACCOUNT NO. 3130

DATE	ITEM	POST. REF.	DEBIT	CREDIT	BALANCE DEBIT	BALANCE CREDIT
20-- Dec. 31	Balance	✔				153 3 4 9 70

ACCOUNT Kris Manuel, Drawing ACCOUNT NO. 3140

DATE	ITEM	POST. REF.	DEBIT	CREDIT	BALANCE DEBIT	BALANCE CREDIT
20-- Dec. 31	Balance	✔			18 4 0 0 00	

ACCOUNT Income Summary ACCOUNT NO. 3150

DATE	ITEM	POST. REF.	DEBIT	CREDIT	BALANCE DEBIT	BALANCE CREDIT

ACCOUNT Sales ACCOUNT NO. 4110

DATE	ITEM	POST. REF.	DEBIT	CREDIT	BALANCE DEBIT	BALANCE CREDIT
20-- Dec. 31	Balance	✔				275 0 6 0 00

ACCOUNT Purchases ACCOUNT NO. 5110

DATE	ITEM	POST. REF.	DEBIT	CREDIT	BALANCE DEBIT	BALANCE CREDIT
20-- Dec. 31	Balance	✔			151 7 4 0 00	

ACCOUNT Advertising Expense ACCOUNT NO. 6110

DATE	ITEM	POST. REF.	DEBIT	CREDIT	BALANCE DEBIT	BALANCE CREDIT
20-- Dec. 31	Balance	✔			5 6 6 4 00	

ACCOUNT Credit Card Fee Expense ACCOUNT NO. 6120

DATE	ITEM	POST. REF.	DEBIT	CREDIT	BALANCE DEBIT	BALANCE CREDIT
20-- Dec. 31	Balance	✔			3 9 1 2 00	

2., 4., 5. **GENERAL LEDGER**

ACCOUNT Insurance Expense   ACCOUNT NO. 6130

DATE	ITEM	POST. REF.	DEBIT	CREDIT	BALANCE DEBIT	BALANCE CREDIT

ACCOUNT Miscellaneous Expense   ACCOUNT NO. 6140

DATE	ITEM	POST. REF.	DEBIT	CREDIT	BALANCE DEBIT	BALANCE CREDIT
Dec. 31	Balance	✔			2 3 1 6 00	

ACCOUNT Payroll Taxes Expense   ACCOUNT NO. 6150

DATE	ITEM	POST. REF.	DEBIT	CREDIT	BALANCE DEBIT	BALANCE CREDIT
Dec. 31	Balance	✔			6 9 1 7 00	

ACCOUNT Rent Expense   ACCOUNT NO. 6160

DATE	ITEM	POST. REF.	DEBIT	CREDIT	BALANCE DEBIT	BALANCE CREDIT
Dec. 31	Balance	✔			18 7 2 0 00	

ACCOUNT Salary Expense   ACCOUNT NO. 6170

DATE	ITEM	POST. REF.	DEBIT	CREDIT	BALANCE DEBIT	BALANCE CREDIT
Dec. 31	Balance	✔			68 1 5 0 00	

ACCOUNT Supplies Expense—Office   ACCOUNT NO. 6175

DATE	ITEM	POST. REF.	DEBIT	CREDIT	BALANCE DEBIT	BALANCE CREDIT

ACCOUNT Supplies Expense—Store   ACCOUNT NO. 6180

DATE	ITEM	POST. REF.	DEBIT	CREDIT	BALANCE DEBIT	BALANCE CREDIT

ACCOUNT Utilities Expense   ACCOUNT NO. 6190

DATE	ITEM	POST. REF.	DEBIT	CREDIT	BALANCE DEBIT	BALANCE CREDIT
Dec. 31	Balance	✔			3 5 2 8 00	

17-6 MASTERY PROBLEM, p. 452

Journalizing and posting adjusting and closing entries; preparing a post-closing trial balance

1., 2., 3., 4.

GENERAL JOURNAL

	DATE	ACCOUNT TITLE	DOC. NO.	POST. REF.	DEBIT	CREDIT	
1							1
2							2
3							3
4							4
5							5
6							6
7							7
8							8
9							9
10							10
11							11
12							12
13							13
14							14
15							15
16							16
17							17
18							18
19							19
20							20
21							21
22							22
23							23
24							24
25							25
26							26
27							27
28							28
29							29
30							30
31							31
32							32

5.

ACCOUNT TITLE	DEBIT	CREDIT

17-6 MASTERY PROBLEM (continued)

2., 4., 5.   **GENERAL LEDGER**

ACCOUNT Cash   ACCOUNT NO. 1110

DATE	ITEM	POST. REF.	DEBIT	CREDIT	BALANCE DEBIT	BALANCE CREDIT
Dec. 31 20--	Balance	✔			25 967 00	

ACCOUNT Petty Cash   ACCOUNT NO. 1120

DATE	ITEM	POST. REF.	DEBIT	CREDIT	BALANCE DEBIT	BALANCE CREDIT
Dec. 31 20--	Balance	✔			500 00	

ACCOUNT Accounts Receivable   ACCOUNT NO. 1130

DATE	ITEM	POST. REF.	DEBIT	CREDIT	BALANCE DEBIT	BALANCE CREDIT
Dec. 31 20--	Balance	✔			9 925 00	

ACCOUNT Merchandise Inventory   ACCOUNT NO. 1140

DATE	ITEM	POST. REF.	DEBIT	CREDIT	BALANCE DEBIT	BALANCE CREDIT
Jan. 1 20--	Balance	✔			331 940 00	

ACCOUNT Supplies—Office   ACCOUNT NO. 1145

DATE	ITEM	POST. REF.	DEBIT	CREDIT	BALANCE DEBIT	BALANCE CREDIT
Dec. 31 20--	Balance	✔			5 555 00	

ACCOUNT Supplies—Store   ACCOUNT NO. 1150

DATE	ITEM	POST. REF.	DEBIT	CREDIT	BALANCE DEBIT	BALANCE CREDIT
Dec. 31 20--	Balance	✔			4 922 00	

ACCOUNT Prepaid Insurance   ACCOUNT NO. 1160

DATE	ITEM	POST. REF.	DEBIT	CREDIT	BALANCE DEBIT	BALANCE CREDIT
Dec. 31 20--	Balance	✔			3 485 00	

ACCOUNT Accounts Payable   ACCOUNT NO. 2110

DATE	ITEM	POST. REF.	DEBIT	CREDIT	BALANCE DEBIT	BALANCE CREDIT
Dec. 31 20--	Balance	✔				9 005 00

2., 4., 5. GENERAL LEDGER

ACCOUNT Employee Income Tax Payable   ACCOUNT NO. 2120

DATE		ITEM	POST. REF.	DEBIT	CREDIT	BALANCE	
						DEBIT	CREDIT
Dec. 20--	31	Balance	✔				4 7 5 00

ACCOUNT Social Security Tax Payable   ACCOUNT NO. 2130

DATE		ITEM	POST. REF.	DEBIT	CREDIT	BALANCE	
						DEBIT	CREDIT
Dec. 20--	31	Balance	✔				7 3 6 56

ACCOUNT Medicare Tax Payable   ACCOUNT NO. 2135

DATE		ITEM	POST. REF.	DEBIT	CREDIT	BALANCE	
						DEBIT	CREDIT
Dec. 20--	31	Balance	✔				1 7 2 26

ACCOUNT Sales Tax Payable   ACCOUNT NO. 2140

DATE		ITEM	POST. REF.	DEBIT	CREDIT	BALANCE	
						DEBIT	CREDIT
Dec. 20--	31	Balance	✔				2 3 4 0 00

ACCOUNT Unemployment Tax Payable—Federal   ACCOUNT NO. 2150

DATE		ITEM	POST. REF.	DEBIT	CREDIT	BALANCE	
						DEBIT	CREDIT
Dec. 20--	31	Balance	✔				1 4 24

ACCOUNT Unemployment Tax Payable—State   ACCOUNT NO. 2160

DATE		ITEM	POST. REF.	DEBIT	CREDIT	BALANCE	
						DEBIT	CREDIT
Dec. 20--	31	Balance	✔				9 6 12

ACCOUNT Anna Cao, Capital   ACCOUNT NO. 3110

DATE		ITEM	POST. REF.	DEBIT	CREDIT	BALANCE	
						DEBIT	CREDIT
Dec. 20--	31	Balance	✔				156 4 5 0 00

ACCOUNT Anna Cao, Drawing   ACCOUNT NO. 3120

DATE		ITEM	POST. REF.	DEBIT	CREDIT	BALANCE	
						DEBIT	CREDIT
Dec. 20--	31	Balance	✔			22 8 0 0 00	

17-6 MASTERY PROBLEM (continued)

2., 4., 5.   **GENERAL LEDGER**

ACCOUNT Inez O'Neal, Capital   ACCOUNT NO. 3130

DATE	ITEM	POST. REF.	DEBIT	CREDIT	BALANCE DEBIT	BALANCE CREDIT
20-- Dec. 31	Balance	✔				153 962 82

ACCOUNT Inez O'Neal, Drawing   ACCOUNT NO. 3140

DATE	ITEM	POST. REF.	DEBIT	CREDIT	BALANCE DEBIT	BALANCE CREDIT
20-- Dec. 31	Balance	✔			23 400 00	

ACCOUNT Income Summary   ACCOUNT NO. 3150

DATE	ITEM	POST. REF.	DEBIT	CREDIT	BALANCE DEBIT	BALANCE CREDIT

ACCOUNT Sales   ACCOUNT NO. 4110

DATE	ITEM	POST. REF.	DEBIT	CREDIT	BALANCE DEBIT	BALANCE CREDIT
20-- Dec. 31	Balance	✔				374 500 00

ACCOUNT Purchases   ACCOUNT NO. 5110

DATE	ITEM	POST. REF.	DEBIT	CREDIT	BALANCE DEBIT	BALANCE CREDIT
20-- Dec. 31	Balance	✔			156 540 00	

ACCOUNT Advertising Expense   ACCOUNT NO. 6110

DATE	ITEM	POST. REF.	DEBIT	CREDIT	BALANCE DEBIT	BALANCE CREDIT
20-- Dec. 31	Balance	✔			6 216 00	

ACCOUNT Credit Card Fee Expense   ACCOUNT NO. 6120

DATE	ITEM	POST. REF.	DEBIT	CREDIT	BALANCE DEBIT	BALANCE CREDIT
20-- Dec. 31	Balance	✔			4 104 00	

2., 4., 5.   **GENERAL LEDGER**

ACCOUNT Insurance Expense   ACCOUNT NO. 6130

DATE	ITEM	POST. REF.	DEBIT	CREDIT	BALANCE DEBIT	BALANCE CREDIT

ACCOUNT Miscellaneous Expense   ACCOUNT NO. 6140

DATE	ITEM	POST. REF.	DEBIT	CREDIT	BALANCE DEBIT	BALANCE CREDIT
20-- Dec. 31	Balance	✔			2 4 7 2 00	

ACCOUNT Payroll Taxes Expense   ACCOUNT NO. 6150

DATE	ITEM	POST. REF.	DEBIT	CREDIT	BALANCE DEBIT	BALANCE CREDIT
20-- Dec. 31	Balance	✔			7 2 3 0 00	

ACCOUNT Rent Expense   ACCOUNT NO. 6160

DATE	ITEM	POST. REF.	DEBIT	CREDIT	BALANCE DEBIT	BALANCE CREDIT
20-- Dec. 31	Balance	✔			18 0 0 0 00	

ACCOUNT Salary Expense   ACCOUNT NO. 6170

DATE	ITEM	POST. REF.	DEBIT	CREDIT	BALANCE DEBIT	BALANCE CREDIT
20-- Dec. 31	Balance	✔			71 2 4 0 00	

ACCOUNT Supplies Expense—Office   ACCOUNT NO. 6175

DATE	ITEM	POST. REF.	DEBIT	CREDIT	BALANCE DEBIT	BALANCE CREDIT

ACCOUNT Supplies Expense—Store   ACCOUNT NO. 6180

DATE	ITEM	POST. REF.	DEBIT	CREDIT	BALANCE DEBIT	BALANCE CREDIT

ACCOUNT Utilities Expense   ACCOUNT NO. 6190

DATE	ITEM	POST. REF.	DEBIT	CREDIT	BALANCE DEBIT	BALANCE CREDIT
20-- Dec. 31	Balance	✔			3 4 5 6 00	

Extra form

	5		6		7		8		9		10		
	ADJUSTED TRIAL BALANCE				INCOME STATEMENT				BALANCE SHEET				
	DEBIT		CREDIT		DEBIT		CREDIT		DEBIT		CREDIT		
1													1
2													2
3													3
4													4
5													5
6													6
7													7
8													8
9													9
10													10
11													11
12													12
13													13
14													14
15													15
16													16
17													17
18													18
19													19
20													20
21													21
22													22
23													23
24													24
25													25
26													26
27													27
28													28
29													29
30													30
31													31
32													32

17-7 CHALLENGE PROBLEM, p. 453

Completing end-of-fiscal-period work

1.

Lighting

Work

For Year Ended

	ACCOUNT TITLE	TRIAL BALANCE		ADJUSTMENTS		
		DEBIT	CREDIT	DEBIT	CREDIT	
1	Cash	24 5 4 0 00				1
2	Petty Cash	3 0 0 00				2
3	Accounts Receivable	10 2 9 8 00				3
4	Merchandise Inventory	251 0 6 8 00				4
5	Supplies—Office	5 9 5 7 00				5
6	Supplies—Store	4 9 1 6 00				6
7	Prepaid Insurance	4 5 5 4 00				7
8	Accounts Payable		10 1 4 3 00			8
9	Sales Tax Payable		1 4 6 0 00			9
10	Alan Dykes, Capital		113 1 2 2 00			10
11	Alan Dykes, Drawing	20 8 8 0 00				11
12	Dona Regan, Capital		109 2 9 8 00			12
13	Dona Regan, Drawing	20 5 0 0 00				13
14	Income Summary					14
15	Sales		293 7 3 0 00			15
16	Purchases	152 7 0 0 00				16
17	Advertising Expense	6 3 7 2 00				17
18	Credit Card Fee Expense	1 2 2 4 00				18
19	Insurance Expense					19
20	Miscellaneous Expense	2 8 4 4 00				20
21	Rent Expense	17 2 8 0 00				21
22	Supplies Expense—Office					22
23	Supplies Expense—Store					23
24	Utilities Expense	4 3 2 0 00				24
25		527 7 5 3 00	527 7 5 3 00			25
26						26
27						27
28						28
29						29

17-7 CHALLENGE PROBLEM (continued)

1.

Solutions _____

Sheet _____

December 31, 20 – –

	ADJUSTED TRIAL BALANCE		INCOME STATEMENT		BALANCE SHEET		
	5 DEBIT	6 CREDIT	7 DEBIT	8 CREDIT	9 DEBIT	10 CREDIT	
1							1
2							2
3							3
4							4
5							5
6							6
7							7
8							8
9							9
10							10
11							11
12							12
13							13
14							14
15							15
16							16
17							17
18							18
19							19
20							20
21							21
22							22
23							23
24							24
25							25
26							26
27							27
28							28
29							29

Extra form

	ACCOUNT TITLE	TRIAL BALANCE		ADJUSTMENTS	
		DEBIT	CREDIT	DEBIT	CREDIT
1					
2					
3					
4					
5					
6					
7					
8					
9					
10					
11					
12					
13					
14					
15					
16					
17					
18					
19					
20					
21					
22					
23					
24					
25					
26					
27					
28					
29					
30					
31					
32					

17-7 **CHALLENGE PROBLEM (continued)**

2.

			% OF SALES

3.

4.

17-7 **CHALLENGE PROBLEM (continued)**

5.

6., 7., 8., 9.

GENERAL JOURNAL

	DATE		ACCOUNT TITLE	DOC. NO.	POST. REF.	DEBIT	CREDIT	
1								1
2								2
3								3
4								4
5								5
6								6
7								7
8								8
9								9
10								10
11								11
12								12
13								13
14								14
15								15
16								16
17								17
18								18
19								19
20								20
21								21
22								22
23								23
24								24
25								25
26								26
27								27
28								28
29								29
30								30
31								31
32								32
33								33

17-7 **CHALLENGE PROBLEM (continued)**

7., 9., 10.   **GENERAL LEDGER**

ACCOUNT Cash   ACCOUNT NO. 1110

DATE	ITEM	POST. REF.	DEBIT	CREDIT	BALANCE DEBIT	BALANCE CREDIT
20-- Dec. 31	Balance	✔			24 540 00	

ACCOUNT Petty Cash   ACCOUNT NO. 1120

DATE	ITEM	POST. REF.	DEBIT	CREDIT	BALANCE DEBIT	BALANCE CREDIT
20-- Dec. 31	Balance	✔			300 00	

ACCOUNT Accounts Receivable   ACCOUNT NO. 1130

DATE	ITEM	POST. REF.	DEBIT	CREDIT	BALANCE DEBIT	BALANCE CREDIT
20-- Dec. 31	Balance	✔			10 298 00	

ACCOUNT Merchandise Inventory   ACCOUNT NO. 1140

DATE	ITEM	POST. REF.	DEBIT	CREDIT	BALANCE DEBIT	BALANCE CREDIT
20-- Jan. 1	Balance	✔			251 068 00	

ACCOUNT Supplies—Office   ACCOUNT NO. 1145

DATE	ITEM	POST. REF.	DEBIT	CREDIT	BALANCE DEBIT	BALANCE CREDIT
20-- Dec. 31	Balance	✔			5 957 00	

ACCOUNT Supplies—Store   ACCOUNT NO. 1150

DATE	ITEM	POST. REF.	DEBIT	CREDIT	BALANCE DEBIT	BALANCE CREDIT
20-- Dec. 31	Balance	✔			4 916 00	

ACCOUNT Prepaid Insurance   ACCOUNT NO. 1160

DATE	ITEM	POST. REF.	DEBIT	CREDIT	BALANCE DEBIT	BALANCE CREDIT
20-- Dec. 31	Balance	✔			4 554 00	

7., 9., 10.   **GENERAL LEDGER**

account Accounts Payable   ACCOUNT NO. 2110

DATE	ITEM	POST. REF.	DEBIT	CREDIT	BALANCE DEBIT	BALANCE CREDIT
20-- Dec. 31	Balance	✔				10 1 4 3 00

account Sales Tax Payable   ACCOUNT NO. 2120

DATE	ITEM	POST. REF.	DEBIT	CREDIT	BALANCE DEBIT	BALANCE CREDIT
20-- Dec. 31	Balance	✔				1 4 6 0 00

account Alan Dykes, Capital   ACCOUNT NO. 3110

DATE	ITEM	POST. REF.	DEBIT	CREDIT	BALANCE DEBIT	BALANCE CREDIT
20-- Dec. 31	Balance	✔				113 1 2 2 00

account Alan Dykes, Drawing   ACCOUNT NO. 3120

DATE	ITEM	POST. REF.	DEBIT	CREDIT	BALANCE DEBIT	BALANCE CREDIT
20-- Dec. 31	Balance	✔			20 8 8 0 00	

account Dona Regan, Capital   ACCOUNT NO. 3130

DATE	ITEM	POST. REF.	DEBIT	CREDIT	BALANCE DEBIT	BALANCE CREDIT
20-- Dec. 31	Balance	✔				109 2 9 8 00

account Dona Regan, Drawing   ACCOUNT NO. 3140

DATE	ITEM	POST. REF.	DEBIT	CREDIT	BALANCE DEBIT	BALANCE CREDIT
20-- Dec. 31	Balance	✔			20 5 0 0 00	

17-7 CHALLENGE PROBLEM (continued)

7., 9., 10.   GENERAL LEDGER

ACCOUNT Income Summary   ACCOUNT NO. 3150

DATE	ITEM	POST. REF.	DEBIT	CREDIT	BALANCE DEBIT	BALANCE CREDIT

ACCOUNT Sales   ACCOUNT NO. 4110

DATE	ITEM	POST. REF.	DEBIT	CREDIT	BALANCE DEBIT	BALANCE CREDIT
20-- Dec. 31	Balance	✔				293 730 00

ACCOUNT Purchases   ACCOUNT NO. 5110

DATE	ITEM	POST. REF.	DEBIT	CREDIT	BALANCE DEBIT	BALANCE CREDIT
20-- Dec. 31	Balance	✔			152 700 00	

ACCOUNT Advertising Expense   ACCOUNT NO. 6110

DATE	ITEM	POST. REF.	DEBIT	CREDIT	BALANCE DEBIT	BALANCE CREDIT
20-- Dec. 31	Balance	✔			6 372 00	

ACCOUNT Credit Card Fee Expense   ACCOUNT NO. 6120

DATE	ITEM	POST. REF.	DEBIT	CREDIT	BALANCE DEBIT	BALANCE CREDIT
20-- Dec. 31	Balance	✔			1 224 00	

ACCOUNT Insurance Expense   ACCOUNT NO. 6130

DATE	ITEM	POST. REF.	DEBIT	CREDIT	BALANCE DEBIT	BALANCE CREDIT

ACCOUNT Miscellaneous Expense   ACCOUNT NO. 6140

DATE	ITEM	POST. REF.	DEBIT	CREDIT	BALANCE DEBIT	BALANCE CREDIT
20-- Dec. 31	Balance	✔			2 844 00	

7., 9., 10. GENERAL LEDGER

ACCOUNT Rent Expense   ACCOUNT NO. 6150

DATE		ITEM	POST. REF.	DEBIT	CREDIT	BALANCE	
						DEBIT	CREDIT
20-- Dec.	31	Balance	✔			17 2 8 0 00	

ACCOUNT Supplies Expense—Office   ACCOUNT NO. 6160

DATE		ITEM	POST. REF.	DEBIT	CREDIT	BALANCE	
						DEBIT	CREDIT

ACCOUNT Supplies Expense—Store   ACCOUNT NO. 6170

DATE		ITEM	POST. REF.	DEBIT	CREDIT	BALANCE	
						DEBIT	CREDIT

ACCOUNT Utilities Expense   ACCOUNT NO. 6180

DATE		ITEM	POST. REF.	DEBIT	CREDIT	BALANCE	
						DEBIT	CREDIT
20-- Dec.	31	Balance	✔			4 3 2 0 00	

ACCOUNT   ACCOUNT NO.

DATE		ITEM	POST. REF.	DEBIT	CREDIT	BALANCE	
						DEBIT	CREDIT

ACCOUNT   ACCOUNT NO.

DATE		ITEM	POST. REF.	DEBIT	CREDIT	BALANCE	
						DEBIT	CREDIT

ACCOUNT   ACCOUNT NO.

DATE		ITEM	POST. REF.	DEBIT	CREDIT	BALANCE	
						DEBIT	CREDIT

17-7 **CHALLENGE PROBLEM (continued)**

10.

ACCOUNT TITLE	DEBIT	CREDIT

11. Inventory Auditing Challenges

REINFORCEMENT ACTIVITY 2 — PART B, p. 456

An Accounting Cycle for a Partnership: End-of-Fiscal-Period Work
The general ledger used in Reinforcement Activity 2, Part A, is needed to complete Part B.

12., 13.

ACCOUNT TITLE	TRIAL BALANCE DEBIT	TRIAL BALANCE CREDIT	ADJUSTMENTS DEBIT	ADJUSTMENTS CREDIT	INCOME STATEMENT DEBIT	INCOME STATEMENT CREDIT	BALANCE SHEET DEBIT	BALANCE SHEET CREDIT

12., 13.

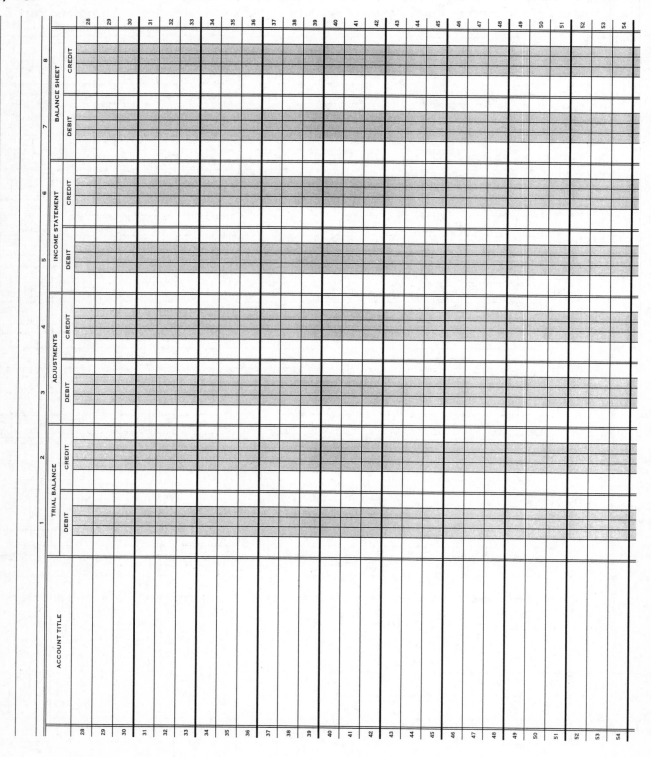

REINFORCEMENT ACTIVITY 2 **PART B (continued)**

14.

			% OF SALES

15.

16.

REINFORCEMENT ACTIVITY 2 **PART B (continued)**

17.

18., 19.

GENERAL JOURNAL   PAGE 13

	DATE	ACCOUNT TITLE	DOC. NO.	POST. REF.	DEBIT	CREDIT	
1							1
2							2
3							3
4							4
5							5
6							6
7							7
8							8
9							9
10							10
11							11
12							12
13							13
14							14
15							15
16							16
17							17
18							18
19							19
20							20
21							21
22							22
23							23
24							24
25							25
26							26
27							27
28							28
29							29
30							30
31							31
32							32
33							33

REINFORCEMENT ACTIVITY 2 PART B (concluded)

20.

ACCOUNT TITLE	DEBIT	CREDIT

Extra form

ACCOUNT TITLE	DEBIT	CREDIT

Extra form

ACCOUNT TITLE	DEBIT	CREDIT

Extra form

Extra form

							% OF SALES

Extra form